WHEN THE GREAT SPIRIT WALKED AMONG US

Four Gospels
One Story

Endorsements

"Our journey as the indigenous, from brokenness and heartache to healing and joy, has been long and tedious. We have faced what some thought were insurmountable odds, but here we are in this century gaining momentum in our recovery, redemption and reconciliation. Along this healing journey, treasures for edification, education and comfort have come along in the exact moment that we have needed them. Such is my feeling about this book. Creator has come to us at the right time with the words of the Gospels written in a way sensitive to who we are as the indigenous of Turtle Island; and in the story form we love and enjoy in our culture. Terry Wildman's gift as a storyteller brings the story of Jesus to life in an authentic way. I am honored to give my full endorsement to *When the Great Spirit Walked Among Us.*"

Warren Petoskey
Odawa/Lakota Elder and Storyteller
Author of *Dancing My Dream*

"*When the Great Spirit Walked Among Us* recognizes the way in which Creator is deeply rooted and grounded in our First Nations people. The language is eloquent and Spirit-filled. One has the sense of hearing a sacred storytelling from the breath of Creator that refreshes and renews the minds of Jesus' followers whether the relationship is newly made or grown sacred over a lifetime. And if one still wonders if there is something more to life, it can be found here, written on the leaves of the Tree of Life."

Kimberlee Medicine Horn, Yankton Sioux
MFA, Poet and Creative Writer

1

"When the Great Spirit Walked Among Us is a breathtakingly beautiful recasting of the Gospel story, here presented in the shape of the American-Indian oral storytelling tradition. It is translation at its finest, moving the message accurately across historical and cultural boundaries, from one great oral storytelling tradition to another. Throughout most of history, the written word has been scarce and expensive. Information was passed along as stories, first by prophets and preachers, later from elders and teachers. They shared it around campfires and cookstoves, faithfully passing on that which they had received themselves. That is why it is such a thrill to be able to recommend this new translation, which is a return to the very first way the Gospel was presented. Its cadences and images evoke simpler times, but times no less perilous than now, when Good and Evil still strive for the hearts and souls of men."

Dr. Timothy P. Jenney, Ph.D.
Host, Accordance Bible Software's Lighting the Lamp
Adjunct Faculty, Regent University, School of Divinity

"From the beginning the story of Jesus has been a translated story. Jesus spoke in Aramaic, but Matthew, Mark, Luke, and John wrote their Gospels in Greek. The story of Jesus is intended to be translated to every tribe, tongue, people, and nation. The fact that translation is intended, not just permitted, serves to show how we must resist any cultural domination of the gospel. Terry Wildman has done a masterful job of rendering the Gospels into the storytelling motif characteristic of Native Americans. It should tell us something important when we realize how beautifully the story of Jesus can be adapted to the style and vocabulary of indigenous people. I deeply appreciate Terry Wildman's retelling of the story of Jesus for First Nations people. I believe the Great Spirit is pleased."

Brian Zahnd
Pastor of Word of Life Church in St. Joseph, Missouri
Author of *Beauty Will Save the World* and *A Farewell To Mars*

2

"Terry Wildman brings his considerable gifts as a storyteller to a masterful retelling of the gospel story that is steeped in the rhythms, forms, and motifs of the indigenous peoples with whom he lives and walks. The First Nations Version makes a simple shift that produces profound effects. The voice that shapes the gospel story for most Americans is the familiar voice of the contemporary church and culture. Hearing the familiar story told with a different voice, an indigenous voice, opens a world of wonderful insights and meanings. This is an elegant retelling of the Gospel story that is sure to engage and excite a broad spectrum of readers."

L. Daniel Hawk, Ph.D.
Professor of Old Testament and Hebrew
Ashland Theological Seminary
Author of *Joshua in 3D: A Commentary on Biblical Conquest and Manifest Destiny*

"I've often wondered what it might look like if Jesus incarnated within another culture. Jesus, a first century Jewish teacher in the corner of Rome's empire, lived, died, and rose as a human being within a specific time and place. What I love about *When the Great Spirit Walked Among Us* is how it translates this gospel story into a language of another context: First Nations! So get swept away into the story of the Great Spirit as he invites us to the blessing way of the Good Road! Read this beautiful retelling of the Scriptures, which is not only beneficial for First Nations communities, but for all who desire to allow the Great Spirit to transform their imaginations!"

Kurt Willems, M.Div. Fresno Pacific
Anabaptist Pastor and Author, kurtwillems.com

"To be an effective bridge builder can be a very difficult task, unless one has knowledge and respect for the conditions at both ends of the bridge. Terry sees clearly the distinctions between the cultures of the White man and the Native American, as well as the religious perspectives of both. He is a humble man, an excellent listener, a peacemaker, and has walked on the soils at both ends of the bridge that he is building. Terry has undertaken a special and substantial project to paraphrase, in a harmony of the four Gospels, the life of Jesus, the Waymaker. Terry has taken texts that were written from an ancient Middle Eastern Jewish tribal perspective and articulately transformed them into the common vernacular of the traditional tribal indigenous peoples. He presents Jesus, as the Creator walking in our midst, in a cultural context that is pre-digested and easy to swallow. For some, this translation will help overcome the critical perception of many indigenous peoples that the Bible is the White man's book. Oh! What would the history of the Americas have been had this bridge-building translation accompanied the European explorers five centuries ago?"

Tom Dooley, Ph.D.
Founder of Path Clearer Inc.
www.PathClearer.com
Author of *Hope When Everything Seems Hopeless*
and *Half Truths are Lies*

"If Creator is the Creator of all, then His Word should be to all. As indigenous people we want to hear the words of Jesus in a way that is relevant to us—to help us walk his Good Road. We too wish to gain wisdom and understanding that comes from the Truth —and have Creator breath His Word on all of us. Thank you Terry Wildman for your diligent work!"

Mike Two Shadows Brennan
Pastor, Sharps Corner Mission
Pine Ridge Indian Reservation
Director, Youth Evangelism Strategies
and Chanku Waste Ranch

When the Great Spirit Walked Among Us

Retold by Terry M. Wildman

Great Thunder Publishing, Maricopa, Arizona

ISBN 978-0-9847706-3-2

The text of this book is from the First Nations Version Project by Terry M. Wildman

www.firstnationsversion.com

This version may differ slightly from other editions of the First Nations Version Project.

Cover design by Mark Sequeira, MJA Studios
Email: mark@mjastudios.com

Acknowledgments

To my loving wife Darlene, thank you for patiently enduring the many hours I spent hidden away in our home studio working on this book. I often become tunnel visioned and tenacious when I am writing, and have a hard time talking about anything else. You not only put up with me, but encouraged me with your support, and the many hours you spent listening to me read aloud as I "tried it out on you." Above and beyond this, you also read and reread the entire book, offering suggestions that have made this story come alive.

To my good friend Keith, the countless hours you spent in research, scouring the texts, offering suggestions, proofreading, and continually pushing me to raise the bar; has made this paraphrase far better than I imagined it could be. Our friendship has grown deeper through this time. Thank you!

I also want to thank Judie Patterson, a new friend who volunteered to read each chapter, and kindly offered punctuation and grammar suggestions.

Chi Miigwech (Big thanks) to the Great Storyteller, Wisdomkeeper, Son of God and True Human Being—Jesus Christ. My friend and Chief who, through his Spirit, walks with me as I attempt follow his Good Road.

Dedicated to the memory of

Richard Twiss

Taoyate Ob Najin
He Stands With His People

This book is a harmony of the four Gospels blended together into a single narrative and retold for Native Americans and all English speaking First Nations peoples.

In the tradition of indigenous peoples the names have been translated to show the beauty of their original meanings. When available, the meaning of the names of places are also included.

The opening prologue called, **First Words**, is a very short summary of the Old Testament, to provide a historical introduction to the time of Jesus.

If you want more information regarding the purpose and philosophy behind this translation you can visit the **From the Author** section in back of this book.

The reader is also encouraged to visit the **Culture and Context** section for more information regarding the historic and cultural setting of the Gospels.

Other Books by Terry M. Wildman

Sign Language:
A Look at the Historic and Prophetic Landscape of America

Birth of the Chosen One

GREAT THUNDER PUBLISHING
Maricopa, Arizona 85139 USA

WHEN THE
GREAT
SPIRIT
WALKED
AMONG US

Four Gospels • One Story

Retold by Terry M. Wildman

www.FirstNationsVersion.com

Great Thunder Publishing

Table of Contents

PROLOGUE

First Words

The Great Spirit

The Great Spirit is known among the First Nations peoples by many names; the Great Mystery, Creator, Grandfather,[1] the Maker of Life, the Giver of Breath, and by many other names from our tribal languages. These names have been chosen in the retelling of this story to honor the simplicity and beauty of our Native understanding of the One Above Us All.

This story tells of the time when the Great Spirit walked among us, retold from the Sacred Book—the greatest story of all. It is about the Great Storyteller, Creator Sets Free,[2] who is the Son of the Great Spirit.

The story begins long before he was born into this world, so before we tell about his birth we must first go back to when the world began.

Creator Makes All Things

In the beginning the Great Spirit made all things seen and unseen.[3] He made the world above and the earth below. He created all the spirit beings to be his messengers and helpers. He also made the sun, moon and stars, and all plants and animals.

The two-winged ones who fly in the sky, the four-legged ones who walk on the ground, every creeping thing that crawls—all were shaped and molded by his hands.

Garden of Beauty and Harmony

Creator made the first man and woman and placed them in the Garden of Beauty and Harmony,[4] to be caretakers of the earth. But the evil serpent,[5] a spirit being who opposed the Great Spirit, twisted the words of Creator. He planted a seed of doubt into their minds, which caused them to not trust Grandfather, so they ate the fruit of the only tree he had told them not to eat.

The life of beauty and harmony was lost and the circle of life was broken. A powerful curse came upon the ground that affected all living things.

By listening to the evil serpent, and disobeying the Maker of Life, they brought death with all its bloodshed, violence and destruction to all the generations of mankind that would follow.

Spiritual and physical death came to all and the hearts of human beings became bad, twisted together with good and evil. They could no longer live in harmony upon the land and began to follow evil ways and hurt and kill one another.

Creator cursed the ancient serpent and made a promise to mankind. He would one day send another human being, born of a woman, who would crush the head of the ancient serpent and restore human beings and all of creation back to the life of beauty and harmony again.

The Great Flood

Many generations passed. Creator's human children had lost their way and the earth became filled with violence. To cleanse the earth a great flood would come and bring an end to all living things. The Great Spirit spared one family and two of each of the animals, along with a few animals to be used for ceremonial offerings. He chose a man named One Who Rests[6] to build a great wooden boat to hold his family and all the animals. The flood came and cleansed the earth. A new day began.

Father Of Many Nations

The Great Mystery knew that good and evil still lived in the hearts of human beings, so he chose a man named Honored Father[7] and made a Peace Treaty[8] with him. He gave him a new name— Father Of Many Nations[9]—because through his descendants Grandfather's blessing way would come to all the clans and families of the earth.

Twelve Tribes of Wrestles With Creator

When Father Of Many Nations and his wife were too old to have children, the Great Spirit gave them a son. They named him He Made Us Laugh,[10] because they laughed when Creator told them they would have a child. He Made Us Laugh had a son who he named Heel Grabber,[11] because he grabbed his twin brothers heel when he was being born. The Great Spirit later gave him a new name, Wrestles With Creator,[12] because he wrestled with a spirit messenger from Creator.

Wrestles With Creator had twelve sons who became twelve tribes. After four-hundred years of captivity and slavery to a foreign nation the Great Spirit set them free through Drawn From The Water,[13] who became the great law-giver.

The Great Spirit made a Peace Treaty with the tribes and gave them their own land, ceremonies to purify them, and feasts to teach them to celebrate his goodness. He also gave them the great law that was carved into tablets of stone, and a Sacred Tent Lodge where they would perform their ceremonies.

The Great Spirit wanted to be their Grand Chief, but the tribes wanted a human chief so they could be like the nations around them. This grieved Creator, but he gave them what they wanted. Most of these chiefs became arrogant and misrepresented the Great Spirit, but there were a few good ones. One of these great chiefs was Much Loved One.[14] He had a good heart toward Creator and the people, even though he, at times, also strayed from the path.

Creator had chosen the tribes to be a light to other nations, but they failed to keep his Peace Treaty, broke his laws, and misrepresented him to others. He sent many prophets to turn the hearts of the tribes back to the right ways, but they did not listen and their hearts became like stone.

Finally, the Great Spirit removed his protection from them and allowed them to be conquered by other nations.

The People of Iron

Through the generations that followed, many powerful nations ruled over the tribes. The most recent was the People of Iron.[15] This government took control of the tribes and had now dominated them for nearly two generations.

The People of Iron forced their treaties on the tribes, but did allow some freedoms. They could practice their own spiritual ways, build gathering houses[16] and maintain a Sacred Lodge[17] to perform their ceremonies and make their prayers.

This government also allowed them to have their own tribal chiefs. But over many years these chiefs became corrupt and were controlled more by the ways of the People of Iron than their ancient Sacred Ways.

The people were oppressed and feared this powerful government of the People of Iron with its many soldiers and weapons of war. They kept praying that the Great Spirit would fulfill the age-old prophecies and send the Chosen One,[18] who they hoped would be a great warrior chief to destroy the People of Iron and set them free.

The right time had finally come for Grandfather to fulfill his ancient prophecies and send his Chosen One.

But he would not come in the way the tribes expected.

"Come, let us sit down in the council house together.
Then face to face you can hear what my heart is saying.
Your bad hearts and broken ways
Have stained your spiritual garments.
A stain so deep, you cannot wash them clean.
But, this is what I will do for you.
I will take your blood-red garments
And wash them until they are as white as snow.
I will wash away the deepest stain
Until you are as clean and white
As the tip of an eagle's wings."

From the Great Spirit
To the tribes of Wrestles With Creator

Isaiah One Eighteen

CHAPTER ONE

Birth of the Chosen One

The Great Storyteller

Long ago, in the time before all days, before the creation of all things…

There was the Story.

The Story was face to face with Creator and was the same as Creator. He was with Creator in the beginning.

The Story made everything there is. Nothing was made except by him.

Life was in him and shined its light on all human beings. This is the true light that comes to all the peoples of the world, and shines on everyone. His light shines into the darkness of this world, and the darkness cannot put it out.

Even though he made all people, not everyone recognized him. Even his own tribe did not welcome or honor him. But all who welcome and trust him receive their birthright as children of the Great Spirit. They are born in a new way, not from a human father's plans, but born from above.

The Story became a human being and lived as one of us—*the Great Storyteller.* We saw how honorable he was. The kind of honor that comes from being an only son to a father, one who is fully trusted and favored.

From his goodness we have all had goodwill poured out on us. Drawn From The Water gave us the great law, but the blessing way and truth came from Creator Sets Free—the Chosen One.

No one has ever seen the Great Spirit, but his only born Son. He is the one who is closest to Grandfather's heart, and has shown us what he is like.

Eye Witnesses

O most honored Friend Of Creator, many have told this story, given to them from those who saw these things with their own eyes; the ones who laid down their lives to pass it on to others.

Since I have heard this story from the beginning, it seemed like a good thing for me to retell it from first to last. In this way you will know for yourself the truth about the things you were taught.

The Good News[19] begins with *the story of* Creator Sets Free,[20] who is the Son of the Great Spirit, *and the Chosen One of the tribes of Wrestles With Creator.*

Creator Sets Free is of the tribe of Give Him Honor. He is a descendant of Father Of Many Nations and the great chief Much Loved One. His ancestors can be followed back through many generations.[21] Fourteen generations from Father Of Many Nations to Much Loved One. Fourteen from Much Loved One to the great removal to the land of Babylon and fourteen more from the great removal to the *birth of the* Chosen One.

Creator Remembers His Promise

It was in the time of the bad-hearted Chief Looks Brave, who ruled the territory of Judea, *the Land of Promise,* that Creator chose to send a powerful spirit messenger[22] to Jerusalem, the Sacred Village of Peace, to a holy man whose name was Creator Will Remember.

He and his wife, Creator Is My Promise, were both descended from the tribe the ceremonial holy people are chosen from. They had deep respect for the Great Spirit. With good and pure hearts they walked a straight path, staying true to the tribal ways and traditions given them by the Great Spirit. They lived in the hill country, in the Land of Promise of the tribes of Wrestles With Creator.

But Creator Is My Promise was barren, unable to have children, and they both were growing old in years.

Creator Will Remember belonged to the clan of He Is My Father, that shared the responsibility of prayers and ceremonies in the Great Spirit's Sacred Lodge that was in Jerusalem.

He was chosen in the traditional way to be the one to enter the Lodge and perform the sweet smelling smoke ceremony for the evening prayer. *Most holy men could only hope for this honor once in a lifetime.* A large number of people gathered outside to pray while he went inside.

As the smoke went up with his prayers, suddenly a messenger from the Great Spirit appeared to him, standing to the right of the altar of incense. Creator Will Remember was troubled when he saw the spirit messenger. He trembled with fear that covered him like a blanket.

"Do not fear!" the messenger said to him. "Your prayers have been heard. The Maker of Life will give you and your wife a son. You will give him the name Creator Shows Goodwill. He will bring great joy to you and many people will be glad that he has been born."

The aroma of the sweet smelling smoke filled the Sacred Lodge as the spirit messenger continued.

"He will be great and honorable in Creator's sight. He will not taste strong drink or wine. Even in his mother's womb he will drink deeply of the Holy Spirit. Because of him many of the children of the tribes of Wrestles With Creator will find the Good Road and return to the Great Spirit's ways."

Creator Will Remember stood silently. His whole being continued to tremble as the messenger finished.

"He will prepare the way for the Chosen One, walking in the same spiritual powers of the prophet Great Spirit Is Creator. He will turn the hearts of many fathers toward their children and many rebellious children will again honor the wisdom of their elders; so that people will be ready to participate in Creator's plan."

When the spirit messenger finished speaking, his words echoed through the Lodge. Still trembling, Creator Will Remember finally found his voice.

Then he questioned the messenger, "We are too old to have children. How can I believe your words?"

The spirit messenger answered, "My name is Creator's Mighty One, his chief messenger. I stand close to the Great Spirit! These blessing words I was sent to speak to you will come to pass, but since you did not believe my words, you will not be able to speak until they are fulfilled."

The people who were praying outside began to wonder why it was taking so long for Creator Will Remember to come out of the Lodge. When he finally came out, unable to speak and making signs with his hands, they understood that he had seen a vision.

When the traditional ceremonies were finished he returned to his home in the hill country. Soon afterward Creator Is My Promise was with child. She stayed at home and for five moons did not show herself to anyone.

She said in her heart, "The Giver of Breath has poured out his blessing ways on me! He has taken away my shame. Now I will have respect in the eyes of my people."

Bitter Tears

When six moons had passed the Great Spirit sent the same spirit messenger, Creator's Mighty One, to another small, out of the way village in the hill country called Nazareth. There he appeared to a young virgin woman named Bitter Tears, who was promised in marriage to a man named He Gives Sons, a descendant of the great chief Much Loved One.

Creator's Mighty One said to her, "Greetings, highly favored one! You are close to the Great Spirit and greatly honored among women."

Bitter Tears was deeply troubled by this greeting and wondered what the spirit messenger would say.

"Don't be afraid," he comforted her. "For you have found goodwill in the eyes of the Great Mystery. You will be with child and give birth to a son. You will call him Creator Sets Free."

It seemed like time stood still, and all creation stopped to listen as the messenger continued to speak.

"He will be greatly honored, the Son of the One Above Us All. He will be Grand Chief like his ancestor Much Loved One and will sit in his place of honor. He will always be chief over the tribes of Wrestles With Creator. His chiefly guidance will never end."

Bitter Tears' voice trembled with emotion, and her eyes grew wide as she looked into the face of the spirit messenger.

She asked, "How will this be, since I have never been with a man?"

Creator's Mighty One answered, "The Holy Spirit will spread his wings over you and his great power from above will overshadow you. This Holy Child born to you will be the Son of the One Above Us All."

To encourage her he said, "Your cousin, Creator is My Promise, who was called barren one, is six moons with child. See! There is nothing too hard for the Great Spirit."

She looked into the face of the messenger and bravely declared, "I am Creator's servant. Let it be for me just as you have said."

Then Creator's chief spirit messenger left her.

Cousins

Bitter Tears quickly put together a traveling bundle and went to visit her cousin, Creator Is My Promise, who lived in a nearby village. When she entered the home of her relatives she greeted her cousin. When Creator Is My Promise heard Bitter Tears' greeting she felt her child jump inside her. She was filled with the Holy Spirit, and with a loud cry she lifted her voice and spoke these blessing words to Bitter Tears.

"The Most Holy One has honored you more than any other woman! The child you carry inside you will bring blessing ways to all people. Why is Grandfather being so kind to me, sending the mother of the Great Chief to visit my home? As soon as I heard your greeting my baby jumped for joy inside me! You have been chosen by the Maker of Life for a great honor, because you believed his words to you."

When Bitter Tears heard this, she was full of gladness and her words flowed out like a song.

"From deep in my heart I dance with joy to honor the Great Spirit. Even though I am small and weak he noticed me. Now I will be looked up to by all. The Mighty One has lifted me up! His name is sacred, He is the Great and Holy One."

Her face seemed to shine as she continued.

"He shows kindness and mercy to both children and elders who respect him. His strong arm has brought low the ones who think they are better than others. He counts coup[23] with arrogant warrior chiefs, but puts a headdress of honor on the ones with humble hearts."

She smiled, looked up to the sky and shouted for joy!

"He prepares a great feast for the ones who are hungry, but sends the fat ones home with empty bellies. He remembers the promise he made to the tribes of Wrestles With Creator, and has shown kindness to the children of Father Of Many Nations."

When she finished they both laughed with joy. With hearts full of gladness they told each other their stories.

For three moons Bitter Tears stayed in the home of her cousin and then returned to her own village.

A Promise Fulfilled

When her time came Creator is My Promise gave birth to a son. When her relatives and close friends heard the good news, that the Great Spirit had been so kind to her, they were glad and rejoiced! Then eight days later, at his naming ceremony, all the relatives wanted to name him after his father.

"No," she said to everyone's surprise. "His name will be Creator Shows Goodwill!" But they said to her, "No one in your family has that name." They made signs with their hands to Creator Will Remember to see what he wanted to name him. He asked for a writing tablet and to their surprise wrote, "His name is Creator Shows Goodwill." Suddenly he could speak again and began to thank the Great Spirit out loud.

Then, with a glad heart he spoke these words the Holy Spirit was giving him to say. "All blessing ways to the Great Spirit of the tribes of Wrestles With Creator! For he has come to rescue his people from a great captivity. In the land of our ancestor, Much Loved One, he has lifted up his coup stick to show his great power to help us."

He lifted trembling hands to the sky and cried out.

"He has remembered his ancient promises made to our ancestors since the beginning of time, and the Peace Treaty he made with Father Of Many Nations. He has come to set us free so we can walk in his good and sacred ways without having to fear our enemies who surround us."

Then he turned to his newborn son and from deep in his spirit, he spoke these blessing words to him.

"And you, my son, will be a prophet from the One Above Us All. You will make a clear path for the coming of the Grand Chief, to show his people that he will heal our broken ways by cleansing us from our bad hearts and releasing us from our wrongdoings. Because Creator is kind and gentle, he will come to us as the sunrise from above, to shine on the ones who sit in darkness and in the land of death's shadow, to guide our feet on the good road of peace."

All the people who heard about this were filled with wonder. Throughout the hills and valleys of Judea they began to speak about what they had seen and heard. All who listened began to say to themselves, "This child must have been born for some great thing."

For it was clear that the hand of the Great Spirit was upon him in a powerful and good way. Creator Shows Goodwill grew strong in body and spirit and stayed in the desert, waiting until the time was right to show himself to the tribes of Wrestles With Creator.

Dream Guidance

Bitter Tears had returned home to be with her family and to He Gives Sons, the man she was promised to in marriage. Before they came together he discovered that she was with child. Because he was a man of honor and did not want to disgrace her, he thought about secretly releasing her from the marriage promise.

As he wondered about these things, a messenger from the Great Spirit appeared to him in a dream and said, "He Gives Sons, son of Much Loved One, do not be afraid to take Bitter Tears to be your wife, because the father of the child is the Holy Spirit."

The dream ended with these words from the spirit messenger.

"She will give birth to a son. You will name him Creator Sets Free, because he will set his people free from their bad hearts and broken ways." This gave full meaning to the words spoken long ago by the prophet, "A young virgin will be with child and give birth to a son. They will call his name Creator Is With Us."

When He Gives Sons awoke, he followed the guidance given him in the dream and took Bitter Tears to be his wife. But he did not have relations with her until after the child was born.

Humble Birth

When the time drew close for Bitter Tears to have her child the government of the People of Iron ordered that the people be numbered and put on government rolls. All the people were required to travel to their ancestral homeland to register.

He Gives Sons and Bitter Tears set out on a long journey to Bethlehem, the village of their ancestor Much Loved One, the great chief.

The journey took several long days and cold nights as they traveled over high hills and through the dry desert. When they arrived tired and weary, they entered the crowded village.

The time for Bitter Tears to have her child was upon her! But no place could be found in the lodging house, so He Gives Sons found a stable where it was warm and dry. There she gave birth to her son. They wrapped him in a warm soft blanket *and laid him on a baby board.* Then they placed him on a bed of straw in a feeding trough.

That night, in the fields nearby, shepherds were keeping watch over their sheep. Suddenly a great light from above was shining all around them. A spirit messenger from Creator appeared to them. They shook with fear and trembled as the messenger said to them, "Don't be afraid, I bring you good news that will be for all nations. Today in the village of Much Loved One a great chief has been born. He is the Chosen One!"

"This is how you will know him," the messenger added, "you will find the child wrapped in a blanket and lying in a feeding trough."

Suddenly a great number of spirit warriors appeared giving thanks to Creator saying, "All honor to the One Above Us All and on the earth let there be peace to all who stay under the shadow of his wings."

When the spirit warriors returned to the world above, the shepherds said to each other, "Let us go and see this great thing the Creator has told to us." So they hurried to the village of Chief Much Loved One and found the child just as they were told, lying in a feeding trough!

They left with glad hearts and began to tell everyone what they had seen. All who heard their story were amazed. The shepherds returned to their fields, giving thanks to the Great Spirit for the wonders they had seen and heard.

Bitter Tears kept all these things hidden in the medicine pouch of her heart and wondered what all this would mean.

Keeping the Traditions

Bitter Tears and He Gives Sons, in keeping with the traditional naming ceremony, on the eighth day gave their newborn son the name Creator Sets Free; the name given to them by the spirit messenger before the child was born.

Then, about one moon later, the time came for them to present their child to the Great Spirit. This was their purification ceremony, an ancient tradition from the great lawgiver Drawn From the Water, who said, "Every male child who is first to open the womb will be holy in the Great Spirit's sight. Bring two turtledoves or two young pigeons[24] to be burned with fire as a sweet smelling smoke offering."

They journeyed to Jerusalem to Great Spirit's Sacred Lodge for this ceremony. When they arrived they were welcomed by Creator Hears, a respected elder who did what was right in the Great Spirit's sight and waited patiently for him to fulfill his promises to the tribes of Wrestles With Creator. The Holy Spirit rested on him and told him he would not die until he saw Creator's Chosen One with his own eyes.

As Creator Hears followed the guidance of the Spirit he arrived at the Sacred Lodge just in time to see He Gives Sons and Bitter Tears bringing their child for the purification ceremony. Creator Hears took the child into his arms and spoke blessing words over him. "O Great Father, I now see with my own eyes the one you have prepared for all Nations; the one who will heal our broken ways and set us free. He will make a clear path for all people to see, and bring honor to the tribes of Wrestles With Creator. Now, just as you have said, I can cross over in peace."

The child's father and mother were amazed at what was being said. So Creator Hears spoke blessing words over them also.

He then turned to Bitter Tears and spoke softly in her ear.

"This child has been chosen for the fall and rising of many in the tribes of Wrestles With Creator. He will be a sign that will be spoken against, exposing the hearts of many."

His voice softened as she looked sadly into his eyes.

He said to her, "Even your own heart will be pierced through like a sharp arrow."

As they pondered his words, a holy woman named Woman Of Goodwill, a tribal elder of many years, welcomed them. She stayed at the Great Spirit's Sacred Lodge night and day with fasting and many prayers. When she saw the child she gave thanks to Grandfather and began telling about the child to all who were waiting for Creator to fulfill his promises to Jerusalem, the Sacred Village of Peace.

After they performed all the ceremonies which Creator's great law required, they set their hearts to return to their home village.

Wisdomkeepers From the East

After the Chosen One's birth in Bethlehem, Wisdomkeepers traveling on a long journey from the East, came to Jerusalem.

They began to ask, "Where is the one who has been born to be Grand Chief of the tribes of Wrestles With Creator? We saw his star where the sun rises and have come to bow down low before him and honor him."

When the bad-hearted Chief Looks Brave, who ruled Judea,[25] heard this he was troubled, along with all who lived in Jerusalem. He called a council of all the chief holy men and law teachers and asked them where the Chosen One was to be born.

"In Bethlehem, the village of Chief Much Loved One," they answered. "This is what the ancient prophecies say, 'But you Bethlehem, O House of Bread, in the land of the tribes of Wrestles With Creator, you have a good reputation, and from you shall come a great chief who will guide my chosen people.'"

Then Chief Looks Brave called a secret council with the Wisdomkeepers to find out when the star first appeared. He then sent them to the village of Chief Much Loved One and told them,

"Look everywhere for the child, find him and tell me where he is, so that I may also come and bow down low before him."

Honoring the Chosen One

When the Wisdomkeepers went their way, they saw the star rising in the East. With glad hearts they followed, until the star stopped and rested over the place where the child was. They were welcomed into the house where they saw the child with his mother, Bitter Tears. They bowed down low to the ground to honor the child. Then they opened their bundles and gifted him with precious gold, sweet smelling incense, and bitter ointment of Myrrh.

The Wisdomkeepers were warned in a dream not to go back to Chief Looks Brave, so they returned to their homeland by a different road.

After the Wisdomkeepers had gone, a spirit messenger warned He Gives Sons in a dream. "Rise up!" he said urgently. "Take the child and his mother and go quickly to the land of Egypt and remain there until I tell you to leave. Chief Looks Brave is searching for the child to kill him!"

That night He Gives Sons took the child and his mother and fled for their lives to the land of Egypt. They remained there until the death of Chief Looks Brave. This fulfilled the ancient prophecy, "I will bring my son from the land of Egypt."

When Chief Looks Brave realized he had been outsmarted by the Wisdomkeepers, he was full of rage and gave orders for all male children in Bethlehem, under two years of age, to be put to death. This fulfilled another age old prophecy, "A sound of weeping and wailing is heard in the high country. A woman is shedding tears for her children. No one can quiet her down, because they are no more."

The Journey Home

After Chief Looks Brave died, a spirit messenger appeared again to He Gives Sons in a dream. He said, "Get up and take the child and his mother and go back to the land of the tribes of Wrestles With Creator. The ones who were trying to take the child's life are dead."

He Gives Sons got up, took the child and his mother and began to go where he was told. On the way, when he heard that the son of Chief Looks Brave had become the new chief, he became afraid.

After being warned in another dream, he took a different path to their home in the North hills, to an out-of-the-way village most people looked down on, called Nazareth. This fulfilled many ancient prophecies, such as the one that said the Chosen One would be *"A small plant out of dry ground"*[26] and *"One looked down upon,"*[27] a Nazarene.

In this village the Holy Child grew strong in wisdom and strength and the people respected him, for the Great Spirit's power and blessing ways were resting on him.

Coming of Age

It was a custom for all the families of the tribes of Wrestles With Creator to journey to Jerusalem to participate in the ancient Passover festival.

This festival celebrated the time when the great lawgiver, Drawn From The Water, had set them free from captivity to the powerful nation of Egypt. He did this by using the great power Creator gave him to perform many signs and wonders.

When Creator Sets Free was twelve years old his family traveled together to celebrate this traditional feast.

When the festival was over his parents began their journey home. Without telling his parents, Creator Sets Free stayed behind in Jerusalem. They thought he was with the other relatives and friends traveling with them. After a long day's journey they began to look for him, but were unable to find him, so they returned to Jerusalem to look for him there.

They returned to the Sacred Village of Peace, searching for him, and on the third day they found him at the entryway of the Great Spirit's Sacred Lodge. He was sitting with the elders, listening to them and asking questions. All who heard his answers were amazed at his wisdom and understanding of the spiritual ways.

His parents were surprised and at a loss for words, but then his mother scolded him, "Son why have you treated us this way? Your father and I were worried and our hearts were heavy as we looked everywhere for you!"

"Why were you looking everywhere for me?" he asked. "I thought you would know to look for me here, in my Father's house, doing what he sent me to do."

But they did not understand the meaning of what he was saying to them. He then returned to Nazareth with them and continued to be a respectful son following the guidance of his parents. But his mother hid all these things deep in the medicine pouch of her heart.

Creator Sets Free, as a young man, continued to grow in wisdom and strength. The people respected him, for the Great Spirit's power and blessing ways were resting on him.

CHAPTER TWO

A Voice in the Desert

He Shows Goodwill

Eighteen long winters had now come and gone. The People of Iron had many new rulers and governors, and the tribes of Wrestles With Creator had a new high holy man[28] for the Sacred Lodge.

Creator's message came down from above and *like a burden basket*[29] it rested on He Shows Goodwill, the son of Creator Will Remember.

The time had come for him to begin his work with the tribes of Wrestles With Creator and prepare the way for the Chosen One.

He was sent by the Great Spirit to tell what he knew about the light *that was coming into the world,* so everyone could believe. He was not the light but came to tell what he saw with his own eyes about the light.

The prophet Creator Will Help Us told about him long ago, "Look! I am sending my messenger ahead of you, to prepare the way. *He will be a* voice howling in the desert,[30] 'Clear the pathways! Make a straight path for the coming of the Grand Chief! The valleys will be filled in. The mountains and hills will be brought down low. The crooked places will be made straight and the rough road smooth. Then all people will clearly see the Good Road that sets them free.'"

Preparing the Way

In the desert places of *the Land of Promise, called* Judea, near the Jordan River, he began to speak out. His message was loud and clear, "It is time to return to the right ways of thinking. Creator's Good Road is close, reach out and take hold of it."

He was performing a purification ceremony[31] for those who were returning to the ways of the Great Spirit; to show they were cleansed from their bad hearts and wrongdoings.

The people came from the village of Jerusalem, from all of Judea and the territory surrounding the Jordan River, to participate in the purification ceremony. Before the ceremony they would admit to their bad hearts and broken ways.

He Shows Goodwill came wearing animal hair garments, with a deer hide sash around his waist. The food he ate was grasshoppers and wild honey.

He noticed the Separated Ones and Upright Ones[32] in the crowd and warned them, "You nest of poisonous snakes!" he cried out. "Who warned you to run and hide from the coming storm? Prove to others, by the way you live, that you have returned to the Good Road. Do you think you can say, 'Father Of Many Nations is our ancestor?' Don't you know the Great Spirit can make these stones into his children? The tomahawk is at the root of the trees. The ones that have no fruit will be cut down and tossed into the fire."

When they heard his words they were afraid and said, "What should we do?"

He answered, "If you have two blankets give one to someone who has none, and the one with food should share it."

There were tribal agents[33] who came to participate in the ceremony, who said to him, "Wisdomkeeper, what should we do?"

"Collect no more taxes than the People Of Iron permit," he answered. *"To take more is to steal from the people and dishonor the Great Spirit."*

When the Lodge soldiers heard this they said, "What about us? What can we do?"

"Be happy with your pay," he answered. "Do not use fear or violence to force money from people and do not accuse them falsely."

When the people heard these words they began to have hope. They wondered if He Shows Goodwill was the Chosen One.

Spiritual Leaders Question Him

Some of the holy men and spiritual leaders from the tribes of Wrestles With Creator were sent from Jerusalem to question He Shows Goodwill.

"Who are you?" they asked.

He knew what they were asking, so he said plainly. "I am not the Chosen One."

"Who are you then?" they demanded. "The Holy man from long ago, Great Spirit Is Creator?"

"No," he answered, "I am not."

"Are you the Prophet who is to come?" they asked.

"No," was his answer again.

So they said to him, "Tell us who you are, so we will have an answer for the ones who sent us. What do you have to say about yourself?"

He Shows Goodwill looked at them, straight in the eyes, and answered, "I am saying the same thing the prophet Creator Will Help Us said, 'I am a voice howling in the desert; make a straight pathway for the Grand Chief.'"[34]

These spiritual leaders were sent by the Separated Ones, so they asked He Shows Goodwill, "Why do you perform the purification ceremony if you are not the Chosen One or Great Spirit Is Creator, or The Prophet?"

He gave them this answer, "I perform the purification ceremony with water, but there is one you do not know, who is right here with you." *He paused for a moment and added softly,* "Even though he comes after me, he is much greater. He has greater honor, for he has always been first. I am not even worthy to bend low and untie his moccasins."

Then he lifted his hands and with a loud voice, cried out! "He is coming to separate the grain from the husks. His harvest basket is in his hands. He will store the good grain in his barn, but the husks he will burn away with a fire no one can put out."

They shook their heads, turned and walked away, with no more questions.

He Shows Goodwill strengthened the hearts of the people with his words as he continued to tell them about Creator's Good News. These things took place in Bethabara at the Jordan River.

Creator Sets Free Comes Forward

The time had come for Creator Sets Free to show himself to all the people. He was now a full grown man of about thirty years. He came from Galilee to the Jordan River, to have He Shows Goodwill perform the purification ceremony.

Creator Sets Free waded out into the water and stood before him, but He Shows Goodwill tried to stop him. "Why are you coming to me?" he said humbly. "I am the one who should come to you."

"This is the way it should be, for now," Creator Sets Free answered. "It is the right thing to do, to bring honor to the Great Spirit."

He agreed to perform the ceremony. As soon as Creator Sets Free came up from the water he saw the sky open. The Spirit of Creator came down like a dove and rested on him. A voice from the sky spoke like distant thunder, "This is my Much Loved Son who makes my heart glad!"

His Vision Quest

Creator Sets Free was now filled with *the power of* the Holy Spirit. He followed the guidance of the Spirit who took him into the desert wilderness, a dry and lonely place filled with wild animals and many dangers. There he would be tested by the ancient evil serpent.[35]

In the story of creation, the first man and woman lived in a Garden of Beauty and Harmony. A sly and crafty serpent came to them and twisted the words of the Great Spirit to deceive them. They listened to the serpent, lost the life of beauty and harmony and fell under the curse of death—both physical and spiritual. This serpent is a spirit being who opposes the good things Creator wants for all human beings.

For forty days and nights Creator Sets Free ate nothing. His body became weak and his hunger grew strong.

When the evil serpent *saw that Creator Sets Free was weak and hungry, he* came to him *and whispered in his ear,* "Are you the Son of the Great Spirit?" *he hissed.* "Prove it by turning these stones into bread."

"It is written in the Sacred Scrolls," Creator Sets Free said, "bread is not mankind's only food. The food that gives us the good life is every word that comes from the mouth of the Great Spirit."

The evil serpent took him to the Great Spirit's Sacred Lodge in the village of Jerusalem. He set him at the very top, high above the village.

"Prove you are the Son of the Great Spirit and jump down from here!" the serpent taunted him. "Do not the Sacred Scrolls also say, 'His spirit messengers will watch over you to keep you from harm. They will even keep your foot from hitting a stone.'"

"Yes," Creator Sets Free said back to him, "but it is also written, 'Do not put the Great Spirit to a foolish test.'"

Once more the serpent took him to a high mountain and in a moment of time, showed him all the great nations of the world and their beauty.

"All of these can be yours!" the serpent said smoothly. "They were given over to me and I can give them to anyone I choose. If you will bow down to me and my ways, they will be yours!"

"Go away from me, you deceiver! For it is written, 'The Great Spirit is the only one to bow down to and serve.'"

The evil serpent *could think of nothing more to test him with, so he* slithered away, to wait for another time.

After that spirit messengers came to give comfort and strength to Creator Sets Free.

Grandfather's Lamb

On another day, He Shows Goodwill and the ones with him saw Creator Sets Free walking toward him from a distance. "Take a good long look," He Shows Goodwill said. "There is Grandfather's Lamb, the one who carries away the bad hearts and heals the broken ways of *all the people in* the world."

The crowd of people looked to see the one He Shows Goodwill was talking about.

"He is the one I said is greater than I, for he has always been first. The reason I perform the purification ceremony with water is to make him known to the tribes of Wrestles With Creator. I now know he is the one, because he who sent me said, 'The man you see the Holy Spirit come down and rest on will perform the purification ceremony with the Spirit.' With my own eyes I saw the Holy Spirit come down from above and rest on him."

The people stared at Creator Sets Free with awe on their faces as He Shows Goodwill finished, by saying, "With my own eyes I have seen that this is the Son of the Great Spirit."

Come and See

The next day, He Shows Goodwill was standing with two of his followers. They saw Creator Sets Free walking nearby. He said to them, "Look! There is Grandfather's Lamb." So they went after Creator Sets Free. When they caught up to him, he saw them and asked, "What are you looking for?"

"Wisdomkeeper,"[36] they asked. "Where are you staying?"

"Come," he said, "and you will see." So they went with him, saw where he was staying and spent the rest of the day with him, for the day was almost over.

The next day one of the men, Stands With Courage, went to find his brother, One Who Hears.[37] When he found him he ran up to him and said, "My brother! We have found the Chosen One!" So he took his brother to meet Creator Sets Free.

The Great Ladder

The next morning Creator Sets Free walked to the territory called Galilee, *which means Circle of Nations.* There he found a man named Friend Of Horses and said to him, "Come, walk the road with me."

Friend Of Horses was from the same village as Stands With Courage and One Who Hears, Bethsaida, *which means House of Fishing.* Friend Of Horses couldn't wait to find his friend Creator Gives and tell him. He *looked everywhere and finally* found him sitting under a fig tree.

"We have found him!" he said *as he ran up to him.* "The one the great lawgiver Drawn From The Water told us about, the one foretold by the prophets of old. He is Creator Sets Free, son of He Gives Sons, from the village of Nazareth."

Creator Gives *crossed his arms and shaking his head,* said to him, "How can anything good come from Nazareth?"

"Come," he said, "and you will see!"

When Creator Sets Free saw Creator Gives walking toward him, he said, "Look, a true descendant of Wrestles With Creator. There is nothing false in him."

Creator Gives was caught off guard, "How do you know me?" he asked.

Creator Sets Free *smiled and* said, "Before Friend Of Horses found you, I saw you under a fig tree."

"Wisdomkeeper!" Creator Gives answered. "You are the Son of the Great Spirit and the Chieftain of the tribes of Wrestles With Creator!"

"You believe me because I said I saw you under the fig tree?" he said to him. "Listen closely to this truth I tell you. You will see much more than this! You will see the sky open wide and the spirit messengers from Creator climbing up and down a great ladder. On the True Human Being[38] they will climb from the spirit world above to the earth below and back again."

CHAPTER THREE

His Great Task Begins

His First Sign

There was a wedding in a small village called Cana, *meaning Place of Reeds*, in the territory of Galilee. Bitter Tears, the mother of Creator Sets Free was there. Creator Sets Free and the ones who walked the road with him were invited as guests to the wedding. Soon after the celebration started they ran out of wine. *This would have been a great embarrassment to the groom and his family. So* the mother of Creator Sets Free said to him, *"Son, they have no more wine."*

"Honored woman," he said to her. "Why are you telling me this? It isn't yet my time."

But his mother, *like mothers often do for good reasons, ignored her son,* turned to the helpers and said, "Do what ever he says."

They looked to him and waited for his instructions.

There were six *traditional* stone water pots used for purification rituals, that could hold large amounts of water. "Fill them to the top," Creator Sets Free told them, "and take some to the head man of the feast." They filled the pots until they could hold no more and did what he said.

The water had turned into wine, but the head man didn't know this. He took a drink and called to the groom, "Everyone serves the best wine first and after the guests have had their fill, they bring out the watered down wine. But *even though you served good wine at first,* you have saved the best wine for last."

The great work of Creator Sets Free began at a wedding festival, with this display of his power. For the Great Spirit was giving his own Son, as his best and last gift, to show his great love to the tribes of Wrestles With Creator.

This was the first of the signs Creator Sets Free performed. When his new followers saw this display of his power, their trust in him grew stronger. All of this happened in the territory of Galilee at the village of Cana.

After this he went with his mother, his brothers and his followers to Capernaum, *meaning Village of Compassion,* where he stayed for a few days.

Crowds Begin to Follow Him

Creator Sets Free traveled throughout Galilee. He was teaching in their gathering houses, telling everyone about the Good Road. He healed every kind of sickness and disease.

The ones tormented with evil spirits were set free, along with people who suffered from seizures. He even healed the crippled and paralyzed among them. His reputation as a healer spread as far as Syria.

Large crowds from all directions began to go after him—too many to number! They came from Galilee, the Ten Villages,[39] Jerusalem, Judea and beyond the Jordan River. They would push, shove and crowd around him.

Seeing the Good Road

The time for the yearly Passover Festival of the tribes of Wrestles With Creator had come. Creator Sets Free made his way to the Great Spirit's Lodge in Jerusalem, the Sacred Village of Peace.

Many people began to believe in him because they saw the powerful miracles he had performed. But he didn't trust himself to them, for he could see right through them. He didn't need any one to tell him about human beings, for he knew the hearts of mankind.

A man named Conquers The People came to Creator Sets Free in secret at night. He was one of the Separated Ones and a head man of the tribes of Wrestles With Creator who sat in the Great Council.

Out of the shadows he whispered, "Wisdomkeeper, we know the Great Spirit sent you to teach us. No one can perform powerful signs like these unless the Maker of Life walks with him."

"Listen closely then, *and I will teach you,*" Creator Sets Free answered, "for no one can see Grandfather's Good Road unless they are born from above.

Conquers The People was surprised by this strange answer. He didn't know what to say, so he asked, "Can a man be born when he is old? Can he enter his mother's womb to be born a second time?"

"I tell you the truth from my heart," Creator Sets Free answered. "One must be born of both water and spirit to find Creator's Good Road. There is a natural birth and a spiritual birth. Are you surprised that I said to you, 'You must be born from above?' Everyone born in this way is like a breath of wind that blows

44

wherever it will. You can hear its sound, but no one knows where it comes from or where it goes."

"How can these things be?" Conquers The People asked.

The light from a nearby fire made the shadows dance about. Creator Sets Free looked gently but firmly into his eyes and continued.

"How can it be that a wisdomkeeper and spiritual leader of the tribes of Wrestles With Creator does not understand these things? Listen closely, I am speaking about things I know to be true, for there is only one who is from the world above—the True Human Being. If you do not believe me when I talk about things on earth, how will you believe me when I talk about the things from the world above?

"Do you not remember when in the desert wilderness, Drawn From The Water lifted up a pole with a serpent on it? This is what will happen to the True Human Being, so people will put their trust in him and have the life of beauty and harmony that does not fade away."

Long ago, when the tribes of Wrestles With Creator were wandering in the desert, they did not listen to the Great Spirit. Poisonous snakes came and bit them and many were dying. Drawn From The Water prayed for them, so Creator told him to put a snake on a pole and lift it up so the people could see it. When they looked at it they were healed and did not die.

Conquers The People remained silent listening to the words of Creator Sets Free.

"The Great Spirit loves this world *of human beings* so deeply he gave us his only born Son. All who trust in him, and his way, will not come to a bad end, but will find the life of beauty and harmony that does not fade away. Grandfather did not send his Son to decide against the *people of this* world, but to set them free from *the worthless ways of* the world.

"The ones who trust in him are released from their guilt, but the ones who turn away from him *to follow the ways of this world,* their guilt remains. For they are turning away from the life of beauty and harmony the Great Spirit offers through his Son.

"My light has shined into this dark world, but because of their worthless ways people loved the dark path more than the light. When they choose the dark path, they don't want others to see, so they hide in the darkness and hate the light. But the ones who are true and do what is right are walking in the daylight so others can clearly see they are on Creator's Good Road."

He Shows Goodwill Steps Back

Creator Sets Free and the ones who walked the road with him went to the nearby countryside in Judea. They stayed there and began to perform the purification ceremony as the people came to the river.

About a two day walk to the north, where there was much water, He Shows Goodwill was also performing the ceremony, at Aenon, *meaning Spring of Water,* near Salem, *which means Peace.*

Some of the followers of He Shows Goodwill began to argue with a local tribal member about the purification ceremony. They took their argument to He Shows Goodwill. "Wisdomkeeper," they said to him, "the one you told us about at the Jordan River is performing the purification ceremony. All of the people are going to him now."

"No one has anything," he answered, "unless it comes down from above. You heard me say, 'I am not the Chosen One.' I was sent to clear the way for him. Like a best man at a wedding, a friend who stands with the groom, I am glad to hear his voice. But it is time for me to step back and for him to come forward, for the bride belongs to the groom—my part is now over.

"I am from earth below, he is the one who comes down from above. I speak from the earth, but he tells us about things from the world above—and who believes him? But the ones who do believe know for sure that he speaks truth from the Great Spirit.

"The Son is the one who has all the fullness of Creator's Spirit and clearly speaks his words. The Father above loves his Son and gives him all things. The ones who trust in his Son have the life of beauty and harmony that does not fade away, but the ones who do not walk in his ways will not have this life. Instead, they will remain *under death,* which makes the Giver of Life angry."

Choosing the Best Part

After their time in the countryside of Judea, *where they were performing the purification ceremony,* they went to the village of Bethany, and lodged at the home of two sisters, one named Head Woman and the other Bitter Tears.

As was his custom Creator Sets Free sat down and began to teach. *The men gathered around him,* and Bitter Tears sat next to him on the floor listening closely to his words. *This would not have been proper for a woman of that culture.*

Head Woman was working hard to get the meal ready for the visitors. When she saw Bitter Tears sitting down, she walked up to Creator Sets Free and said, "Wisdomkeeper, don't you care that my sister has left me to work alone? Tell her to help me."

"Head Woman, O Head Woman," he said, "I know many things worry and trouble you. Set your heart on the one thing that matters. That is what Bitter Tears has done, and I will not take it from her."

He Shows Goodwill Put In Prison

He Shows Goodwill had begun to speak out against Chief Looks Brave, who ruled the territory of Galilee, because he was with his brother's wife. He rebuked him for dishonoring the sacred law of their people, and for many other things. One day Chief Looks Brave had him arrested, put in chains and locked away, adding this to his many other wrongdoings.

Looks Brave would have put him to death, but he knew the people honored He Shows Goodwill as a prophet. He also feared him, for he knew he was a holy man who walked in a sacred manner, so he kept him safely locked away. From time to time Looks Brave liked to sit and listen to He Shows Goodwill, even though his words troubled him.

Many people were beginning to walk the road with Creator Sets Free and were coming to him, *at the Jordan river,* for the purification ceremony, although it wasn't him but his followers who were performing the ceremony. He now had more followers than He Shows Goodwill.

When Creator Sets Free found out the Separated Ones knew of this, and when he heard that He Shows Goodwill was imprisoned, he left that place to return to Galilee.

On the way he had to travel through the territory of Samaria.

Many of the people of Samaria were mixed bloods and despised by the tribes of Wrestles With Creator. They had their own Sacred Lodge and ceremonies and didn't respect the tribal members or consider Jerusalem to be a holy place. Both of them would go out of their way to keep from having contact with the other.

Living Water For a Samaritan Woman

The sun was beating down from high above the head of Creator Sets Free as he journeyed through Samaria. He became weary and stopped to rest by a watering hole near the place called Sychar, *which means Village Burial Site.* This was the ancient watering hole of Heel Grabber. It was on a piece of land Heel Grabber had passed down to his son, He Gives Sons.

Creator Sets Free sat down to rest about the sixth hour of the day, while the ones who walked the road with him went to the nearby village to find some food. A Samaritan woman came to the well to draw water, *at the time of day when no else would be there.* But Creator Sets Free saw the woman and said to her, "Would you give me some water to drink?"

The woman did not know what to say, *because a traditional man would never speak to a woman in public,* and because the tribes of Wrestles With Creator have no dealings with the Samaritans.

She found her voice and asked, "Why would you ask me for a drink, seeing I am a woman and a Samaritan?"

"If you only knew about Creator's good gift," he answered, "and who it is that asks you for a drink, you would ask him for living water and he would give it to you."

She said to him, "This watering hole is deep, and you have no way to draw out the water. Where will you get this living water? Are you greater than our ancestor Heel Grabber, who gave us this well, and was the first to drink from it with his children and animals?"

"The ones who drink from this well, will thirst again," he answered. "But the ones who drink the water I give, will never thirst. This water will become a river flowing from inside them, giving them the life of beauty and harmony that does not fade away."

"Please give me this water," she said to him, "so I will never thirst again, or need to walk this long path to get a drink."

He said to her, "Go to your husband and bring him here."

"I have no husband," she answered.

"Yes, that is true," he said. "You have had five husbands, and the man you are with now is not your husband."

Her eyes grew wide as she lifted a trembling hand to her mouth. "Oh! I see—you are a prophet," she said back to him. "Our ancestors honored and served Grandfather on this mountain. But your people say the only place to make our prayers and perform our ceremonies is in Jerusalem, the *so-called* Village of Peace."

This was a very old argument between the Samaritans and the tribes of Wrestles With Creator.

"Honored woman, trust my words," he said to her. "Your people honor and serve him, but in ways they do not fully understand. We honor and serve him with understanding, for the Good Road[40] has been entrusted to the tribes of Wrestles With Creator.

"But the time is coming when all who honor and serve the Great Mystery, will not need to do so in this mountain or in Jerusalem. The Father is looking for the ones who will honor him in spirit and truth—and the day for this has now come. The One Above Us All is spirit, and all who honor and serve him must do so in a spiritual manner."

"I know the Chosen One will come," she said, "and when he comes he will make all things clear to us."

Creator Sets Free *looked deeply into her eyes and* said, "I am the Chosen One, the one who is speaking to you now."

Just then his followers returned. They wondered why he was talking to a woman, but no one said to her, "What do you want?" or to him, "Why are you talking to her?"

The Harvest is Now

The woman left her water pouch, went to the village and told the people, "Come and see this man who knows everything about me. Could he be the Chosen One?"

The people of the village went out to find him. Meanwhile, the ones who walked the road with him said, "Wisdomkeeper, please eat!"

"I have food to eat you do not know about," he said.

His followers whispered to each other, "Did you bring him anything to eat?"

He knew what they were saying, so he said to them, "What feeds me is to do the will of the one who sent me, and to finish his work. It has been said, 'Is it not four moons until the harvest?' No! Open your eyes! The harvest is upon you now! The ones who reap the harvest are rewarded because they are gathering grain for the life of beauty and harmony that does not fade away. Both the ones who plant the seed and the ones who harvest will celebrate together. This is a true saying, 'one plants and another reaps.' I send you to reap where others have done the work of planting, and now you will join their work."

Soon the people from the village arrived. Many believed in him because the woman had said, "He knows everything about me." They asked him to stay, so he remained there for two more days. When they heard him speak many more believed in him. They said to the woman, "We believe now, not just because of your words, but because we have heard him ourselves. We now see that this is the one who will change the world and set all people free."

He Heals the Son of a Government Official

After the two days he continued on his journey to Galilee. The people of Galilee welcomed him, because they had seen the powerful things he did at the Passover festival.

He stopped at the village of Cana where he had turned the water into wine. At a village *almost a days walk away,* the son of a government official was sick and near death. The man came to Creator Sets Free and asked him to come and heal his son. Creator Sets Free *looked around at the crowd and* said, "Why do you need to see signs and wonders before you will believe?"

"Honored One," the man spoke with desperation in his voice. "Please come before my child dies!"

"Go home!" Creator Sets Free said to him. "Your son will live."

The man believed him and left to go home. On the way his servants met him and told him his son was getting stronger. He asked them the hour when this occurred. "Yesterday, at the seventh hour, the fever left him," they answered. The father knew it was the same time that he was told, "Your son will live," so he and his family believed.

This was the second sign Creator Sets Free performed in Cana, having come from the southern territory of Judea to Galilee. As Creator Sets Free visited the many villages in Galilee, the power of the Holy Spirit was resting on him. Stories about him spread from village to village. He taught in their gathering houses and everyone spoke well of him.

But that would soon change.

CHAPTER FOUR

Early Opposition and Conflict

His Own Village Rejects Him

Creator Sets Free returned to his boyhood village of Nazareth. As was his tradition, he entered the gathering house on the Day of Resting[41] and stood up to read from the ancient scrolls. The head man handed him the scroll with the words from the prophet Creator Will Help Us. He opened the scroll and began to read.

He spoke with deep respect in his voice as he held the scroll in a sacred manner. His words were strong and clear and his eyes were bright and full of life as he read.

"The Spirit of Creator has come to rest on me. He has chosen me to bring good news to the ones who have nothing. He has sent me to mend broken hearts and tell captives they have been set free; to make the blind see again and lift up the ones who have been pushed down—to make it known that the Year of the Blessing Way[42] has come at last!"[43]

He rolled up the scroll, returned it to the head man and sat down. All eyes turned and rested on him, to see what he would say. *He looked around at them and spoke clearly and firmly,* "Today these words you have heard have found their full meaning." And he began to teach and share his wisdom with them.

At first they were amazed at the power and beauty of his words. *But soon the meaning of his words sunk into their hearts and the mood of the people began to change.*

"Where did he get this medicine?" they complained. "Who taught him to do these powerful signs and wonders? Isn't this the son of Bitter Tears and He Gives Sons, the wood carver? Aren't his many brothers[44] and sisters here among us?"

So he said to them, "I am sure you will say to me, 'Healer, use your medicine on yourself.' And you will say, 'We want to see you do the powerful signs we have heard about, here in your own village.' But the truth is, a prophet is given much honor except in his own village, among his own clan, and in his own house."

Those who were listening continued to grumble out loud, shaking their heads and rolling their eyes.

"Listen carefully," he said to them. "There were many widows in the land of Wrestles With Creator during the days of the prophet Great Spirit Is Creator. It was a time of great hunger and food was hard to find. It had not rained for more than three years. But Great Spirit Is Creator was not sent to any of these widows; instead he was sent to a widow in Sidon, *an outside nation.*[45] And there were many with an unclean skin disease in the days of the prophet Creator Saves Us, but none were healed and cleansed except for an outsider from Syria, *the head soldier of the enemy's army.*"[46]

The people in the gathering house were insulted and furious at his words. Together they herded him out to the village hillside to throw him off the cliff, but he slipped through the crowd and went on his way.

He was amazed and troubled by their unbelief and could do no mighty work among them, except to put his hands on a few sick people and heal them.

Ancient Prophecies Fulfilled

He left Nazareth and stayed in Capernaum, on the Sea of Galilee, teaching in their gathering houses on each Day of Resting.

Capernaum was in the territory of the tribes of Honored Dwelling and I Will Wrestle. The ancient prophecy of Creator Will Help Us had finally found its full meaning, "In the territory of the tribes of Honored Dwelling and I Will Wrestle, toward the great waters beyond the Jordan River, to Galilee where many Nations dwell; the ones who sit in darkness, where death casts a great shadow, have seen the light of a new sunrise."[47]

From that time forward Creator Sets Free began to speak out, "The time has come, the Good News is here! Turn back to the right ways of thinking. Creator's Good Road is close, reach out and take hold of it."

Fishing for Human Beings

Here is what happened at the Sea of Galilee, also called Lake of Gennesaret, *which means Village of Treasure.*

Creator Sets Free was walking by the shoreline when he saw two fishermen throwing out their nets. They were One Who Hears and Stands With Courage. He walked up to them and said, "Come, walk the road with me."

He walked a little further down the shore and saw two other brothers, Heel Grabber and He Shows Goodwill, the sons of Gift From Above. They were in the canoe with their father mending their fishing nets. He said to them, "Come, walk the road with me."

A great number of people pressed in close to Creator Sets Free to hear him speak the words of the Great Spirit. He was standing on the shore by the two fishing canoes. He climbed into the canoe belonging to One Who Hears and asked him to push out a little from the shore. He then sat in the canoe and taught the large gathering of people.

When he had finished speaking he said to One Who Hears, "Push out further into the deep water and throw in your nets for a catch."

"Wisdomkeeper," he answered, "we have been fishing all night and caught nothing, but because it is you who ask, I will do it."

They threw the net out into the water *and before they knew what was happening the net became heavy. They struggled with the weight of it and began to pull it in,* but the net was so full of fish it began to tear. They called out to the other canoe for help. The men came and began to pull in the nets. *Fish of every size poured into the two canoes* until they were so full they began to sink. When the fishermen with him saw what happened, they were filled with wonder and awe at the great catch of fish.

One Who Hears fell to his knees in front of Creator Sets Free. "Wisdomkeeper!" he groaned, "go away from me! For I am a bad-hearted and unholy man."

"Do not fear!" Creator Sets Free told him. "Come, walk the road with me, and from now on your nets will be full of human beings."

When they returned to the shore they left everything and began to walk the road with him. Gift From Above and the hired men in the canoe, watched as his two sons dropped their nets and walked away to become followers of Creator Sets Free.

What New Medicine is This?

On the following Day of Rest, he took the ones who walked the road with him to the gathering house at Capernaum and began to teach the people. Suddenly, a man controlled by an unclean spirit cried out loud, "AAAIIIEEE! Creator Sets Free from Nazareth. What are you doing here? Have you come to put an end to us? I know who you are! You are the Holy One from the Great Spirit!"

Creator Sets Free rebuked him, "Be silent!" he said. "Come out of him!" The unclean spirit shook the man, threw him to the ground and howling with a loud voice, came out of him.

The people were in awe and began to ask each other, "What is he teaching? What new medicine is this? He even tells the unclean spirits what to do—and they do it!" They were amazed at his manner of speaking, for he spoke boldly as one with authority, unlike the other spiritual leaders. His reputation spread like wildfire into the territory of Galilee and to all the surrounding territories.

He Took Away Our Sickness

As soon as they left the gathering house they went to the home of One Who Hears and his brother Stands With Courage. Heel Grabber and He Shows Goodwill were with them.

The wife of One Who Hears was there. Her mother was sick in bed with a bad fever, so they asked Creator Sets Free to help her. He went and stood by her, told the fever to go, and it left! Then he took her by the hand and lifted her up—she was healed. *With a glad heart* she went to prepare a meal for them.

Later that day, when the sun was going down, many sick people were brought to him. He touched them all and healed them. Many were set free from evil spirits. As the spirits left them they howled with loud voices saying, "You are the Chosen One, Creator's own Son!" But he rebuked them, and didn't let them speak, for they knew who he was.

All this was done to bring full meaning to the ancient prophecy, "He helped us in our weakness and took away our diseases."[48]

One day, early before the sunrise, he found a quiet, out of the way place to be alone and pray. His closest followers found him and said, "Everyone is looking for you!"

He said to them, "It's time to go to the other villages and tell them the Good News."

But the crowds found him again and would not let him go. He said to them, "I was sent to tell about the Great Spirit's Good Road. You must let me go to other villages, so they can also hear."

A Man With Skin Disease is Cleansed

While he was in one of these villages, a man with a skin disease all over his body came to Creator Sets Free. He humbled himself, bowed down and pleaded with him, "Honored One!" he cried. "If you want to, you can heal and cleanse me."

Creator Sets Free, stirred with compassion, reached out and touched the man. "I want to!" he said. "Be cleansed!" And right away the disease left him and he was healed.

Creator Sets Free sent him away at once. "Tell no one!" he said. "Go and show yourself to a holy man and have him perform the cleansing ceremony given to us by the great lawgiver Drawn From The Water.

The man didn't follow his instructions. Instead, he spread the news about his healing far and wide. The reputation of Creator Sets Free began to grow among the people as word about him spread.

The crowds came from everywhere to find him. Soon, he wasn't even able to show his face in the local villages, so he went again into the desert wilderness to pray.

Spiritual Leaders Offended

On another day Creator Sets Free was teaching at a house in Capernaum. Word got out that he was there. The house was so full of people there was no more room, even the doorway was blocked. The Separated Ones and the scroll keepers had come from Judea, Jerusalem and all the surrounding villages.

The healing power of the Great Spirit was resting on Creator Sets Free.

Four men came carrying a paralyzed man on a sleeping mat, to bring him to Creator Sets Free, but they couldn't get past the crowd. In their desperation, they climbed up to the rooftop and broke through the roof. They lowered the paralyzed man down, sleeping mat and all, right in front of Creator Sets Free. When he saw their faith in him, he said to the paralyzed man, "Young man, you are released from *the things in your heart that are not true to the Good Road."*

The spiritual leaders began to grumble among themselves, "Who is this man to speak against the Great Spirit with such disrespect? Who but the Maker of Life can release a man from his wrongdoings?"

In his spirit, Creator Sets Free knew what they were thinking and said to them, "Why are your hearts full of dark thoughts? Is it easier to tell a paralyzed man, 'Get up and walk,' or to say to him, 'You are released from your wrongdoings.'"

The room became quiet as he waited for an answer, then he said to them, "This is how you will know that the True Human Being has the right to forgive bad hearts and wrongdoings on this earth." He turned to the paralyzed man and said, "Get up, roll up your sleeping bundle and walk home." Right away the man stood up in front of them and did what he said, giving thanks to the Great Spirit for his healing.

Great respect and awe filled the hearts of all who were in the house. They were saying, "Who has ever seen this kind of mysterious and powerful medicine." They gave thanks to the Great Spirit for giving such great authority to a human being.

Eating With Outcasts

After this he taught again by the lake shore. As he walked by he saw a tribal agent sitting at his tax booth.

Tribal agents were often tribal members who were given the right to collect taxes for the People of Iron. They could force their own people, under the threat of violence, to pay them. To make a living they would take more than the People of Iron required. But many of them became greedy and took even more than they were permitted. They were hated and looked down on by the people.

The name of this tribal agent was He Brings Together. Creator Sets Free went to him and said, "Come, walk the road with me." He got up from his booth, left it all behind, and began to walk the road with him.

He Brings Together hosted a great feast for Creator Sets Free. *He invited all his friends to come.* Tribal agents were there and many outcasts from the village. They were all sitting at the table with Creator Sets Free.

The Separated Ones called certain people outcasts. They used their strict interpretation of the law as a way to point them out. These outcasts were not permitted to enter the gathering houses. They were looked down on and despised by the Separated Ones. Outcasts included tribal agents, prostitutes, people who ate and drank too much, the ones with diseases that made them ceremonially unclean, and anyone who was not a member of the tribes of Wrestles With Creator.

When the Separated Ones saw Creator Sets Free eating with outcasts, they complained to his followers saying, "Why does your wisdomkeeper keep company with outcasts?"

Creator Sets Free overheard them and said, "People who are well do not need medicine. I have come for the ones who can see they need help, not for the ones who think they don't."

New Skins for New Medicine

It was a common practice, among the tribal people, to go without food for prayer and other spiritual reasons. Sometimes it was done out of sadness and sorrow for a friend or a family member's troubles.

Some of the followers of He Shows Goodwill and the Separated Ones were going without food, so they asked Creator Sets Free this question, "Why do your followers feast, instead of going without food, and praying often, like we do?"

A gentle smile came across the face of Creator Sets Free, and with a sigh, he answered them, "Do you expect wedding guests to be sad and go without eating when the groom is hosting a feast? The time will come when he is gone, then they will be sad and go without eating."

They still didn't understand, so he said to them, "No one uses a new piece of cloth to patch an old garment, it would shrink and make the tear worse. No one puts new wine into an old wineskin, for the new wine would burst the skins. New and fresh wineskins are what is needed, but the ones who have a taste for the old don't want the new."

He said this to show that the old ways of the spiritual leaders did not reflect the beauty of the new way he was bringing.

Chief of the Day of Resting

On another Day of Resting, Creator Sets Free and his followers were walking through a field of grain. The men were hungry, so they plucked some grain, rubbed the husks off in their hands and began to eat. When the Separated Ones saw what they were doing, they said to him, "Why do your followers do what is not permitted on the Day of Resting?"

He answered them, "Have you not heard about the time long ago when the great chief, Much Loved One, was hungry? How he and his followers went into the Sacred Lodge and ate the ceremonial bread? Only the holy men are allowed to eat this bread.

"Have you not read in the great law that the holy men who perform the ceremonies in the Sacred Lodge are permitted to ignore the sacredness of the Day of Resting—without blame?

"Listen to me! The one standing before you is greater than the Sacred Lodge! If you understood this saying, 'I want compassion, not ceremonial offerings,' you would not have blamed the innocent.

"Human beings were not made for the Day of Resting. Instead, the Day of Resting was made for human beings. The True Human Being is chief over the Day of Resting!"

Human Beings or the Day of Resting?

Creator Sets Free went to their gathering house to teach. A man was there with a shriveled and useless hand. The Separated Ones kept a close eye on Creator Sets Free to see if he would heal the man, so they could accuse him. *Testing him* they asked, "Is it permitted to heal on the Day of Resting?"

Creator Sets Free knew what they were scheming, so he said to the man, "Come, stand here, where everyone can see you." So the man did what he said. Then Creator Sets Free asked them, "On the Day of Resting, is it permitted to help or to harm, to rescue or destroy?" They just looked at him and said nothing.

There was fire in his eyes as he looked around the room. His anger turned to sorrow when he saw their hearts of stone. He turned to the man and said, "Stretch out your hand." He stretched it out and it was the same as his good hand!

Creator Sets Free rebuked them, "Is there anyone here who would not help his sheep out of a ditch it fell into, even on the Day of Resting? Are human beings worth less than sheep? That is why it is permitted to do good on the Day of Resting!"

The Separated Ones stormed out in a fit of rage. They went straight to the Friends of Chief Looks Brave[49] to conspire with them about what to do with Creator Sets Free. But he knew their plans, so he left that place. A large number of people went with him and he healed all who were sick.

Grandfather's Chosen Servant

Creator Sets Free and the ones who walked the road with him went to the seaside. Word about him drew large crowds from Galilee, Judea, Jerusalem, and the territory beyond the Jordan River. He asked his followers to keep a canoe close by, in case the crowd pressed in too close.

His reputation as a healer made the sick desperate to touch him. When the ones with evil spirits saw him they would fall down at his feet and cry out, "You are the Son of the Great Spirit!" As he forced the spirits out he silenced them and then told the people not to tell anyone who he was.

Another ancient prophecy of Creator Will Help Us had now found its full meaning, "Here is the one I have chosen, who does all I ask and makes my heart glad. I have made my stand with him and love him as a father loves a son. My Sacred Spirit will rest on him and give him a message that will right the wrongs done to all people. He will not make loud arguments on the village pathways, *but will speak with humble dignity.* He will not break a bruised reed. He will not snuff out a smoldering fire. Everything he has promised, he will do. All Nations will hear of his reputation and put their trust and hope in him."[50]

Working on the Day of Resting

A short time later Creator Sets Free went *again* to the Sacred Village of Peace, to another traditional feast for all the tribes of Wrestles With Creator.

Creator Sets Free entered Jerusalem by the Sheep Gate, near a pool of water called Bethesda, *meaning House of Kindness.* There were five covered entryways, where a great number who were sick, blind, or could not walk or stand would lay. They were waiting for the swirling of the water. *According to tradition,* from time to time a spirit messenger would go down into the pool and make the water swirl. Then the first one to get in the water would be healed.

A man was there who had been ill for thirty-eight winters. Creator Sets Free saw him lying there. Aware that he had been sick for a long time, he asked him, "Do you want to be healed?"

"Honored One," the man answered. "When the water swirls there is no one to help me into the pool and someone else gets there first."

"Get up!" he said to the man. "Take up your sleeping bundle and walk." *The man felt his body begin to change. Strength surged into his legs and arms.* He got right up, rolled up his bundle and walked.

Creator Sets Free healed this man on the Day of Resting. The strict, traditional tribal members saw the man carrying his bundle. "It is the Day of Resting," they said to him. "You are not permitted to carry your sleeping bundle."

He said to them, "The one who healed me told me to take up my bundle and walk."

"Who is the man who told you this?" they asked. But the man who was healed didn't know who he was. Creator Sets Free had left because too many people were there.

Later on, Creator Sets Free saw the man in the Sacred Lodge. "Look! You are healed," he said to him. "Now that you have been set free, do not use your freedom to walk a path that leads to brokenness."

The man went back to the strict traditional people and told them it was Creator Sets Free who had made him well again. Because of this the spiritual leaders were giving Creator Sets Free trouble and wanted to put him to death, because he was healing on the Day of Resting.

Creator Sets Free made it clear to them, "My Father is working, so I am working also."

This made them want to kill him all the more. For he not only showed no respect for the Day of Resting, he also was making himself out to be equal with the Great Spirit—calling him his own father.

Equal Honor Belongs to the Son

Creator Sets Free continued to explain his relationship with the Father.

"Listen closely," he said. "The Son only does what he sees the Father doing, for the Father and the Son do the same things. The Father loves the Son and shows him everything he does. He will show him great and powerful medicine, things that will fill you with wonder. You will see the Son give life to whoever he wants and bring the dead back to life again—just like the Father does.

"The Father doesn't make the final decision about anyone. He has given that decision to the Son. He did this so all will honor the Son in the same way they honor the Father. The ones who do not honor the Son, do not honor the Father who sent him.

"Hear what I am saying, the ones who listen to me and trust the one who sent me, have the life of beauty and harmony that does not fade away. The final decision about their end has been made, for they have already crossed over from death to life.

"The time has now come when the ones who are dead will hear the voice of Creator's own Son—and all who hear it will live. Just as all life comes from the Father, in the same way he has made all life come from the Son.

"Listen closely, the final decision about everyone has been given to the Son, because he is the True Human Being.

"Don't look so surprised! For the day is dawning when the dead and buried will hear his voice and come out of their graves. The ones who have done good will rise to a new life, but the ones who do what has no worth will rise to a bad end.

The Father and the Son

"I do nothing on my own, and listen before I make decisions. What I choose is right because I am not seeking my own way, but the way of the one who sent me. If I am the only one who speaks for myself then my words are empty, but there is another who speaks for me, and what he says is true.

"You sent messengers to He Shows Goodwill and he told you the truth about me, but I do not need a human being to speak for me. He Shows Goodwill shined like a burning torch and for a short time you were glad to walk in his light. Now, to be set free from your broken ways, you must listen to me. My words carry more weight than his, and are proven by the things I do. I have done the things the Father sent me to do. That is all the proof that is needed.

"The Father is the one who sent me, and he is the one who speaks for me. But, since you have never seen his form or heard his voice, you do not trust the one he sent, so his words take no root in you.

"You search the Sacred Scrolls, for you think they will give you the life *you want*—but they tell my story. Why do you refuse to come to me for the life of beauty and harmony?"

The spiritual leaders had heard enough! They just shook their heads and started to walk away.

Creator Sets Free said to them, "I came representing my Father, yet you show me no respect. But I am not looking for honor or respect from you, for you are empty inside and the love of the Great Spirit has no place in you. But you will honor the one who comes representing himself. If the honor you seek is from each other, and not from the only Creator—how will you believe?

"I have not come to tell the Father how wrong you are. It is Drawn From The Water, the one you have put your hope in, who will do this. If you trust him, then you should trust me, for he told my story. But if you do not believe his words, how will you ever believe mine?"

But the spiritual leaders would not listen to him and turned away. After this Creator Sets Free returned to Galilee.

CHAPTER FIVE

The Good Road

He Chooses Twelve Message Bearers

The crowds were growing larger. The task of healing and helping this great number of people was too much for Creator Sets Free to do alone. He knew that he needed help from the ones who were walking the road with him.

He went by himself to a mountain where he prayed all night to the Great Spirit. In the morning, on the mountain side, he gathered the ones who had been walking the road with him. He chose twelve of them and called them message bearers.[51] They would walk close to him and learn from him, so he could send them out to tell others about the Good News. They would have the power to heal the sick and set people free from evil spirits.

Here are the names of the ones he chose.[52]

First there was One Who Hears and his brother Stands With Courage. Then he chose two brothers that he called Sons of Thunder; Heel Grabber and He Shows Goodwill, the two sons of Gift From Above. Next there was Friend Of Horses and Son Of Ground Digger along with Gift From Creator and He Brings Together, the tribal agent. Then he chose Heel Grabber, son of First To Change, along with Close To My Heart and One Who

Listens—called Man On Fire. And last of all Speaks Well Of, who later betrayed him.

Creator Sets Free, the twelve message bearers and a large number of his followers went down from the mountain to where the ground is flat. From all the directions, a great number of people came *to hear him speak and to be healed.* The ones tormented by unclean spirits were there also. Great power flowed out from him and healed them all!

Wisdom From the Mountainside

After healing the sick and setting people free from unclean spirits, Creator Sets Free went back up to the mountainside and sat down. His twelve message bearers and others who walked the road with him, gathered around him along with all the people.

When he saw their great numbers, he was deeply moved in his spirit. He knew they were pushed down with no one to help, and scattered about like sheep that have no shepherd to watch over them. He looked into their faces with great compassion, took a deep breath and began to teach *about the Land of Grandfather's Good Road.*

Eight Blessing Ways

"The blessing way rests on the ones with broken spirits; the Good Road belongs to them.

"The blessing way rests on the ones whose hearts have fallen to the ground; he will lift them up and give them comfort.

"The blessing way rests on the ones who walk softly and in a humble manner; the earth, land and sky will welcome them and always be their home.

"The blessing way rests on the ones who hunger and thirst for wrongs to be made right; they will eat and drink until they are full.

"The blessing way rests on the ones who are kind to others; their kindness will find its way back to them—full circle.

"The blessing way rests on the ones with clean and pure hearts; they will see the Great Spirit.

"The blessing way rests on the ones who make peace by living in the way of harmony; it will be said of them, 'They are the children of the Great Spirit!'

"The blessing way also rests upon the ones who are hunted down and mistreated, lied about and spoken against, looked down on with scorn and contempt; all because they have chosen to walk the good road with the True Human Being.

"When this happens let your hearts be glad and jump for joy; this is the same way they treated the prophets and holy people of long ago. You are walking in their moccasins now! There is great honor waiting for you in the Land of Creator's Good Road."

Four Ways to Sorrow and Trouble

Here is what he said to the privileged among the people.

"Sorrow and trouble will come to you who store up possessions for yourselves, for you have already had a life of ease.

"Sorrow and trouble will come to you who eat your fill now; you will go hungry later.

"Sorrow and trouble will come to you who are laughing about this now; you will have your trail of tears.

"Sorrow and trouble will come to you when others say only good things about you, for that is what our ancestors said about the prophets who told lies.

His Followers Are Salt and Light

"The ones who walk the road with me are *of great worth. As they walk the Good Road they are* the salt of the earth, *bringing cleansing and healing*[53] *to all.* Fire will test the salt in everyone, *for all ceremonial offerings*[54] *made with fire are seasoned with salt.* Salt is a good thing, but if it loses its saltiness how will it get its flavor back? That kind of salt is of no worth and is thrown out. Make sure the salt in you has a good taste, that you may live in harmony with one another.

"The ones who who walk the road with me are a light shining in this dark world. A village on a hill cannot be hidden. No one puts a lamp in a hole below the floor, or under a basket. Instead it is lifted up high on a pole, so all who are in the house can see it. Let your light shine by doing what is good and right. When others see, they will give honor to your Father—the One Above Us All.

The True Meaning of the Great Law

"When you hear my words you may think I have come to undo the great law given by Drawn From The Water and the words of the prophets. But I have come to honor them and show everyone their true meaning. I tell you the truth, as long as there is a sky above and an earth below, not even the smallest thing they have said will fade away, until everything they have said has found its full meaning and purpose.

"Any one who turns away from these instructions and tells others to do the same, will be looked down on, as a small-one, in the Land of Creator's Good Road. But the ones who do them and teach others to do the same, they will be looked up to as great-ones.

"I will say this to you, unless you have a better reputation than the spiritual leaders, you will not find the Good Road from above."

Creator Sets Free then began to help the people see the full meaning and purpose of the law and the prophets.

The Way to Respect Others

"You have heard that our ancestors were told long ago, 'Do not take another person's life,[55] for whoever does will have to give an answer for it.'

"But I tell you, every one who is angry toward a fellow human being will have to give an answer for it. If they speak with disrespect to someone, saying 'you hollow head,' they will face the tribal council. If they curse someone by saying 'you *damn* fool,'[56] they may end up in the Valley of Smoldering Fire.[57]

"If you are offering a ceremonial gift, and there remember that someone has something against you, leave your gift and go make things right. Then you can come back and finish the ceremony.

Harmony with fellow human beings is more important than ceremonial offerings.

"If someone has a complaint against you and takes you before the village council, work out an agreement before you get there. You know how to decide things for yourself. The council might decide against you and turn you over to the ones who have the power to put you in prison, where there is no way out until the debt is paid in full."

The Way to See A Woman's Worth

The women in the time of Creator Sets Free were dominated by the men and were often treated like property and looked down on with disrespect.

So he said to the men, "You have heard the saying, 'You must not have relations with anyone you are not married to.'[58] But I tell you this, any man who looks at a woman and wants his way with her, has already done so in his heart.

"This is not how the Great Spirit wants us to see our sisters. If your right eye sees in this way[59] then gouge it out and throw it away. If your right hand does harm to her[60]—cut it off and throw it away. It is better to lose a part of your body, than for your whole body to be thrown into the Valley of Smoldering Fire.

"Drawn From The Water has said if you put away your wife you must give her divorce papers.[61] Let me tell you why. Any one who puts away his wife, *without giving her divorce papers,*[62] makes her unfaithful *when she remarries, unless she was unfaithful already.* Then anyone who marries her is marrying another man's wife.

The Way To Speak the Truth

"You have heard the ancestors were told, 'When you make a solemn promise, you must keep it to honor the Great Spirit.' But I say to you, do not make any solemn promises. Do not say, 'I promise by the world above,' for it is Creator's seat of honor, or 'I promise by the earth below,' which is the resting place for his feet. Or 'I promise by the Sacred Village Of Peace,' for it belongs to the Great Spirit Chief. Do not even say, 'I promise by my own head.' Can you make even one hair on your head become white or black? Your simple 'yes' or 'no' is enough. To say more is *to speak with a forked tongue* like the ancient evil serpent.

The Way to Respond to Evil

"You have also been told, 'Take an eye for an eye and a tooth for a tooth.'[63] But I tell you, do not fight back. *Evil will not be defeated by more of the same.* If someone strikes the side of your face, turn to him the other side also.

"If someone takes you to council for your shirt, give him your vest also. If a soldier of the People of Iron forces you to carry his bundle one mile, *show the strength of your heart and* carry it two.

"Do not turn away from the one who wants to borrow from you. If someone asks for something, be generous and give it to them, and don't ask for it back.

The Way to See Your Enemies

"You have been told to love only your own people and to despise others as your enemy.[64] But I tell you, treat all people with love and respect, return blessing for cursing, do good to the ones who hate you, and send up good prayers for the ones who make trouble for you and bring you pain.

"This will show that you are children of your Father from above, who sends his rain on the ones who do right and the ones who do wrong. If you love and show respect only to the ones who do the same, what credit is that to you? If you welcome only friends, how are you different from others? Even tribal agents and outcasts do these things.

"I say to you again, show love to your enemies, do good to them and give without asking for something in return. Do for others what you would like done for you. In this way you will be fully grown children walking in the steps of your Father above, who is perfect in all his ways.

The Way To Do Good

"Beware of doing good just so people can see you, for then you will receive no honor from your Father, the Creator. When you give gifts to the poor and do good things for others, do not brag about it on the village pathways or in the gathering houses, like those who put on a false face, pretending to be something they are not. I tell you truly, they honor only themselves and they will get nothing more.

"But when you help others who are in need—do it in secret. Do not even tell your left hand what your right hand is doing. Then your Father who sees all things will honor you.

The Way to Pray

"When you send your words to the Great Spirit, do not be like the ones who love to stand up and pray with a loud voice, in the gathering houses and along the village pathways, hoping to be seen by others. They have their reward already. Instead, find a hiding place where no one can see or hear you and send your prayers to your Father in secret. He will see what you have done and honor you.

"When you pray, do not be like the outside Nations, who use empty words over and over again, thinking their many words will help them be heard. Your Father, the Creator, already knows what you need even before you ask.

The Way to Fast

"When you go without food to seek spiritual things, do not be like the ones who put on a false face. They hang their heads down and darken their faces to look like they are going without food. They only want people to notice them and think they are spiritual. Do you not see? They already have their reward. There is no honor in this. When you go without eating, put on your headdress and wash your face, so others won't notice. But your Father from above will see in secret, and he will honor you.

The Way to See Possessions

"Take care not to trust in earthly possessions that can be spoiled by worms, eaten by moths, or stolen by others. Instead, share your possessions with the ones in need, walking the Great Spirit's good path, where nothing can be lost or stolen. Then you will have a money pouch for the world that is coming. For where you store your possessions is where your heart will be."

Among the tribes of Wrestles with Creator a greedy person was said to have a bad eye and unable to see the Good Road. A generous person was said to have a good eye, full of light and able to clearly see the Good Road.

So he said to them, "Light shines into the body through the eyes. If your eyes are clear, your whole being is full of light, like a torch that gives light to your path. But, if your eyes are bad, then your whole being is full of darkness. If the only light you have is darkness, then the darkness is very great. Make sure your eyes are full of light and not darkness, then you will walk the Good Road with firm steps.

"No one can be loyal to two chiefs. You will have to choose between them. You will either hate one chief and love the other, or honor one and resent the other. You cannot be loyal to the Great Provider and to possessions at the same time.

"This is why I am telling you not to be troubled about getting enough to eat or drink, or what to wear. Is eating, drinking and clothing yourself all there is? Does your life not have more meaning than this?

"Look to the two-winged ones who soar on the wind. Do they plant seeds and gather the harvest into a storehouse? No! But the Great Spirit gives them plenty to eat. Do you not know he cares even more for you? Will worrying about getting enough to eat help you live any longer?

"Why do you trouble yourself with what to wear? Have you seen how the wild flowers grow in the plains and meadows? Do you think they work hard and long to clothe themselves? No! I tell you not even the great chieftain Stands In Peace, wearing his finest regalia, was dressed as well as even one of these.

"If Grandfather covers the wild grass in the plains with such beauty, which is here today and gathered for tomorrow's fire, will he not take even better care of you? Why is your faith so small? There is no need to say, 'What will we eat? What will we drink? What will we wear?' This is what the Nations *who have lost the Good Road* have given their hearts to, but your Father from above knows you need these things.

"If you will make Creator's Good Road your first aim, representing his right ways, he will make sure you have all you need for each day. There is no need to worry about tomorrow. Trust Grandfather for each day as it comes.

"Do not fear, for even though you are a small flock, it makes your Father's heart glad to give you the Good Road!"

The Way to Help Others See

"When you point out the faults in others, Creator will point out your faults. The way you treat others will come back to you, full circle. Release others from their wrongdoings and Creator will release you from yours. The amount you measure out to others is the amount that comes back, like a basket that has been filled to the top, shaken down and packed together, until it overflows.

"Here is a wise saying—how can a blind person guide another who is blind? Will they not both stumble and fall? The one guided cannot rise above his guide, but will be just like him—*blind.*

"*Think of it this way,* how can you see the speck of wood in someone else's eye when you can't see a log in your own eye? How can you say, 'Here, let me help you,' when you can't see that you need even more help? Stop pretending to be something you are not!

"If you will be honest about yourself, you will then see clearly to help others. Forgiving and *helping others in this way is a sacred task, but do not let your good be spoken of as worthless.*[65] Take care not to give what is sacred to the ones[66] who will turn on you and treat you with disrespect. For who would toss an eagle feather into the dirt[67] to be trampled on.

The Way to Enter the Good Road

"Here is the meaning of what I have been saying; whatever good thing you want others to do for you, is what you should do for them. This is the whole purpose of the instructions given by Drawn From The Water and the words spoken by the prophets.

"This is *Creator's Good Road,* a small gate and a narrow path that leads to the good life; only a few walk this road. But the gate is large and the path is wide that leads to a bad end—many walk this road.

"Some who walk this wide road represent themselves as sheep, but inside they are hungry wolves. Watch out for these false prophets. *How will you recognize them?* Do grapes come from a thorn bush or figs from thistles? Will a rotten tree give good fruit or a healthy tree bad fruit? No! Healthy trees give good fruit and rotten trees give bad fruit. When you see the fruit of their ways, you will know them. Trees with bad fruit are cut down and used to make a fire.

"The human heart is like a medicine pouch. The ones who walk the narrow road will speak from the good medicine stored in their hearts. The ones who walk the wide road will speak from the bad medicine stored in their hearts. For when the heart is full the mouth speaks.

"Listen closely, not everyone who calls me their Great Chief is walking the Good Road. On that day, when everything comes full circle, many will say to me, 'O Great Chief, did we not speak for you, force out evil spirits, and do great things all in your name—representing you?' But this is what I will have to say to them, 'Who are you? Go away from me, you who do what you know is wrong —for you never truly knew me'.[68]

"It is the ones who walk in my ways that will find their way onto the Good Road—this is what my Father wants.

Final Words

"The ones who listen to me, and walk in these ways, are like a wise man who built a lodge. He dug deep into the sand to find solid rock to build on. The rain poured down, the streams flowed, and the strong winds came. They all beat against the lodge, but it stood strong against the storm. Nothing could shake it, for it was built solid on the rock.

"The ones who hear my words but do not walk in these ways, are like another man, a foolish one, who built his lodge on top of the sand. When the storm came against it, the lodge crashed to the ground, and all that was in it was lost."

Creator Sets Free was finished for the day with his teachings and wise stories. All the people were amazed and had great respect for him. He was not like the other spiritual leaders and scroll keepers. He spoke with true wisdom and dignity, showing he had the right to represent the Great Spirit.

CHAPTER SIX

From Village to Village

A Soldier From the People of Iron

When Creator Sets Free was finished speaking, he came down from the mountainside. The large crowd of people went with him into Capernaum. A young boy who served a head soldier[69] of the People of Iron was sick and near death. The head soldier had heard about Creator Sets Free, so he asked some elders from the tribes of Wrestles With Creator to go to him.

When the elders found Creator Sets Free they began to plead with him to come and heal the head soldier's servant. They said to him, "The head soldier cares deeply for this young boy who is suffering and unable to move his body. He is a man of honor who loves our nation and has built a gathering house for us. He is worth helping."

"I will come and heal the boy," he said. *"Take me to him."*

They were not far from the house when the head soldier saw them coming. He sent some messengers to say to him, "Honored one, I don't want you to bring trouble on yourself by coming into my house. That's why I didn't come to you myself. If you will only speak a word, my servant will be healed. I too am a man under orders and have many soldiers under me. I say to this one 'go' and he goes, and to another 'come' and he comes. My soldiers do what I say."

Creator Sets Free was amazed at this answer. He turned to the large crowd that was with him and said, "I have never seen such great faith, not even among the tribes of Wrestles With Creator. He is only one of the many people, from all the nations, who will come from every direction[70] to sit in a grand lodge and feast with our ancestors. They will sit down with Father Of Many Nations, He Made Us Laugh, and Heel Grabber in the Land of Creator's Good Road. But the sons and daughters, for whom the feast of the Good Road was first prepared, will be forced out into the night. Outside in the dark of the night, they will howl with tears and grind their teeth together in anger and frustration."

Then he turned back to the messengers and told them, "Return to the house and say to the head soldier, 'Because of your faith in me, the boy will be healed.'" When they returned to the head soldier, they found the servant well.

The Son of a Widow

Not long after this, he and the ones who walked the road with him went to the village of Naim, *which means Harmony*. A large crowd of people trailed behind him. As he came near the village gate, he met a procession coming from the village. They were carrying the body of a young man who had died. The young man's mother was weeping, for she loved him dearly, and as a widow had no one else to care for her. When Creator Sets Free saw her he felt great compassion and said, "Don't weep, *Grandfather has seen your tears.*"

He walked up to the ones who were carrying the young man. *They stopped and waited to see what he would do.* Creator Sets Free reached out his hand and laid it on the young man who was dead. "Young man," he said out loud, "rise up!" To the amazement of all he sat up and began to talk. Creator Sets Free then gave him back to his mother. *Her weeping turned to joy as she threw her arms around her son and kept kissing his face.*

Great fear and trembling fell on the crowd and they gave honor to Creator and said, "A great prophet has been sent to us! The Giver of Breath has come to visit his people!" News about this traveled far and wide into all of the surrounding villages and territories.

A Spiritual Leader

A spiritual leader from the Separated Ones, named One Who Hears, invited Creator Sets Free to a meal. So he went to his house and joined the guests at the table. There was a loose woman in the village, an outcast, who heard that Creator Sets Free was eating with the spiritual leader. So she went to the house and brought with her a small pottery jar of sweet smelling oil. She came up behind Creator Sets Free and began to weep at his feet. Her tears fell on his feet and she wiped them with her hair. Then she kissed his feet and rubbed the oil on them.

When the spiritual leader saw this, he said to himself, "If this man were a true prophet he would see who is touching him. He would know what kind of woman this is—an outcast!"

Creator Sets Free *knew what he was thinking and* said to him, "One Who Hears, I have something to say to you."

"Wisdomkeeper," he answered. "Say what you will."

"Two men owed a debt to the same person. One owed him five hundred coins of silver, the other fifty. Neither of them had enough to pay him back, so he released them from their debt. Which one do you think will love him the most?"

"I suppose it would be the one who owed him the most."

"You have answered well." Creator Sets Free told him.

Then he turned to the woman and said to One Who Hears, "Do you see this woman? When I entered your house you did not offer me water to wash the dust from my feet. But she washed them with her tears and wiped them with her hair. You did not welcome me with a kiss, but this woman is still kissing my feet. You did not put oil on my head, but she has rubbed sweet smelling oil on my feet. I tell you, she is forgiven and set free from her brokenness, because of her great love. But small is the love of one who has been forgiven only for small things."

Creator Sets Free looked at her with kindness in his eyes. "You are forgiven!" he said to her. "Your faith has released you from your past. Go in peace."

The other guests at the table began to grumble to each other and say, "Who is this man who thinks he can forgive wrongdoings."

Women of Honor

After this Creator Sets Free began to walk from one village to another telling stories about Creator's Good Road. The twelve he had chosen were with him and also some women who had been healed and set free from evil spirits. One was Bitter Tears of the village of Magdala, who had been set free from seven evil spirits. Another was Woman Of His Goodwill, the wife of the head man of the household of Chief Looks Brave. And then there was Water Flower and many other women who helped out with their own goods.

All My Relatives

Creator Sets Free entered into a house and a large crowd gathered there. There were so many that he and his followers were not even able to eat. When his relatives heard about this they went to find him and take him away from there, thinking he had lost his mind.

As Creator Sets Free was teaching, a woman from the crowd raised her voice and said to him, "Creator's blessing way is on the womb that birthed you and the breasts that nursed you!"

"That may be," he answered her. "But a greater blessing belongs to the ones who listen to the word of the Great Spirit and walk in his ways."

When his mother and brothers found him, they were unable to get to him because of the great number gathered there, so they waited outside and sent for him. Word came to the people sitting around him, so they said, "Your relatives are here, waiting outside to see you."

"Who are my relatives?" he asked, as he looked around the circle of people. Then he lifted his hands toward his followers and said, "Here they are! The ones who walk in the ways of the Great Spirit are my relatives; my mother, brothers and sisters."

CHAPTER SEVEN

Stories About the Good Road

Hidden and Secret Things

The Great Storyteller was about to tell his stories to the people. He took his followers aside to help them understand the purpose of the stories. He said to them, "The prophets said long ago, 'I will tell many stories, stories of the ancient ways, things hidden since the time of creation.'

"So you see, the hidden things of old will be uncovered and the secret things of old will be made known. No one would put a lamp under a blanket, but would lift it up high on a pole for all to see. The ones who have ears to hear will understand."

The Stories Begin

Later the same day Creator Sets Free left that place and found a quiet spot to sit by the Sea of Galilee. Once again, people from all directions gathered around him. The number of people was so great that he entered a canoe and pushed out from the shore. The people gathered at the shoreline on the waters edge *and sat down to listen.*

The Great Storyteller began to teach the people using many stories about the Land of Creator's Good Road.

"What is the Land of Grandfather's Good Road like?" he asked. "What can I compare it to? What story will help us see its meaning?

Four Kinds of Soil

"Listen!" he said. "A seed planter went to plant some seeds and began to scatter them about on the ground.

"Some seeds fell on the village pathway, but people walked on them, and the two-winged ones pecked at the seeds and ate them all.

"Some of the seeds fell on the rocks where there was only a little dirt. The plants sprouted up quickly but when the sun came out they dried up because they had no roots.

"Other seeds fell into the weeds, and thistles sprouted around the seeds and choked the life out of them. None of these plants grew for a harvest.

"But some seeds fell on good ground, grew strong, and gave a harvest of thirty, sixty, and even one-hundred times more than what was planted. If you have ears, you will hear and understand."

Meaning of Four Kinds of Soil

After hearing this the ones who walked the road with him asked, "What is the meaning of the seed planter story?"

"If you don't understand this story, then how will you understand any of my stories?" he answered. "Listen closely and I will tell you the meaning.

"The seed in this story is the message from the Great Spirit about his Good Road.

"The village pathway represents the ones who hear but do not understand the message. The evil serpent sneaks up and snatches it away from them. Their faith never has a chance to grow.

"The rocky ground represents the ones who hear and receive the message with a glad heart, but because they have no roots, their faith is shallow and does not last. As soon as the message brings them trouble or opposition, they stumble and fall away.

"The weeds and thistles represent the ones who have heard the message, but they are too busy worrying about their earthly existence. This makes them stray away from the good road, wanting more and more possessions, thinking this will make them happy. The message is choked and their faith stops growing.

"The good ground represents the ones with good and pure hearts. When they hear and understand the message, they hold on to it and keep it safe in the medicine pouch of their hearts, waiting patiently, *with a quiet spirit*, until it grows into a harvest."

The Weeds in the Garden

Creator Sets Free told the people another story. He said, "Creator's Good Road is like a man who scattered good seed in his garden. But during the night, while his family slept, an enemy snuck in and scattered bad seeds in with the good ones. When the plants began to grow, the weeds also grew with them.

"When the helpers saw the weeds, they said to the man, 'Didn't you plant good seeds in your garden? Where did these weeds come from?'

"The man answered, 'An enemy has done this.'

'Should we go and dig out the weeds?' the helpers asked.

'No,' the man said, 'they are too hard to tell apart now. You might dig out the good plants with the bad. Wait until it is time for the harvest. At that time I will say to you, "First go and gather the weeds into bundles for burning, then gather the grain into my storehouse."'"

Meaning of the Weeds in the Garden

When he was finished, Creator Sets Free sent the crowds away, and went into the house where they were staying. The ones who walked the road with him went in with him and asked, "Tell us the meaning of the story about the good and bad seeds in the garden."

"The True Human Being is the one who plants the good seeds," he answered. "The garden is *all the nations of* the world. The good seeds are the children of the Good Road. The weeds are the children of the evil serpent, the one who plants the bad seeds. The harvest is when all things come full circle, and the helpers are spirit messengers.

"When all things come full circle, the True Human Being will send his messengers to remove the stumbling stones from the Good Road, along with all who hold on to their bad-hearted ways. They will be gathered into bundles and used to feed the fire of the oven. They will weep many tears and grind their teeth together in anger and frustration. Then the ones who are upright in heart will shine like the sun in the Land of Creator's Good Road.

"The one with ears, should hear and understand.

Separating Good and Bad

"Here is another way to see the Good Road. A large fishing net is let down into the great waters. Many different kinds of fish are caught in it. When it is filled up the fishermen pull it to shore. Then they sit down and separate the good fish into baskets and throw away the bad fish.

"It will be the same when all things come full circle. The spirit messengers from Creator will be sent to separate the ones who are upright in heart, *who are on the Good Road,* from the ones who have bad hearts. The bad-hearted ones will then be thrown into the oven of fire where they will weep with many tears and grind their teeth together in anger and frustration.

The Good Road Will Cover the Earth

"Here is another way to see the Good Road," he said. "It is like a man who plants a seed into the earth. Day or night, awake or asleep, the seed grows without the man knowing how or doing anything. The earth makes the seed grow without any help, first the stem, then the head, and finally the grain appears. Once it is ripe it is harvested.

"The Good Road is also like a man who plants a single grain of mustard seed, *an herbal medicine, one of* the smallest of seeds. But when planted in a garden,[71] it grows larger than all the other plants *and takes over the garden.* It becomes a great tree with many branches, large enough for the two-winged ones who soar in the sky to find lodging in its shade.

"Again, think of the Good Road like the yeast a grandmother uses when she makes bread dough. She mixes a little yeast into a large amount of flour. Then the yeast spreads throughout the dough causing it to rise.

The Good Road is of Great Worth

"The Good Road is like a hidden treasure a man finds buried in a field. He quickly buries it back into the ground. He is then happy to go and trade everything he has for that field.

"The Good Road is also like a trader in goods who is looking for the finest of pearls. When he finds one of great worth he trades all his goods so he can have it."

The Reason for the Stories

Creator Sets Free would only use stories like these to speak to the large crowds. He would tell them as much as they were able to hear. Then in private he would tell the full meaning of the stories to the ones who walked the road with him.

Later, when the twelve message bearers, and other followers were alone with him, they said, *"Wisdomkeeper, tell us again* why you use stories to teach the people."

He answered them, "To you the honor has been given to understand about the mysterious ways of Creator's Good Road. This honor is not given to those who are not ready for it. The ones who understand will gain wisdom and be ready for more—much more. But the ones who do not understand or walk in the ways of wisdom, will lose even the little they have.

"These are the ones the prophet Creator Will Help Us spoke of when he said, 'They have eyes that do not see and ears that do not hear.[72] Their hard and stubborn hearts have made their ears dull and their eyes dim. If they would only see with their eyes and hear with their ears, they could open their hearts to the Maker Of Life and he would heal them.'[73] This is why I speak to them in stories.

"The blessing way has come upon you, for you have eyes to see and ears to hear. I tell you the truth, there were many prophets and holy men who wanted to see what you see and hear what you hear, but never did."

Then he asked them, "*Now* do you understand the things I am saying to you?"

"Wisdomkeeper," they said, "we do understand."

He *smiled and* said to them, "Every scroll keeper, who has learned the way of Creator's Good Road, is like the head of a family, an elder who opens the medicine pouch of his heart, sharing wisdom that is both new and old; *bringing new understanding to the old ways.*"

CHAPTER EIGHT

Powerful Medicine

Power Over Violent Storms

The day was ending and the sun would soon set. Seeing how large the crowd was, Creator Sets Free said to his followers, "Let's cross over to the other side of the lake." They sent the crowd away, climbed into a few canoes and pushed off from the shore.

Tired from a long day, Creator Sets Free went to the back of the canoe, laid down on a soft blanket and fell into a deep sleep. *His followers let him sleep and continued to row across the lake. A dark and menacing storm began to move in quickly and the sound of distant thunder rolled over the waters. They paddled harder trying to get to shore before the storm hit.* But the storm overtook them and threatened to sink the canoes. They struggled to keep upright against the wind and waves, but water was filling the canoes.

In *desperation* they woke him from his sleep and cried out, "Wisdomkeeper! Don't you care that we are fighting for our lives? Help us!"

He awoke from his sleep, stood up and rebuked the wind and the raging water. "Silence!" he said *to the wind and the waves.* "Calm down and be still."

At his words the wind stopped blowing and the waves calmed down. Great peace fell upon the surface of the waters. He looked at his followers and said to them, "Why are you afraid? Is your faith so small?"

They were greatly amazed and trembled with fear. They *shook their heads and* whispered to each other, "Who is this man? Even the wind and the waves listen to him."

Power Over Evil Spirits

When they finished crossing the lake they came to the territory of the Gerasenes. As soon as he stepped from the canoe a man from the village was there. This man had been tormented with evil spirits for many winters. The people of the village had tried to capture him and tie him down, even with chains, but he overpowered them and broke their chains. He escaped, tore off his clothes and wandered about in the desert and hills, wailing and cutting himself with stones. No one dared to pass through that area.

The man saw Creator Sets Free from a distance, ran up to him, fell down before him and began to wail. Creator Sets Free said to the man, "Come out of him you unclean spirits!"

"Creator Sets Free, Son of the Great Spirit, what are you doing here?" the evil spirits cried out through the man. "Are you here to torment us before the time? I beg you to promise by the Great Spirit that you will not."

Creator Sets Free asked, "What is your name?"

"Our name is Many Soldiers,"[74] the evil spirits answered, "for our numbers are great. We beg you not to send us far away from here into the dark and bottomless pit. Instead, send us into the herd of pigs, that we may enter them." They said this because a large herd of about two-thousand pigs were feeding on a nearby mountainside.

"Be gone!" he said, giving them permission.

The evil spirits left the man and entered into the herd of pigs. Then the whole herd stampeded down the mountainside headlong into the Sea of Galilee and drowned in the deep water. The ones who were watching over the pigs rushed away, shaken and afraid. They went to the nearby village and told everyone all that happened.

As word spread, people came from the villages and the countryside to see for themselves. There they found the man who had the evil spirits, sitting quietly at the feet of Creator Sets Free. He was clothed and in his right mind. They listened to the story of how the man was set free and healed. This filled them with fear, so they begged Creator Sets Free to go away from their land.

Creator Sets Free and his followers returned to the canoes to depart. The man who had been set free from the evil spirits begged them to take him along. Creator Sets Free would not permit it and said to the man, "Return home to your family and friends. Tell them all the good and kind things the Great Spirit has done for you."

The man went his way and told his story far and wide in all the territory of the Ten Villages. He gave honor to Creator Sets Free for the great things he had done, and all who heard were amazed.

A Desperate Request

Creator Sets Free and his followers canoed back to the other side of the lake. A great crowd was already there, waiting for him at the seashore. A man named He Gives Light, the head man of the local gathering house, pushed his way through the crowd and fell down on his knees in front of Creator Sets Free.

"My little girl is almost dead!" he cried out urgently. "She is twelve years old and my only daughter. Please, I beg of you, come to my house, lay your hands on her that she may live and be healed!"

Creator Sets Free agreed to come and went with him. The crowd also trailed along, pressing in around him from all sides.

Who Touched Me?

There was a woman in the crowd who had been bleeding for more than twelve years. She spent all she had on medicine men who were not able to heal her, and she was getting worse. When she heard about Creator Sets Free she pressed through the crowd and came up close behind him. She reached out her hand and touched the fringe of his outfit, for she had said to herself, "If I can only touch his clothes, I know I will be healed."

She touched him and right away the blood stopped flowing and she felt in her body that she was healed. Creator Sets Free stopped, turned and looked around the crowd and said, "Who touched me?"

The ones who heard him shrugged their shoulders and began to look around, but no one came forward.

One Who Hears and the others said to him, "Wisdomkeeper, the crowds are pushing and shoving you. How can you say, "Who touched me?"

"Someone touched me," he said out loud. "I felt power go out from my body."

The woman knew she could hide no longer. She came forward trembling with fear and fell down at his feet. In front of all the people she told the story of why she touched him and how she was healed.

Creator Sets Free looked at her with kindness in his eyes and said, "Take courage daughter, your faith has made you well. Go in peace."

Power Over Death

As they continued on, some messengers from the home of the head man of the gathering house came. *With sad faces* they said to him, "There is no need to trouble the Wisdomkeeper any longer, your little girl has died." *The man's heart fell to the ground and grief began to creep over him.*

Creator Sets Free overheard and quickly said to him, "Don't be afraid, simply trust me and all will be well."

Then he sent the crowd away and only One Who Hears, Heel Grabber and He Shows Goodwill, his most trusted message bearers, were permitted to go with him. As they came near the house the sound of flute players along with weeping and great wailing could be heard. Creator Sets Free said to them, "Why are you making such noise? Do not weep, the child is not dead. She only sleeps."

They scorned and laughed at him, for they knew she was dead.

"Out of my way!" he said. Then he put them all out of the house, except his most trusted message bearers and the father and mother. He went into where the girl lay, took hold of her hand and said in his native language, "Talitha Cumi," meaning "Little girl, wake up!"

She drew in a great breath as her spirit returned to her body. She stood up and began to walk. Her father and mother stood there, amazed beyond words, *weeping for joy. Their little girl was alive!* Creator Sets Free had them give her some food. Then he told them firmly not to tell anyone what had happened. Even so, the story about this spread far and wide.

Faith In His Power

Creator Sets Free left the house of He Gives Light and two blind men went after him. They were calling out to him, "Be kind to us, descendant of Much Loved One." The blind men, *with the help of others*, went with him into a house, so Creator Sets Free asked them, "Do you believe I can make your eyes whole?"

"Yes, Wisdomkeeper," was their answer.

He reached out, touched their eyes and said to them, "Your trust in me will make it so."

They staggered back and rubbed their eyes. He had healed them. They could see! Creator Sets Free gave them a strong warning and said, "Tell no one about this." But *in their excitement,* they didn't listen, and told the news far and wide about what Creator Sets Free had done for them.

As Creator Sets Free went from there, someone brought a man to him who could not speak because of an evil spirit. When the spirit was forced out of him, the man began to speak. All the people were amazed and said, "In all the history of the tribes of Wrestles With Creator no one has ever seen this kind of powerful medicine."

But the spiritual leaders from the Separated Ones said, "The ruler of evil spirits gives him the power to do this."

He Shows Goodwill Doubts

Reports about Creator Sets Free came to He Shows Goodwill, who was still in prison. He sent two of his followers to ask Creator Sets Free a question. The messengers found him and watched as he healed the sick and diseased, gave sight to the blind and set many free from evil spirits. Then they asked him the question from He Shows Goodwill, "Are you the one we are waiting for, or should we look for someone else?"

He told them, "Go back to He Shows Goodwill and tell him about the things you have seen with your own eyes and heard with your own ears. The blind can see again, the lame can walk, the ones with skin disease have been cleansed! Ears that cannot hear have been opened and the poor have been told the Good News! Even the dead have come back to life again!"

Creator Sets Free sent them back to him with these last words, "Creator's goodwill rests on the ones who do not stumble and leave the path because of me."

A True Prophet and Much More

When the messengers left, Creator Sets Free spoke to the people, "What were you looking for in the desert wilderness? A frail reed blowing in the wind? Did you see a man in soft clothes? No! The ones who wear soft clothes live soft lives. Were you looking for a true prophet? Yes! He is a true prophet but also much more! He is the one spoken of in the Sacred Writings, 'Look! I am sending my messenger ahead of you. He will make a clear path.'

"I tell you the truth, He Shows Goodwill is a true human being. No one born of a woman has ever been greater, but now the smallest one who walks Creator's Good Road is greater than he is.

"The great law and the prophets spoke until He Shows Goodwill came. If you can accept it, he is Great Spirit Is Creator, the one the prophets said would come. From his time until now, Creator's Good Road has been proclaimed, but people are attacking it *and trying to force their way upon it.* If you have ears to hear, you will understand.

"This generation, what can I compare them to? They are like children at a trading post, teasing each other, saying, 'You didn't dance when we played the drum! You didn't cry when we played a sad flute song.'

"He Shows Goodwill did not feast, or drink wine, but they say 'He has an evil spirit.' The True Human Being comes feasting and drinking and they say, 'He eats too much and is a drunk, a friend of tribal agents and outcasts!' But wisdom can see right through the behavior of her children."

When the people and tribal agents heard this, they agreed that the ways of the Great Spirit are true and right, for they had received the purification ceremony of He Shows Goodwill. But the spiritual leaders turned away from the Great Spirit's plan for them, for they had refused the ceremony of He Shows Goodwill.

More Help Is Needed

Creator Sets Free continued to walk about and visit the villages. He taught in their gathering houses and helped people to understand about the Creator's Good Road. He healed people from every kind of sickness and disease.

When he saw the great number of people needing help, he was moved in his spirit with great compassion for them. He knew they were pushed down with no one to help, and scattered about like sheep with no shepherd to watch over them.

So he said to the ones who walked the road with him, "There is a great harvest in front of us, but there aren't enough helpers. Pray to the Great Spirit Chief of the harvest, so he will send out more helpers into the fields."

He Gathers His Message Bearers

He then gathered his twelve message bearers together to prepare them for the great harvest. He gave them authority over evil and unclean spirits, to force them out of people and to heal all kinds of sickness and disease. *They would now represent his Good Road as they went ahead of him.*

He said, "It is not the time to go to the outside Nations or to the villages of the people of Samaria. Instead, go to the lost sheep of the tribes of Wrestles With Creator.

"This is what I want you to say, 'Creator's Good Road is close, reach out and take hold of it!'

"Heal all who are sick, cleanse the ones with skin diseases, and force evil spirits out of people. Give away the things I have given to you and ask no price for your service.

Instructions for the Message Bearers

"Take no trading goods with you or coins for your money pouches. Take no traveling bundle, or extra clothes to wear. The ones who work hard in the great harvest fields deserve to be fed and cared for.

"Whenever you enter a village find an honorable person who will give you lodging. When you come to their home, greet the family with respect and bring your blessing of harmony and peace to them. If they receive it, stay with them until it is time to move on.

But if they don't invite you in, then your blessing of peace will return to you.

"If no one in that village welcomes you, or listens to your blessing words, then go from there and shake the dust from your moccasins. The truth is, on the day when the end of that village is decided, it will be worse for them than it was for the ancient villages of Sodom and Gomorrah."

He Warns of Hard Times Ahead

"Look and listen! I am sending you out like sheep into a pack of wolves, so be as crafty as serpents but as harmless and gentle as doves. Look out for men with bad hearts, for they will bring you before their councils, and whip you with leather straps in their gathering houses. You will be dragged before government rulers and will tell them what you know about me.

"When this happens, do not be afraid and do not worry about what you will say, or how you will say it. When that time comes, you will be given the words to say, for it is not you who will speak, but the Spirit of your Great Father speaking in you.

"Brother will betray brother, and parents will betray their children, even to death. Children will turn against their parents and put them to death. The time will come when all will hate you because you represent me, but remember, the ones who never give up and make it to the end of the road will be made whole.

"If they hunt you down in one village, go to the next one. From my heart I tell you, the True Human Being will come to you before you finish going through all the villages in the land of the tribes of Wrestles With Creator.

"Remember I said to you, 'A follower is not greater than the one he follows, and a helper is the same as the chief he serves.' If they show no respect to the Chief of the Lodge calling him Ruler of the Flies,[75] will they not treat the members of his Lodge even worse?

Do Not Fear Your Opponents

"Do not fear the false faces of the spiritual leaders. It is time to follow my example. Make your stand against their lies and shine the light of my Good Road on their dark paths. For the light shines in the darkness and the darkness cannot put it out.

"Have no fear, for they can only kill the body. The one who should be feared is he who can bring an end to your entire being in the Valley of Smoldering Fire.

"Two sparrows can be traded for a small copper coin, and five sparrows for two coins. Not one of these can fall to the ground unless your Father, the Creator, sees it. Are you not worth more to him than many sparrows? He knows the number of hairs on your head, so do not fear the ones who stand against you.

"When you represent me before others and I will represent you before the spirit messengers and my father. But the ones who disown me, will be disowned before them."

The Message Bearers are Sent Out

Creator Sets Free had finished instructing his twelve message bearers. He sent them out two by two, and then left to go to many more villages, to tell them the Good News.

The twelve went out into the Great Harvest, just as they were instructed. They told the people to turn their hearts back to the ways of the Great Spirit and to believe the Good News. They forced out the evil spirits and poured oil on the sick and healed them.

A Day of Sorrow

He Shows Goodwill was still in prison at the hands of Chief Looks Brave. Looks Brave had a new wife who wanted He Shows Goodwill put to death, but he would not do it. She waited for an opportunity and it finally came on Looks Brave's birthday.

A great feast had been prepared for a celebration. Many nobles, government officials and head men of Galilee were there. The daughter of Looks Brave's new wife came in and danced before them. All the guests were pleased. Chief Looks Brave was so pleased with her dance, that he made a solemn promise to her in the hearing of all his guests, "Ask anything of me and I will give it to you, up to half of all that I rule over."

She went out to her mother and said, "What shall I ask for?"

Now was the time! With a sly smile she answered, "Ask for the head of He Shows Goodwill."

The girl returned to the feast and said to Looks Brave, "Give me, here and now, the head of He Shows Goodwill in a basket."

He could not believe his ears! The heart of Looks Brave fell to the ground. He feared He Shows Goodwill, for he knew him to be a holy man, and that the people honored him as a prophet. He did not want to put him to death, but he knew he could not refuse her, because he had made a solemn promise in front of all the guests. He *reluctantly* ordered a soldier to have him beheaded. They gave his head to her in a basket, so she took it to her mother.

Now, when the followers of He Shows Goodwill heard about his tragic death, they came for his body and buried it properly. When they were finished they went to find Creator Sets Free, to tell him what had happened. When he heard how He Shows Goodwill had been put to death, he found a canoe and went off to a deserted place to be alone for a while. But the crowds of people went after Creator Sets Free and when he came to shore they were waiting for him. He felt deeply for them, so he healed the ones who were sick.

The Message Bearers Return

The twelve message bearers returned from their journeys. *They pushed through the great crowd and found Creator Sets Free.* They began to tell him all the things they had done and taught, but the crowd was pressing in around them, giving them no rest, or even time to eat a meal.

Creator Sets Free said to them, "Lets find a quiet place to rest." So they left in a canoe on the Sea of Galilee[76] to go to a deserted place, near the village of Bethsaida, to be alone. The crowd of people saw where they were going and ran by foot ahead of them, and were waiting for them when they arrived.

When Creator Sets Free saw the great crowd of people, his heart went out to them again. He saw that they were like sheep with no shepherd to watch over them. He welcomed them and took the time to tell stories and help them understand many things about Grandfather's Good Road. He also prayed for them and healed the ones who were sick.

He Feeds Five Thousand

It was late in the day and night was coming, so his followers said to him, "This is a deserted place and the day is almost over. Lets send the people away to the villages in the countryside so they can find food to eat."

Creator Sets Free looked around at the great crowd of people— over five-thousand! He then looked at Friend Of Horses and said, "Where will we find enough food to feed all these people?" He said this to test him, for he already knew what he would do. *He put his hands on the shoulders of Friend Of Horses and smiled.* "You feed them!" he said.

Friend Of Horses took a step back and looked at him with wide eyes. He wasn't sure if Creator Sets Free was serious or not. "What!" he blurted out, "How could we feed so many? Eight moons worth of gathered food would only give them enough for one small bite apiece. Do you want us to go and try to buy enough to feed them all?"

Stands With Courage, one of the twelve, *tried to be helpful* and said, "Here is a boy with five loaves of bread and two small fish, but how would that possibly be enough?"

Creator Sets Free said to them, "Have the people gather together in groups and sit down on the grass."

So they did what he asked. The people began to scoop up their children and belongings and gather together, some in groups of fifty and others in groups of one hundred.

Creator Sets Free waited patiently for them to finish. When they were all settled down, he had the ones who walked the road with him bring baskets and stand in a circle around him.

He took the five loaves of bread, given by the little boy, *and held them up to the sky.* He gave thanks to the Great Spirit and began to break the bread into smaller pieces and gave them to his followers to give to the people. In the same manner he also divided the two fish and they were given out to the people. Everyone ate until they were full!

When they were done eating he instructed them to gather the leftovers of fish and bread, so nothing would go to waste. It took twelve baskets to hold it all. The number of men in this great gathering of people was about five thousand!

The people began to realize what had happened. This was a powerful sign that Creator Sets Free had just performed. *They began to wonder who this man was who could do such amazing things.*

Like wildfire, the hopes and dreams of generations began to rise in their hearts and minds. They were saying to one another, "This must be the Prophet, spoken of long ago, who would come into the world!"

Creator Sets Free knew in his spirit that the people were about to take him by force, to make him their Grand Chief. He urged his followers to get into a canoe and sent them away to the other side of the Sea of Galilee. Then he left the crowd and went to a quiet place on the mountainside, to be alone and pray, for he knew it would soon be time for the yearly Passover Festival in Jerusalem.

He Walks on the Water

His followers were still in the canoe rowing across the sea. Darkness was beginning to creep across the waters. *Lighting flashed in the distance and the sound of thunder rolled across the sky.* A strong wind blew in over the waters. The waves grew large and pounded against them, *threatening to overturn the canoe.* They were pulling hard on the oars trying to make headway, but had only traveled part way across by early morning. They were still a long way from land.

Creator Sets Free came down from the mountainside and watched from shore as they struggled. He stepped onto the great lake and began go out toward them, walking on the surface of the water. He came near them and was about to pass them by. When they saw him, they began to wail and cry out in fear, for they thought it must be a ghost *or some kind of spirit.*

Creator Sets Free *heard their cries and* called out to them, "Do not fear, take heart, it is I!"

"Wisdomkeeper, is it you?" One Who Hears shouted back to him. "If so, tell me now to come to you on the water."

"Come!" he said to him *without any hesitation.*

With reckless abandon One Who Hears climbed over the side of the canoe and began to walk on the water toward him. *The wind howled and the waves splashed against him as he made his way toward Creator Sets Free.* When he saw the wind and felt the waves, fear took hold of him. He began to sink, and cried out, "Wisdomkeeper, help me!"

Creator Sets Free quickly reached out and took hold of him. "Man of little faith," he said. "What made you hold back and doubt me?"

The wind stopped blowing as the others welcomed him into the canoe. His followers stared at each other in awe and amazement. Even the miracle with the bread and the fishes hadn't prepared them for this, for their hearts were still too hard and stubborn to see clearly. They all kneeled before him, saying, "Truly, you are the Son of the Great Spirit."

He Arrives at Gennesaret

Suddenly they were at the shore by the village of Gennesaret. They climbed out of the canoe, tied it up and went ashore.

As soon as they came ashore the people saw them and recognized Creator Sets Free. They quickly ran to tell all the villages. The people came from all around carrying the sick on sleeping mats to where they heard he was. Wherever he went they trailed behind him, into the villages and countryside. They laid the sick down at the market places and begged him to let them touch the fringe of his clothes—and all who touched him were healed.

Looking for the Wrong Food

It was now morning on the other side of the Sea of Galilee where Creator Sets Free had fed all the people with the bread and fish. The people there began to gather at the shore looking for him, for they knew he had not left in the canoe.

They couldn't find him so they took some nearby canoes from some people who had just come across from Tiberias. They climbed into the canoes and crossed over to Capernaum.

When they arrived on the other side they found Creator Sets Free at the local gathering house. They came to him and said, "Wisdomkeeper, how did you get here?"

Creator Sets Free *ignored their question and* said to them, "From my heart I tell you the truth, you are not looking for me because of the powerful sign you saw, but only because you filled your bellies with food. Why do you work so hard for food that fades away? You should work for the food that gives you the life of beauty and harmony that does not fade away. The True Human Being will give you this food, for he has the Father's full approval.

"What does Great Spirit require us to do *for his approval?*" they asked.

"This is what he requires," he answered. "Put your trust in the one he has sent."

Bread From the World Above

"What powerful sign will you show us, that we should trust in you?" they asked. "What sign will you perform? When our ancestors were wandering in the desert they ate bread, just as the Sacred Writings say, "From the world above he gave them bread to eat."

"From my heart I tell you the truth," Creator Sets Free answered, "Drawn From the Water did not give you the bread from the world above. It is my Father who gives you the true bread that comes down from the world above. This bread gives life to the world."

"Wisdomkeeper," they said, "From now on give us this bread."

Creator Sets Free smiled, held out his arms to them and said, "I am the bread of life that came down from the world above. The ones who come to me will hunger no more, the ones who trust me will thirst no more."

He lowered his arms and with with a heavy heart he continued, "But even as I told you before, you have seen me but you still do not trust in me. The ones my Father has given to me will come to me. They are a gift from my Father that I will always keep.

"I came down from the world above, from the one who sent me. I came to do what he wants, not what I want. What my Father wants is for me to keep safe the ones he has given to me, and bring them back to life again when the circle is complete.[77] The ones who see who the Son truly is, will put their trust and hope in him and have the life of beauty and harmony that does not fade away. I will bring them back to life again at the end of all days. This is what the one who sent me wants."

Upon hearing this they complained, "Who is this 'Bread from the world above?' Is this not the son of He Gives Sons? We know who his mother and father are. How can he say 'I came down from the world above?'"

"Stop grumbling to each other," he answered. "No one comes to me unless they accept the help my Father gives them. I will then bring them back to life at the end of all days. The Sacred Writings from the prophets of old tell us, 'There will come a time when the Great Spirit will instruct everyone.' That is why the ones who hear and listen to the Father come to me.

"The only one who has seen the Father is the one sent from the Great Spirit. This one has clearly seen the Father. I tell you from my heart, the ones who trust in me have the life of beauty and harmony that does not fade away.

"I am the bread that gives this life. Your ancestors ate bread in the desert wilderness and they died. Here, standing before you, is the bread that comes down from above. The ones who eat this bread will not die. I am the living bread from above; the ones who eat this bread will live beyond the end of all days. And this is the bread that I will give as a gift to *all the people of* the world—my human body."

His words caused a great division among them, and they began to argue with one another. "*What is he saying?* How can this be?" they asked. "Will he give us his flesh to eat?"

"From my heart I tell you the truth," he answered. "The only way to have the life of beauty and harmony, is to eat from the human body of the True Human Being and drink from his blood. Then, at the end of all days, I will bring you back to life. My body is true food, my blood is pure drink. The ones who eat my body and drink my blood have the life of beauty and harmony in them, the same kind of life I have.

"In the same way the living Father sent me, and gave me his life, the ones who feed on me will have my life. The bread from above is not like the bread our ancestors ate—and then died. This bread gives the life of beauty and harmony that does not fade away."

These are the words he spoke to the people in the gathering house at Capernaum.

Many Followers Walk Away

When the ones who walked the road with Creator Sets Free heard this, many of them said, "These words are too hard to hear, who can even listen to them?"

Creator Sets Free knew in his spirit what was troubling them, so he said, "Do these words make you stumble from the path? What will you do when you see the True Human Being going back up to where he came down from?

"Life comes from the Spirit, not from the human body.[78] My words have the Spirit of Life in them—but some of you have no faith *in who I am*."

He said this because he knew, from the beginning, the ones who did not believe and who would betray him.

He then finished by saying, "That is why I said no one can come to me on their own, but only if they receive the help my Father gives them."

When they heard this, many who followed him turned and walked away. Creator Sets Free looked at the twelve and said, "Do you also want to walk away?"

"Wisdomkeeper," One Who Hears answered him, "who else would we walk the road with? You have the words that give the life with no end. We have come to trust in you and know that you are the Holy One from the Great Spirit."

Creator Sets Free said to them, "Even though I chose all twelve of you, one of you is an enemy."[79] He was talking about Speaks Well Of, one of the twelve, who would later turn on him and betray him.

CHAPTER NINE

Son of the Living Creator

His Reputation Grows

The reputation of Creator Sets Free *had spread far and wide, until it finally* reached Chief Looks Brave. Some were telling him that He Shows Goodwill had come back to life from the dead. Others were saying that the ancient prophet, Great Spirit Is Creator, had been seen again, and some said that one of the prophets of old had come back to life from the dead.

Chief Looks Brave was very troubled and wondered, "Has He Shows Goodwill, who I put to death, come back from the world of the dead with powerful medicine?" So he decided to look for Creator Sets Free, to see for himself who he was.

Man-made Traditions

Some of the Separated Ones and scroll keepers came to Creator Sets Free from Jerusalem. *They were still looking for ways to accuse him and make him look bad in the eyes of the people.*

The Separated Ones and many of the tribal people will not eat until they ceremonially wash their hands and forearms, following the traditions of the elders. They will not eat at the market place unless they first wash their bodies. They also follow many other traditions, like the washing of drinking cups, bowls, and even the benches they sit on.

Creator Sets Free and the ones who walked the road with him were eating a meal together. When the Separated Ones saw them eating without ceremonially washing their hands, they complained to Creator Sets Free and said, "Why do your followers not keep the traditions given by the elders and wash their hands before they eat?"

"Your false faces do not fool me!" he said *loud enough for all to hear.* "The prophet Creator Will Help Us was talking about you when he said, 'These people honor me with their lips but their cold hearts are far away from me. Their prayers are empty and their ceremonies are for show. The things they tell others to do are only rules made up by human beings.'[80]

"You ignore Creator's instructions and use your traditions to make yourselves look good to others. The great lawgiver told you this, 'Give honor to your father and mother,' and 'The ones who dishonor them should be put to death.' But your tradition says, 'If you give to the Great Spirit the gifts that were meant for your father and mother, you no longer have to honor them.' This is only one of the many ways you use your traditions to do away with the instructions given by the Great Spirit."

His followers said to him, "Don't you know what you said insulted the Separated Ones?"

"Every plant that has not been planted by my Father will be pulled out by the roots," he answered. He also warned them, "The Separated Ones are blind guides, the ones who follow them are also blind and they will both fall into a ditch. *You will do well to stay away from them.*"

What Is Impure?

Creator Sets Free then gathered the people around him and said, "Listen with your hearts and understand what I tell you. There is nothing you can take into your mouth that will make you impure. It is what comes out of your mouth that makes you impure."

Later when they entered a house away from the crowds, One Who Hears asked him the meaning of his words.[81]

"Why do you not understand?" he answered. "When food enters the mouth it goes into the stomach, not the heart, and then out of the body."—and so Creator Sets Free declared that nothing you eat can make a person impure.

"It is what comes out from the mouth, from deep inside, that makes people impure," he instructed them further. "From their bad hearts and broken ways comes things like the taking of lives, unfaithful marriages, shameful desires, stealing, lying and speaking against the Great Spirit. It is these things that make a person impure, not failing to wash one's hands."

He Heals the Daughter of an Outsider

Creator Sets Free traveled through the territory of Tyre and Sidon. He wanted to keep away from the crowds, so he found a house to stay in, out of sight. But soon a woman came to him who had a daughter with an impure spirit in her. She had heard about Creator Sets Free, so she came to him and fell down at his feet.

"Honored One, descendant of Much Loved One!" she cried out *in desperation*. "Have pity on me, for my daughter is tormented with an evil spirit!" This woman was from a nation outside of the tribes of Wrestles With Creator. She was a Greek, born in Phoenicia of Syria.

Creator Sets Free gave no answer to the woman. His followers begged him to send her away for she was bothering them with her loud crying.

He then said to the woman. "I was sent only to the lost sheep of the tribes of Wrestles With Creator."

The woman moved closer to him, she bowed down and pleaded, "Honored One, help my daughter!"

"I must feed children of *Father Of Many Nations* first," he said, "The children's portion would not be given to their pets."

"That is true, Honored One," she answered him, "but even the children's pets under the table can eat the crumbs that fall on the ground."

"Honored Woman," he said to her, "your answer shows your great faith! Go home to her. What you have asked for is done; she is free of the evil spirit."

The woman went home and found her daughter resting on her sleeping mat. She was healed, the evil spirit had left her.

The Crowds are Amazed

Creator Sets Free left and journeyed through the area of the Ten Villages. He came to the Sea of Galilee again and walked to a nearby mountainside and sat down.

The people who lived there brought a man who could not hear or speak right. They begged Creator Sets Free to lay his hands on him. So he took the man away from the crowd. When he was alone with him, he put his fingers into the man's ears and said in his native language, "Ephphatha!" which means "be opened."

A look of surprise came over the man's face as his ears opened. He could hear *voices and sounds from all around him.* He opened his mouth and as he spoke everyone could understand him clearly.

Creator Sets Free instructed the people to tell no one, but they spread the news far and wide. Everyone was full of joy, wonder and amazement. "He has done well!" they announced. "He even heals the ones who cannot hear or speak!"

When the news spread, once again great crowds of people came, bringing to him the lame, the blind, the injured, and many more. They laid them down at the feet of Creator Sets Free, and he healed them all. The crowds were filled with wonder and amazement, and gave honor and thanks to the Great Spirit of the tribes of Wrestles With Creator.

Four Thousand Fed

Creator Sets Free spent the next three days healing the sick and injured. People came from the Ten Villages and surrounding area where many Nations lived. The number of people had grown to over four-thousand.

Creator Sets Free said to the ones who walked the road with him. "I am concerned for all these people, for they have been with us for three days with no food. Some of them have come from a great distance, and if I send them away hungry they might lose their strength."

"This is a deserted place," they said. "Where could we find enough food to feed all these people?"

"How much food do we have?" he asked.

"We have seven loaves of bread and a few small fish," they answered.

Creator Sets Free instructed all the people to sit down on the ground. He took the seven loaves and the fish, gave thanks and broke them into pieces. He gave them to his followers and they set them in baskets before the people.

The people hungrily took portions of bread and fish and sat down to eat in groups on the ground. The baskets of bread and fish stayed full until they all had a portion to eat.

Everyone ate as much as they wanted, and when they were done eating his followers gathered up the left overs—seven baskets full! They had fed four thousand men and also women and children. After feeding them all he sent them back to their homes.

Blind to the Signs

After this Creator Sets Free and his followers got into their canoes, crossed the Sea of Galilee and went to the village of Magdala *on the west side of the sea.* When they arrived they were met by a number of Separated Ones and Upright Ones. *They had come from Judea to find Creator Sets Free and challenge him.*

"Show us a powerful sign from the world above," they demanded, looking for an argument.

Creator Sets Free was weary of their ongoing attacks, but as always he was able to answer them with great wisdom.

He *turned and looked to the west and* said. "When the sun is setting you say, 'The sky is red. It will be a good day tomorrow.'"

He turned to the east, looked to the sky and said, "At the sunrise you say, 'The sky is dark and red. Today will be a bad day.'"

He turned back west again, "When a cloud rises in the west you say, 'It will rain soon,' and so it does."

Then last, he turned to the south and said, "The wind blows from the south and you say, 'It will be a hot day,' and so it is."

Then he turned to the spiritual leaders and said, "You who wear false faces! You understand what the earth and sky are saying, but you are blind to the message of the season you live in."

He groaned from deep in his spirit and said to them. "Why do the bad-hearted and unfaithful people of today look for signs? I tell you the truth! The only sign they will be given is the sign of the prophet Wings Of Dove."[82]

Beware of Bad Teaching

After saying this he climbed into a canoe with his followers and went to the other side of the sea again. They arrived *hungry and ready to eat,* but they had only one loaf of bread, for they had forgotten to bring more.

Creator Sets Free said, "Be on the lookout for the yeast of the Separated Ones who put on a false face. Watch out for the yeast of the Upright Ones, and of the Friends of Looks Brave."

His followers tried to figure out why he said this. They said to each other, "Is it because we forgot to bring more bread?"

Creator Sets Free knew their thoughts. "Why are you thinking like this?" he said. "Why are you worried that you forgot to bring bread? Is your faith so small? Are your hearts still hard? Have you no eyes to see with and no ears to hear with?"

His words were almost harsh and frustration showed on his face as he tried to make things clear.

"Have you forgotten so soon?" he asked. "How many baskets of broken pieces were left over when I fed the five thousand?"

"Twelve," they answered.

"How many when I fed the four thousand?"

"Seven," they said.

His eyes pleaded with them as he spoke, "Then why do you worry about how much bread you have? Can you not see I am talking about the yeast of the Separated Ones and the Upright Ones?— not about bread."

They finally understood he was talking about the teachings of the Separated Ones and the Upright Ones, not about yeast in bread.

He Heals a Man Born Blind

They walked on to the village of Bethsaida. As they came into the village they saw a group of men leading a blind man down the road. They brought the blind man to Creator Sets Free and begged him to lay his hands on him.

"He took the blind man by the hand, *away from the crowd*, to the outside of the village. Creator Sets Free spit *on his own hand and rubbed it* into the man's eyes. He then laid his hands *gently* on him and asked, "Can you see?"

The man looked around and said, "I can see people, but they look like trees walking around."

Creator Sets Free put his hands over the man's eyes again, and when he opened his eyes a second time, he could see clearly. He then sent the man home and instructed him not to go into the village.

The Father Reveals His Son

One morning, on the way to the territory of Caesarea Philippi, after praying together with the ones who walked the road with him, he asked them, "Who do the people think I am? What are they saying about the True Human Being?"

They looked around at each other and said, "Some say you are He Shows Goodwill who performed the purification ceremony. Others say you might be one of the many prophets of old[83] come back to life from the dead."

Creator Sets Free lowered his voice and spoke with a more serious tone. "So tell me," he asked them. "How do you see me? Who do you say that I am?"

Silent faces stared back at him. They began to look at each other and some looked down to the ground. The moment of truth had come, but no one dared to speak. Then suddenly a voice pierced through the silence.

"You are the Chosen One!" One Who Hears answered, "the Son of the living Creator."

Creator Sets Free *smiled at him and* said, "One Who Hears, son of Wings Of Dove,[84] the blessing way has come upon you. You did not hear this from human beings. It was my Father who opened your ears.

"For this reason, I give you the name Stands On The Rock.[85] *Even though you are only a small stone, what you have said will be* the rock on which I will form my Council of Wisdomkeepers[86], and the gates of the Dark Underworld of Death[87] will not stand against them."

He looked around the circle at the faces of his followers as they listened closely to him.

"I am opening the ways of the Good Road before you.[88] Whatever you say yes or no to on earth will reflect the wisdom of the world above."

His words seemed to echo into the distance as they took in what he had said.

He then warned them not to tell anyone that he was the Chosen One.

Finding True Life

He then began to tell them clearly what was going to happen. "The True Human Being must go to Jerusalem, the Sacred Village of Peace," he told them, "where the elders, the head holy men,[89] and the scroll keepers will turn their faces from me. They will have me put to death, but I will come back to life on the third day."

Stands On The Rock *grabbed him by the arm and* rebuked him, saying, "Wisdomkeeper! Don't even think it! This must never happen to you!"

"Go away from me evil serpent!"[90] he said to Stands On The Rock. "You have become a stone to trip over and make me stumble on my path. Your thoughts are against the Great Spirit, for his ways are not the ways of human beings."

Stands On The Rock was stunned by the rebuke of his Wisdomkeeper. What could he say? He hung his head and stepped back as a crowd of people began to gather around Creator Sets Free.

"To walk the road with me," Creator Sets Free said as the crowd gathered, "you must turn away from your own path, and always be ready to carry your tree pole with me *to the place of ultimate sacrifice.* The ones who hold on to their lives will not find life, but the ones who are willing to let go of their lives, for me and my message, will find the true life. How will it help you to get everything you want, but lose the true life? Is there anything in this world worth trading for it?

"There are bad-hearted and unfaithful people living today, who are ashamed to make their stand with me and my message. The day will come when the True Human Being will show the power and beauty of his Father and his holy spirit messengers. On that day, he will be ashamed of these people and not make his stand with them. What they have done with their lives, good or bad, will decide their end.

"From my heart I tell you the truth, there are some of you standing here today, who before you die, will see the True Human Being coming in the power of the Good Road."

Listen to my Son Now

About six days later, Creator Sets Free took Stands On The Rock, Heel Grabber and his brother, He Shows Goodwill, up on a great high mountain to be alone and pray. They climbed high into the mountainside, and when they reached the top Creator Sets Free began to send his words to the Great Spirit. His followers, *worn out from the long climb,* fell asleep. While they slept, the appearance of Creator Sets Free began to change. His clothes turned white as snow, whiter than anyone on earth could make them.

His followers awoke and shook the sleep from their eyes. They stared in wonder at Creator Sets Free with his face and clothes shining. They also saw two other bright and shining men standing with him. It was the prophet of old, Great Spirit Is Creator and the ancient lawgiver Drawn From The Water. They were talking to him about his crossing over from this life to the next, that would take place in Jerusalem. When they finished talking, the men with him turned to go.

All his followers were afraid, not knowing what to do or say. Stands On The Rock spoke *without thinking,* "Wisdomkeeper!" he said. "This is a good place to stay. Let's make three teepees, one for you, one for Drawn From The Water, and one for Great Spirit Is Creator."

From above a bright cloud began to fall on them. Their knees trembled with fear as the cloud surrounded them. A voice spoke from the cloud, saying, "This is my much loved Son, the one who makes my heart glad. Listen to him!"

They all fell on their faces in fear, but Creator Sets Free laid his hands on them and said, "Do not fear! Stand to your feet." When they looked around, the cloud was gone, the men were gone, all they could see was Creator Sets Free standing in front of them.

As they walked down the mountainside he instructed them to tell no one what they had seen until after the True Human Being had come back to life from the dead. So they told no one, but wondered what this "coming back to life from the dead" meant.

During the long walk down the mountain, they asked him, "Why do the scroll keepers say that Great Spirit Is Creator must be the first to come?"

"It is true," he answered. "Great Spirit Is Creator was the first to come, and he returned all things to their original purpose. So yes, he has already come—but no one recognized him. They did whatever they wanted with him, just as the Sacred Writings foretold. It is also foretold that they will treat the True Human

Being in the same way, they will look down on him and turn their faces away from him."

Then his followers understood he was talking about He Shows Goodwill who performed the purification ceremony.

Help Our Weak Faith

It was the next day when they finished coming down from the mountain. A large crowd had surrounded the other followers of Creator Sets Free, *who had not gone up the mountain.* The scroll keepers were in the crowd confronting his followers with questions. When the people saw Creator Sets Free they were filled with excitement and ran to greet him.

Creator Sets Free made his way through the crowd and went right to the scroll keepers. "Why are you here?" he questioned them. "What do you want from my followers?"

Before they could answer him a man stepped out from the crowd and fell on his knees in front of him. "Wisdomkeeper!" he said *with desperation in his voice.* "I came here with my son to find you. He has an evil spirit that keeps him from speaking. He often becomes stiff and the spirit will grab hold of him and throw him to the ground, then foam comes from his mouth and he grinds his teeth together. I asked your followers to force this spirit to go from him, and they tried but failed."

"Your generation is bent and twisted—with no faith!" Creator Sets Free said. "How much longer will I have to be with you and put up with you? Bring the boy to me."

As they were bringing the boy to him the evil spirit took hold of him and threw the boy to the ground. The people struggled to keep hold of him as he twisted and squirmed. Foam began to come from his mouth *and the people moved away from the boy as Creator Sets Free walked up to him.*

Creator Sets Free turned to the boy's father and asked, "How long has he been this way?"

"From the time he was a child," the father answered. "The evil spirit has thrown him into the fire and into the water. Be kind to us and help us, if you can."

"What do you mean, 'If you can?'" he said. "Nothing is too hard for the one who has faith."

The father of the boy began to weep and cried out loud, "I do believe! Help my weak faith."

Creator Sets Free saw that the crowd was now pushing in closer to see, so he rebuked the evil spirit. "Spirit that makes one unable to speak or hear," he said firmly, "I tell you to leave this boy and never enter him again."

The boy wailed and his body twisted and turned on the ground as the evil spirit was forced out of him. The boy settled down and the wailing ceased. He became still like one who is dead. Some of the people said, "He is dead!" But Creator Sets Free took hold of his hand and stood him on his feet. The boy was set free from the evil spirit. Then Creator Sets Free gave him back to his father. The people were struck silent and amazed at this awesome display of the Great Spirit's power and might.

Later when Creator Sets Free was alone with his followers, they asked him, "Why couldn't we force the evil spirit out of him?"

"It is because of your weak faith," he answered.

"Wisdomkeeper!" they asked. "Please make our faith stronger."

"I tell you from my heart," he said to them, "if you had faith as small as a mustard seed, you could tell this mountain to move from here to there, and it would listen to you. You could also say to this sycamore tree, 'Come out by the roots and be planted in the sea,' and it would do what you say. Nothing would be too hard for you. But it takes praying and going without food, to make you ready to force out a spirit of this kind."

He Reminds Them of What is Coming

From there Creator Sets Free took his followers through Galilee. He stayed away from the crowds so he could take time to further instruct his followers. They were still struck with wonder at the things he was doing, *and were now sure he was the Chosen One who would defeat the People of Iron.*

To prepare them for what was ahead, he told them again about what would happen to him *in Jerusalem, the Sacred Village of Peace.* "Let these words sink deep into your ears," he said. "The True Human Being will soon be taken and handed over to men who will kill him, but on the third day he will come back to life from the dead."

But still they did not understand. The meaning was hidden from them. Their hearts would not let them believe what they heard with their ears. His words filled them with sorrow and dread, and they were afraid to ask him what it all meant.

Dues For the Sacred Lodge

Capernaum was the village where Stands On The Rock lived. Some men who collected the money for the Great Spirit's Lodge walked up to Stands On The Rock and said, "Does your Wisdomkeeper pay his dues for the Lodge?"

"Yes, he does," Stands On The Rock answered them.

When he returned to his house, before he could say a word about what happened, Creator Sets Free said to him *using his family name,* "Tell me, One Who Hears, do the rulers of this world collect taxes or dues from their own family members or from others? How do you see it?"

"From others," Stands On The Rock answered.

Creator Sets Free said to him, "So then, the family members don't have to pay, but to keep from insulting them we will pay. Go to the lake and open the mouth of the first fish you catch, and you will find a silver coin. Use that to pay the dues for both of us."

Who is the Greatest?

Another time, as the followers of Creator Sets Free were walking about, they began to argue with each other over which one of them was the greatest. When they got back to the house, Creator Sets Free asked them, "What were you arguing about as we walked on the road?" *But they just looked around at each other, not wanting to answer him.*

Creator Sets Free knew their thoughts, so he gathered the twelve of them together, sat down with them and said, "The ones who want to be first in line must go to the back and put others first."

"Then who is the greatest in the Land of Creator's Good Road?" they asked.

Creator Sets Free had a small child come to him. He stood the child in front of them, next to himself. "I tell you from my heart," he said to them, "unless you become like a little child you will not find the pathway onto the Good Road. The ones who humble themselves, like this little child, will become great ones in the Land of Creator's Good Road."

Then he lifted the child up into his arms and said, "When you represent me and welcome a little child, you are welcoming me. When you welcome me, you are not only welcoming me, but also the one who sent me. That is what I mean when I say, 'the smallest of all will become the greatest of all.'"

He then laid one of his hands *gently* on the child's head and said, "This world of sorrow and pain will make many stumble, but how terrible it will be for the ones who go along with it. It would be better to be thrown into the deep waters with a great stone tied to your neck, than to cause even one of these little ones, who trust me, to stumble on the path.

"Do not look down on them, for they have great value *in the eyes of Creator.* Their spirit messengers always behold the face of my Father, the one who is above us all."

Walk the Road With Me

As they traveled on, a scroll keeper came up to Creator Sets Free. "Honored One," he said, "I will follow you wherever you go."

He answered the man, "The foxes live in their holes, the two-winged ones who fly above us live in their nests, but the True Human Being has no place to lay his head."

Creator Sets Free turned to another man and said, "Come, walk the road with me."

"Honored One," he said, "let me first go home to my father *until it is time* to bury him."

"Let the ones who are dead bury their own dead," he said to the man. "*You are alive*, go and tell others about the Good Road."

Another said to him, "Honored One, I will walk the road with you, but first let me go home and prepare my family."

Creator Sets Free told him, "The ones who start walking Creator's Good Road and then turn back are not ready."

CHAPTER TEN

The Great Chief of the Harvest

Creator Sets Free Walks the Talk

His work on earth was coming to an end, and Creator Sets Free would soon be returning to the world above.

His most difficult task lay ahead of him. He knew he must make his way to Jerusalem, where he would be rejected by his own people and condemned to die a horrible and painful death. As he had told others not to turn back, he knew he had to finish walking the path his Father, the Great Spirit, had set before him.

So he *drew strength from deep within and* made up his mind to go to Jerusalem, the Sacred Village of Peace, and fulfill his Father's purpose.

The Great Harvest

After this, Creator Sets Free chose seventy men from the ones who walked the road with him. He sent them out two by two, to prepare the way for him in the villages he was about to visit.

He told them the same things he told the twelve when he sent them out, "There is a great harvest before us, but there aren't enough helpers. Pray to the Harvest Chief, so he will send more helpers. I am sending you to represent me. You will be like lambs walking among wolves. Take no traveling bundle with you, no trading goods, not even a second pair of moccasins. Go straight to the places I am sending you, waste no time greeting other on the way.

"When you lodge with someone, say to them first, 'Peace be to this house.' If people of peace live there, you will be welcomed; if not, your blessing of peace will return to you as you leave. Stay with the ones who welcome you, there is no need to move around from house to house. Eat whatever they set before you, for the ones who work hard are worth feeding. Offer healing prayers for any who are sick, and say to them, 'Creator's Good Road has come close to you.'

"If you enter a village and no one welcomes you, go into the village pathways and say, 'We must wipe the dust of your village from our *clothes* as a sign against you, for Creator's Good Road has come close to you, *but you would not welcome it.'* I tell you the truth, that village will face a worse end than the village of Sodom, on the day when their end is decided.

"The ones who welcome you, welcome me. The ones who send you away are sending me away. The ones who send me away, send away the one who sent me."

The Danger of Rejecting His Message

Creator Sets Free began to warn about what would happen to the villages that saw his greatest signs and wonders, but did not receive his message.

"Sorrow and trouble will come to you Chorazin, *O Village of Secrets,* and the same for you Bethsaida, *O House of Fishing.* If the ancient villages of Tyre—*the Rock,* and Sidon—*the Hunting Grounds,* had seen the powerful signs you have seen, they would have turned their hearts back to Creator's ways. It will be worse for you in the day when you face your end.

"As for you Capernaum, *O Village of Comfort,* do you think you will be lifted up to the world above? No! You will be brought down low, to the Dark Underworld of Death. Long ago the people of the village of Sodom—*the Burning Place*, would have thrown dirt and ashes on their heads and turned their hearts back to the Maker of Life, if they had seen the powerful signs you have seen. The day of their end will be better than yours."

So, after he said these things the seventy went out, two by two, to all the villages.

The Wrong Spirit to Follow

Creator Sets Free sent some other messengers ahead to Samaria to find lodging, but the people of Samaria would not welcome him, for they knew he was on his way to Jerusalem *and wanted nothing to do with the people there.*

When Heel Grabber and He Shows Goodwill found out he was not welcome there, they said, "Wisdomkeeper, do you want us to call down fire from above to burn them up, like the prophet Great Spirit Is Creator did?"

Creator Sets Free rebuked them, "You do not know what spirit you are listening to, for the True Human Being came to help people, not hurt them."

After that, they walked *silently* with him toward another village.

Welcome the Gifts Others Bring

On the way, He Shows Goodwill *came close to him and* said, "Wisdomkeeper, we saw a man forcing out evil spirits using your name. We told him to stop, because he doesn't walk the road with us."

"Do not stop him," Creator Sets Free told them. "No one who can do works of power in my name will suddenly turn against me. The ones who are not against us are for us. The ones who welcome my message bearers, welcome me. The ones who welcome me, welcome the one who sent me.

"If you welcome a prophet for who he is, you will receive the gifting he brings. If you welcome a good hearted person for who he is, you will receive the good that he brings.

"Listen closely, even a drink of water, given to the least of the ones who walk my road, is of great value. What is done for them will never be lost."

The Road of Forgiveness

Creator Sets Free then began to teach his followers how to walk the Good Road when there is conflict with others.

"Guard your hearts *in your dealings with one another and always be ready to forgive.* If your brother or sister wrongs you, go to them alone and tell them. If they listen, then you have won them back. If they cannot see the wrong, then go with others who have seen it, at least two or three, so they will also hear them. If they still will not listen, take them before the village council.[91] If they will not hear the village council, then they will be the same to you as an outcast or a tribal agent. *You have lost your brother or sister, but still treat them with the same dignity and respect you have seen from me.*

"For It takes two or three, who have seen with their own eyes, to agree about a decision like this. My followers must gather together, under the guidance of my Spirit, representing who I am.

Then, whatever they ask is what my Father will do. For what has been decided in the world above must be your guide for the decisions you make on the earth below.

"Look first to yourself, *at what is in your own heart.* If your brother or sister has wronged you then tell them face to face, if they turn around and ask forgiveness, then release them."

"Wisdomkeeper," Stands On The Rock asked, "how many times can my brother or sister wrong me and I still forgive? Is seven times enough?"

"Not just seven times," Creator Sets Free answered, "but seventy times seven. Even if they have a change of heart and ask seven times in one day—forgive."

"Wisdomkeeper," they begged, "help our weak faith!"

A Story About Forgiveness

Creator Sets Free then told a story to help them see deeper into the ways of forgiveness.

"Creator's Good Road is like a ruler who wanted to collect the money owed to him by his hired servants. One owed him ten thousand silver coins, more than he could pay in a lifetime. The ruler ordered the man, his family and all he owned to be sold to pay for the debt. The servant fell to his knees before him and said, 'Ruler, give me time and I will repay all that I owe!'

"The ruler felt sorry for the servant, set him free and released him from his debt.

"But that same servant went to one of his fellow servants who owed him only a few copper coins, maybe two weeks wages. He took hold of the man's throat and said, 'Pay me all that you owe!'

"The man humbled himself, bowed down and pleaded, 'Please, give me more time and I will repay you!'

"But the man would not even listen. He threw him into prison until he could pay all that he owed. When his fellow servants saw this, it made their hearts fall to the ground. They went to the ruler and told him the sad story.

"The ruler had the man brought to him and said, 'How could your heart be so cold? I forgave you all your debt because you begged me to. Why would you not do the same for your fellow servant?' The ruler was angry with him and put him in prison to be punished until his debt was paid in full."

Creator Sets Free looked deep into the eyes of the ones who walked the road with him and said, "My Father is warning you; the same thing will happen to the ones who, from their hearts, fail to forgive their fellow human beings."

The Harvesters Report Back

The seventy that were sent out by Creator Sets Free returned. Their hearts were overflowing with joy as they reported back to him. "Wisdomkeeper!" they said. "Even the evil spirits did what we said when we spoke to them in your name, representing you."

Creator Sets Free *looked up to the sky and back down at them and said,* "With my own eyes I have seen the evil serpent, like lightning, falling down from the world above. I have given you authority over snakes and scorpions and over all the power of this enemy. Nothing will be able to harm you."

But then he gave them some words of wisdom, "It is good to have glad hearts about these things, but what should make your hearts truly glad is to have your names carved into the rock cliffs of the world above."

The Holy Spirit filled the heart of Creator Sets Free with joy. "O Great Father, maker of the earth and sky," he prayed, "you have hidden these things from the ones who are wise in their own eyes, but have shown them to the humble of heart. Yes, my Father, it has made your heart glad to see this day come."

Then he turned to the ones who walked the road with him and said, "My Father has put everything into my hands. Only the Father knows the Son and only the Son knows the Father. No one can truly know the Father, in his fullness, unless the Son makes him known.

Creator Sets Free lifted his eyes to the horizon as if he was speaking to all the world.

"Come close to my side, you whose hearts are on the ground, you who are pushed down and worn out, and I will give you rest. Learn from me, for I am gentle and humble of heart, and you will find rest for your troubled thoughts. With my help the heavy load you bear will become light and easy to carry."

Then he turned back to his twelve *message bearers* and said to them, "You have been given a great honor to see these things. There were many prophets and holy men who wanted to see and hear the things you have, but did not."

A Sly Scroll Keeper Sets a Trap

A scroll keeper, *one who was skilled in his knowledge of the great law,* came to Creator Sets Free to test him and trap him in his words.

"Wisdomkeeper," he said. "What path must I walk to have the life beyond all days?"

He answered him, "What do the Sacred Scrolls say? Tell me, how do you see it?"

The scroll keeper spoke from the words of the great law, "You must love the Great Spirit from deep within, with the strength of your arms, the thoughts of your mind, and the courage of your heart,[92] and you must love your tribal members in the same way you love yourselves."[93]

"You have answered well, "Creator Sets Free said back to him. "If you walk this path you will live."

But the scroll keeper, wanting to look good to others, asked him, "Who are my tribal members?"

He Turns the Trap with a Story

Creator Sets Free answered him with a story.

"There was a man walking on the road from Jerusalem to Jericho. On the way he was attacked by thieves who beat him, stripped him of his clothes and left him bleeding and near death. Now it happened that a holy man was on the same road, not far behind. When he saw the man, he went around him on the other side of the road. Not far behind him was another man, also from the tribe holy men are chosen from. When he saw the wounded man, he did the same as the holy man.

"Then a man from Samaria[94], who was also walking the road saw the wounded man. *Even though he was not a tribal member, but a mixed blood despised by the tribal people,* he felt pity for the man. He helped him by pouring good medicine on his wounds and wrapping them in a cloth. He put the man on his own animal and took him to a lodging house to care for him.

"The next day, when the man of Samaria was leaving, he gave the keeper of the lodge a few coins and said, 'Use this to care for this man and when I return I will pay you for anything more that is needed.'"

Creator Sets Free then looked at the scroll keeper and said, "Which one of these three was a tribal member to the man?"

The scroll keeper answered, "The one who was kind to him."

"Go," Creator Sets Free said, "and walk in the same way."

He Gives His Followers a Prayer

Another time after Creator Sets Free had finished praying, one of his followers said to him, "Wisdomkeeper, teach us how to pray, in the same way He Shows Goodwill taught his followers."

Creator Sets Free *smiled and* said to them, "*When you send your words to the Great Spirit,* here is how you should pray.

"O Great Father, the one who lives above us all, your name is sacred and holy. Bring your Good Road to us, where the beauty of the world above is reflected in the earth below. Provide for us day by day—the elk, the buffalo, and the salmon; the corn, the squash, and the wild rice; all the good things we need every day to feed our families. Release us from the things we have done wrong, in the same way we release others for the things done wrong to us. Guide us away from selfish desires, that tempt us to stray from your Good Road, and rescue us from the evil one and his worthless ways.

"Your Good Road with its great beauty and power shines like the sun, to the time beyond the end of all days."

Never Give Up When You Pray

"Let your prayers rise like smoke to the Great Spirit—he will see and answer you. Every step is a prayer, and as you dance upon the earth the way will open before you. Search for the ancient pathways and you will find them. Answers will come to the ones who ask, good things will be found by the ones who search for them, and the way will open before the ones who keep dancing their prayers."

Creator Sets Free took a loaf of bread and a fish from a basket. He lifted the bread up high for all to see.

"What father, if his son wanted bread, would give him a stone to eat?"

Then he lifted the fish up high.

"If he asked for a fish would he give him a snake, or for an egg would he give a scorpion? Even fathers with bad hearts give good gifts to their children. Will not the Creator, who is your Father from above, give good gifts to his children? Yes! He will give to them the Holy Spirit and other good gifts."

"Suppose you went to a friend in the middle of the night and said, 'I need three loaves of bread! A relative of mine has made a long journey to see me and I have nothing for him to eat.' But he says to you, 'Quit bothering me! I can't help you, my children and I are all in bed.' Don't give up! If your friendship isn't enough, then he will do it just because you are bold enough to keep asking."

The Spiritual Leaders Accuse Him

They brought a man to him who could not see or speak and was tormented by an evil spirit. He healed him and the man could see and speak again. The large crowd was amazed and said, "Could this be the promised descendant of the ancient Chief Much Loved One?"

But some spiritual leaders and scroll keepers who had come from Jerusalem were there. When they heard what the people were saying, they said, "No! His power over evil spirits comes from the Ruler of the Flies,[95] the one who rules all evil spirits."

Creator Sets Free knew what they were thinking and said, "A nation warring against itself comes to a bad end. A village or clan warring against each other will not survive. If the evil serpent is against himself how will he continue to rule?

"If it is by his power that I tell evil spirits what to do, by what power do your children do these things? They are the ones who will decide against you. If I force out evil spirits by the finger of the Great Spirit then Creator's Good Road has come close to you.

"Who can enter the house of the strongman, who is dressed in war garments with many weapons, and take away his goods? Only one who is stronger can attack and defeat him. He then strips him of his war garments and the weapons that he trusted in and divides the goods among the people.

"In this war there is no unclaimed territory. The one who is not fighting with me, fights against me. The one who does not help me gather, scatters and makes things worse.

"I tell you the truth, all the wrongdoings and evil speaking the many generations of mankind have done, can be forgiven them. Anyone who speaks against the True Human Being, can be forgiven. But speaking evil of the Holy Spirit will not be forgiven, in this present world, nor in the one that is coming.

"A tree has either good fruit or bad, for it is known by its fruit. You nest of poisonous snakes! How can you who are evil speak any good things? What is in your hearts will come out of your mouths. Good people speak from the good medicine stored in their hearts. Evil people speak from the bad medicine stored in their hearts. I say to you, when the day comes for the final decision, human beings will have to give an answer for every worthless word spoken. The words that come out from your hearts will decide for or against you when you stand before the Great Spirit."

He said this because the spiritual leaders accused him of having an evil spirit, so he told them this story.

"When an evil spirit goes out of a person it wanders through dry and desolate lands, looking for a place to rest. When it finds none it says, 'I will go back to the house I left.' It returns to find the house empty, swept clean and put in order. The spirit then finds seven other spirits, more evil than itself, who all go in and live there, making the person worse than before.

"This is how it will be for the generation of people living today."

Bad Hearts Demand a Sign

More people began to gather around him, adding to the size of the crowd. The spiritual leaders, seeing the crowd, wanted to test him in front of the people. "Wisdomkeeper," they demanded, "show us a *powerful* sign from the world above, to prove who you are."

Creator Sets Free *turned their words back on them, "After all the powerful things you have seen me do, how can you demand to see more!* Only a bad-hearted generation *with false faces and* unable to believe, would say such a thing. The only sign that you need is the sign of the prophet Wings Of Dove. Just as he was in the belly of a great fish for three days and nights, the True Human Being will be in the womb of the earth, and come out on the third day."

"When the time comes for the final decision to be made about the people living today, the people of Nineveh will stand in agreement against them. What they did will show your guilt, because they changed their hearts and ways when they heard the message of Wings Of Dove. Look! One greater than Wings Of Dove stands before you now.

"The female chief of the south[96] will also be there to stand against the people of today, and what she did will show your guilt, for she journeyed from a land far away to listen to the wisdom of the great chief Stands In Peace.

"Look! One greater than Stands In Peace is standing right in front of you."

CHAPTER ELEVEN

The Growing Conflict

Festival of Huts

Creator Sets Free had left Judea because the spiritual leaders there wanted to put him to death. To avoid conflict with them he had been staying in the territory of Galilee. But now it was almost time for the Festival of Huts in Jerusalem, which all the tribes participated in.

This festival was celebrated at the end of the harvest. The tribes were instructed to make temporary shelters made from tree branches. In this way they remembered the time after they had been set free from their captivity in Egypt, when their ancestors migrated in the desert wilderness under the care of the great chief, Drawn From The Water.

The brothers of Creator Sets Free came to him and said, "You should leave here and go back to Judea for the Festival. This way more of your followers will see the powerful signs you can do. Why don't you show everyone who you are? The ones who want to be well known do not hide in secret. You should show all the world who you are." But they said this *to mock him,* because they didn't believe in him.

Creator Sets Free answered them, "You are free to go anytime you want, for the people there do not hate you. But they do hate me, because I show them their bent and crooked ways. You can go to the festival, but I am not going now—it is not my time yet."

After he said this he stayed behind in Galilee, until his family left. Then he went to the festival, not openly, but in secret.

Looking for Him at the Festival

Tribal members from all the directions came to the Festival. The Sacred Village of Peace was crowded and overflowing with thousands of people walking, donkeys pulling carts and merchants selling their crafts.

Many were looking for Creator Sets Free at the festival. The people who had gathered there were whispering and wondering about him. "Where is he?" they asked.

Some of them said, "He is a true human being with a good heart." But others were saying, "No! He is leading the crowds down a false path."

No one was saying these things out in the open, because they feared what the tribal leaders might do to them.

Why Do You Want to Kill Me?

Creator Sets Free *came secretly to the Festival and stayed away from the crowds.* He waited until the midpoint of the Festival and went to the Sacred Lodge and began to teach.

The people were amazed at his teaching. "Where did he get this wisdom and understanding?" they asked. "He hasn't studied under our wisdomkeepers or attended our learning houses."

Creator Sets Free answered them, "The wisdom I share is not my own, but comes from the one who sent me. The ones who desire to walk in the ways of the Great Spirit will understand my wisdom comes from him. The one who represents himself is seeking his own honor. The one who represents the one who sent him is true and upright and there is nothing false in him.

"Drawn From The Water *was representing the Great Spirit when he* gave you the law. *You did not try to kill him.* Why do you want to kill me?"

"You must have an evil spirit!" they answered back. "Why else would you think we are trying to kill you?"

He answered them, "I did one work—I healed a man. You were amazed to see such power, but you were offended because this was done on the Day of Resting.

"Do you not see? Drawn From The Water gave you the cutting of the flesh[97] ceremony, handed down to him from the ancestors. Sometimes this ceremony is performed for a baby boy on the Day of Resting. If this is permitted on the Day of Resting, then why are you angry with me for healing a man on that day? Do not decide things by their outward appearance. Instead, make your decisions in a good way, looking beyond what you see with your eyes."

How Could He be the Chosen One?

Some of the people were saying, "Isn't this the one they are seeking to put to death? Look, he speaks boldly to all and they have nothing to say to him. Do the spiritual leaders think he is the Chosen One? But how could this be? When the Chosen One comes no one will know where he comes from, but we know where this man is from."

Creator Sets Free then lifted up his voice in the courtyard of the Sacred Lodge and cried out, "You may think you know me and where I am from, but I know where I am truly from—the Father. He is the one who sent me. You do not know who I am or where I am from, because you do not know him."

Soldiers Sent to Arrest Him

The spiritual leaders were looking for a way to arrest him, but no one could even lay a hand on him, for it was not yet his time. Many of the people chose to believe in him. They said, "When the Chosen One comes will he do more powerful signs than this man has done?"

When the Separated Ones and the head holy men heard what the crowds were saying about him, they sent the lodge soldiers to arrest him.

"I will be gone soon," he said to them. "I am returning to the one who sent me. You will look for me, but you will not find me. Where I am going you cannot follow."

The tribal members began to grumble, "Where will he go that we can't find him? Will he go to where the tribal members live among the Greeks? Will he teach them there? What does he mean by saying, 'You will look for me, but will not find me,' and, 'Where I am going you cannot follow?'"

The Source of Living Water

It was now the last and greatest day of the Festival of Huts.

It has been said that on this day, by ancient tradition, a holy man would be chosen to take a golden pot to the Pool of Siloam and fill it with water. He would then bring the water to the Sacred Lodge for a special ceremony and celebration. The holy man would take the water to the great alter, then at the sound of the ram's horn, called the shofar, he would pour out the water on the altar. They would recite the words of the prophet Creator Will Help Us, "With glad hearts we will draw from the wells, water that will set us free."[98]

After the ceremony Creator Sets Free stood before the people and cried out with a loud voice, "The ones who thirst must come to me and drink! Put your hope and trust in me. I am the one the Sacred Writings spoke of when they said, 'Rivers of living water will flow out from inside him.'"[99]

He was saying this about the Spirit, who would soon be given to the ones who believed in him. The Spirit had not yet been poured out, for Creator Sets Free had not yet risen to his place of honor and beauty.

Conflict About Who He Is

When they heard these words, many of the people gathered there were saying, "This must be the Prophet," but others were saying, "*No!* He is the Chosen One."

But some did not agree and said, "How can this be? Will the Chosen One come from Galilee? Do not the Sacred Writings tell us that the Chosen One will be a descendant of Much Loved One and come from Bethlehem, the same village he was from?"

So the people could not agree about him. The lodge soldiers were amazed by his words and could not bring themselves to arrest him. They returned to the head holy men and the Separated Ones, who asked them, "Where is he? Why didn't you arrest him?"

The Soldiers answered, "No one has ever spoken like this man!"

"Has he turned you from the path also?" they said. "Not even one head man or spiritual leader from among the tribes believes in him. These people are ignorant of the Sacred Writings given by Drawn From The Water. They are under a curse!"

Conquers The People, the same one who came to Creator Sets Free in secret at night, was one of the spiritual leaders. He *boldly* said to the other leaders, "Can we judge this man according to our laws, without giving him a chance to stand before the council and give an answer for what he does?"

The other spiritual leaders *scorned him and* said, "Are you also from Galilee? Look into the Sacred Writings for yourself. You will see that no prophet comes from Galilee."

The Festival of Huts was over and the people all returned to *the peace and safety of* their own homes, but Creator Sets Free went to the Mountain of Olives *to find lodging there.*

Conflict Between Law and Compassion

Early in the morning at the sunrise, Creator Sets Free returned again to the Sacred Lodge. All the people began to gather around him, so he sat down and *once again* began to teach *and tell his stories.*

Across the plaza a cloud of dust was rising from a group of people who were walking toward Creator Sets Free as he was teaching. They were forcefully dragging a woman along with them. He could see her tears and the look of terror on her face.

It was the scroll keepers and the Separated Ones. They brought the woman to Creator Sets Free and forced her down on the ground in front of him and all the people.

"Wisdomkeeper," they said, "we found this woman in the very act of being unfaithful to her husband. Drawn From The Water instructed us in the great law to throw stones at her until she dies. What do you have to say about this?" They were putting him to a test, so they could have a way to accuse him.

The crowd was silent and waited to see what he would say.

Creator Sets Free remained silent. He bent over and with his finger wrote something in the dirt. *When he didn't answer right away they became angry. "Tell us!" they demanded. "What do you have to say?"*

He looked up at them and said, "The one who has done no wrong should be the first to throw a stone at her." He then bent over and again began to write in the dirt with his finger.

When they heard his words they all stood there silently. Then, beginning with the elders, one at a time they dropped their stones and walked away. Soon all were gone except for Creator Sets Free and the woman. He stood up and looked at her. "Honored woman," he said. "Where are the ones who were accusing you? Is there no one who finds fault with you?"

The woman *looked up timidly into his eyes and* said, "No one, Wisdomkeeper."

"Then I also find no fault with you," he said to her. "You may go your way, but take care not to return to this broken path you have been walking."

Conflict Between Light and Darkness

After the woman left, the people began to gather around him again, so he lifted up his voice and said to them, "I am the light shining on all *the people of* the world. The ones who walk with me will not stumble in the darkness but will have the light that gives them life."

When they heard this, the Separated Ones said to him, "When you say these things about yourself, you are the only one who says they are true. If no one else speaks for you, then we cannot receive your words."

Creator Sets Free answered them, "If I am the only one who speaks for myself, my words are still true. I know where I came from and where I am going. You are the ones who do not know where I came from or where I am going.

You are deciding about me with weak human minds.[100] I am not deciding about anyone, but even if I did, my decisions would be true, for I do not stand alone. My Father who sent me is the one who stands with me. Your law tells you it takes the word of two people to know the truth. So then, I speak for myself and the Father speaks for me also."

"Who is your Father?" they said back to him.

"You do not know me or my Father," he told them. "If you knew me, you would know who my Father is."

The people began to argue among themselves about him.

So he lifted up his voice again and said, "You are not able to go where I am going. When I am gone you will *wander in the darkness* looking for the Chosen One,[101] and your bad hearts will lead you down the path of death *and destruction.*"

The people said to each other, "Is he going to kill himself, since he says he's going where we cannot follow?"

So he said to them, "You are from below and belong to this *dark world*. I am from above and *the darkness of* this world has no place in me, for I am the light of the world. Unless you believe that I AM[102] who I say I am, you will come to a bad end. That is why I said that you will wander in the darkness until you die."

When they heard this, they said to him *in anger,* "Who do you think you are?"

He answered, "From the beginning I have been telling you who I am. I have many more things I could say and decide about you, but I only speak the true words of the one who sent me."

But no one understood that he was talking about the Father.

So Creator Sets Free said to them, "When you lift up the True Human Being and nail him to a tree pole, then you will know that I am who I say I am. For I only do and say the things taught to me by my Father. The one who sent me is with me now. He has never left me alone, for I always do the things that make his heart glad."

Conflict About Freedom

Many began to trust in him as they listened to his words. Creator Sets Free said to the tribal people who believed in him, "If you walk in my footsteps and follow my teachings, you will truly be my followers. Then you will see and understand the truth that sets all people free."

But they questioned him, "We are the descendants of Father Of Many Nations and have never been anyone's slave. How can you say, 'You will be set free?'"

"From my heart I tell you the truth," he answered them. "All who walk in the broken ways of this world become slaves to their bad hearts. A slave is not a member of the family and will not always live with the family. But a son of the family always has a home.

"The freedom the Son gives you is the way of true freedom.

Conflict Over Fatherhood

"I know you are the descendants of Father Of Many Nations, but still you want to put me to death, because my message has no home in you. I am telling you the things my Father has shown me, but you are doing the things your father has shown you."

"Father Of Many Nations is our father," they said back to him *in anger.*

Creator Sets Free said to them, "If you were truly the children of Father Of Many Nations you would do the same things he did. Instead, you want to put to death the one who has told you truth from the Great Spirit. This is not what Father Of Many Nations did. You are doing the same things your father does."

"We were not born from an unmarried woman—*like you,*" they said *with contempt.* "We have but one Father—the Great Spirit."

The Battle Lines Are Drawn

Creator Sets Free told them, "If the Great Spirit was truly your Father, you would show respect and love to me, for I came from him. I did not send myself, he is the one who sent me.

"Why can't you hear what I am saying to you? Are my words too soft? *Then I will speak more clearly.* Your father is the ancient evil serpent. You are doing what he wants, for he was the first to take the life of another. He stands outside of the truth, because truth has no home in him. He speaks with a forked tongue and twists his words. His lies show who he truly is. He is a liar and the father of all that is false.

"Even though I am telling you the truth you do not believe me. Which one of you can show that I have done anything wrong? The ones who come from the Great Spirit can hear his words. The reason you do not hear me, is because you are not from him."

"Now we have the right to call you a Samaritan and one who has an evil spirit," they said to him *in anger.*

He answered them back, "I have no evil spirit. I honor my Father, but you dishonor me. I am not trying to honor myself, but there is one who honors me and he has the last word. From my heart I tell you the truth, death will not have the final word for the ones who walk in my message."

"Now we are sure you have an evil spirit," they said. "Father Of Many Nations and all the prophets crossed over to death. How can you say that the ones who walk in your word will not taste of death? Do you think you are greater than Father Of Many Nations and the prophets? Who are you making yourself out to be?"

Creator Sets Free answered them, "If I honor myself, then I have no honor. The one who honors me is my Father, the one you say is our Creator. You do not truly know him, but I do. If I were to say, 'I don't know him,' I would be a liar, like you! But I know him deeply and walk in all his ways. Father Of Many Nations looked ahead to my day, he saw it and it made his heart glad!"

"How could you have seen Father Of Many Nations?" they asked, *shaking their heads.* "You have not even seen fifty winters."

"From my heart I tell you the truth, " he answered. "I was there before Father Of Many Nations was born— for I AM."

The people had heard enough! They picked up stones to throw at him, but he hid himself *in the crowd,* passed them by and walked away.

Who Is Blind and Why?

After getting safely away from the Lodge, he saw a man blind from birth *sitting by the pathway. They stopped near the man and* the ones who walked the road with him asked, "Wisdomkeeper, why was this man born blind? Was it his wrongs or his parent's that caused this?"

"It was not his parents or him that caused this," he told them. "But his blind eyes will now see the beauty of the Maker of Life. While the sun still shines we must be doing what he wants. A time of darkness is coming when no one will do what he wants. But as long as I am in the world, I will be its light."

After saying this he spit on the ground. Then he made mud from his spit and rubbed it on the man's eyes and told him to go and wash in the pool of Siloam, *which means Sent.*

With the help of others, the man did what Creator Sets Free said. When they arrived at the pool, he cupped his hands, drew water up to his face, and washed the mud out of his eyes. He opened his eyes, blinking hard as the light of day burst in—he could see!

Full of excitement and joy he ran back to where he had been to show everyone what had happened. The people who lived near him and others who knew he was blind saw him and said *in amazement,* "Could this be the blind man who sat and asked for handouts?"

Some were saying it was him, others said he only looked like him, but he said, "I am the one!"

So they asked him, "How did your sight return to you?"

He said, "A man named Creator Sets Free[103] made some mud and rubbed it on my eyes. He told me to go to the pool of Siloam and wash. So I did what he said, and now I can see."

"Where is he?" they asked.

"I don't know where he is," the man answered.

They took the man to the Separated Ones to see what they would say. The Separated Ones asked him how he was healed. He said to them, "He rubbed mud on my eyes, I washed off the mud and now I can see."

The Separated Ones became angry because Creator Sets Free had made mud and healed the man on the Day of Resting. "This man cannot be from the Great Spirit," they said. "He does not honor the Day of Resting."

But others were saying, "How can someone with a bad heart perform powerful signs like these?"

The spiritual leaders could not agree, so they said to the blind man, "You are the one he healed, what do you have to say about him?"

The man answered them, "He must be a prophet from the Great Spirit."

The spiritual leaders could not believe the man had been blind. So they found his parents and asked them, "Is this your son who you say was born blind? How does he now see?"

His parents were afraid of the spiritual leaders, who had said that anyone who says Creator Sets Free is the Chosen One would be banished from the gathering house. So they gave them this answer, "Yes, this is our son and he was born blind, but we do not know how he sees, or who opened his eyes. He is a full grown man, ask him. He will tell you for himself."

The spiritual leaders now had to admit it was a true miracle. They went back to the man who was blind and said to him, "Give honor to the Great Spirit for healing you, not to Creator Sets Free, for we know he is an outcast with a bad heart.

"I do not know if this man has a bad heart," he answered them. "All I know is, I was blind—but now I see."

They asked the man again, "What did he do to open your eyes?"

He said to them, "You didn't listen the first time I told you. Why do you want to hear it again? Do you also want to become one of his followers?

This made the leaders angry so they tried to insult the man.

"You are his follower!" they said disrespectfully. "We follow Drawn From The Water, for we know the Great Spirit has spoken to him, but we do not know where this man is from."

The man answered them, "This is a strange thing! You, who are spiritual leaders, do not know where this man comes from, yet he is the one who opened my eyes. The Great Spirit does not listen to people with bad hearts, he listens to the ones who humbly serve him and do what is right. From the creation of the world no one has ever seen a man healed who was born blind. If he is not from the Great Spirit he could not have done this."

The Separated Ones were furious! How could this man talk back to them like this?

They *puffed up their chests and* said, "You were born an outcast and you think you can teach us?" Then they threw him out *and banned him from his gathering house.*

When Creator Sets Free heard that they had put the man out of the gathering house, he went to him and said, "Do you believe in the True Human Being?"

"Tell me who he is," the man answered, "and I will believe in him."

"I am the True Human Being," Creator Sets Free said. "The one who is talking with you now."

The man bowed down low to him and said, "Honored One, I believe!"

Creator Sets Free *put his hands gently on the man's head and* said, "It is for the ones like you that I came into this world—so the blind will see—and that the ones who see, may know they are blind."

Some of the Separated Ones overheard what he said to the man. "Are you saying that we are blind?" they asked.

"If you were truly blind you would have no guilt," he answered them. "But since you claim to see, your guilt remains."

The Good Shepherd

Creator Sets Free told this story to the Separated Ones, for they were blind guides, leading the tribes of Wrestles With Creator down a false path and to a bad end.

"Listen closely, *and I will tell you a story about a sheep pen with many sheep.* There is a *good* shepherd who watches over the sheep. The shepherd comes to the gate and the gatekeeper opens the way, *for he knows the shepherd cares for the sheep.* The sheep know the shepherd's voice, for he calls each of them by name, and they follow him as he leads them in and out of the sheep pen.

"Thieves and outlaws do not use the gate, but climb over the fence into the sheep pen. The sheep run away from these thieves and outlaws, for they do not know the voice of a stranger."

Creator Sets Free could see that the Separated Ones did not understand, so he told them the meaning of the story.

"Listen closely," he said. "I am the gatekeeper for the sheep. All who put themselves before me are thieves and outlaws—*false shepherds.* My sheep do not listen to them.

"I am also the gate for the sheep. The ones who enter by me will be safe *and well cared for.* Following the shepherd, they will go in and out and find good food to eat.

"But thieves enter only to take away life, to steal what is not theirs, and to bring to ruin all they cannot have. But I have come to give the good life, a life that overflows with beauty and harmony.

"I am the Good Shepherd, *the one who watches over the sheep.* I will lay down my life for them. The ones who watch the sheep, only for pay, will run away when a wolf comes. Then the wolf preys upon the sheep and scatters the flock. The ones who do it only for pay are not true shepherds, for they do not care for the sheep, *but only for themselves.*

"I am the Good Shepherd, the one who lays down his life for the sheep. The Father knows me and I know him. In the same way, I also know each one of my sheep and they know me. I have other sheep who are not from this flock. I will go and find them, and they will *also* hear my voice. Then there will be only one flock, with one shepherd.

"My Father has a great love for me, for I lay my life down to take it back up again. No one takes my life from me, for I lay it down on my own. I have the right to lay my life down and the right to take it back up. It is my Father who gives me this right."

Creator Sets Free said these things at the Sacred Lodge where he was teaching, near the storehouse where they keep the ceremonial gifts.

The people began to argue among themselves about him. Many were saying, "He has lost his mind and has an evil spirit. Why do we even listen to him?" At the same time others were saying, "These are not the words of someone with an evil spirit. Can an evil spirit open blind eyes?"

And so, there was much disagreement about him among the people.

Creator Sets Free, knowing the mood of the people, left Jerusalem, for the conflict had grown too strong. He decided go back to the villages in Galilee, near his home, and continue his work there for a while.

CHAPTER TWELVE

More Stories About the Good Road

Beware of Greed

As Creator Sets Free was leaving Jerusalem, a great number of people had gathered around him and his followers. There were so many that they were tripping and falling over each other.

Someone from the crowd pushed forward and said to him, "Wisdomkeeper, tell my brother to give me my part of what our father left to us."

Creator Sets Free said to him, "Who made me the one to decide this between you and your brother? Watch your step, greed is getting in your way. Remember, one's life is not made up of many possessions."

There were many people in the crowd who heard what he said about possessions, so he told this story to help them see more clearly.

"A man with many possessions had a field that was growing a great harvest of food. 'What will I do with all this food?' he said to himself. 'I don't have room in my storage barns for this great harvest.'

"The man thought about it and then said to himself again. "I know what I will do, I will tear down my old storage barns and build larger ones.' Then I will have enough to last me many winters, then I will take my rest, eat, drink and celebrate.'

"But this is what the Great Spirit said to him, 'Why are you being so foolish? This is the day you will cross over and give an answer for your life. The food you have stored up for yourself will now belong to others.'"

Creator Sets Free let the people think about the story, and then he said, "This is how it will be for the ones who keep more than they need for themselves. They may have many earthly possessions, but will miss the life of beauty and harmony that comes only from the Maker of Life.

"So empty your money pouches and share with the ones who have little. Then your money pouches will be filled with true possessions for the world to come. These will never grow old and fade away, no one can steal them, and no moth can ruin them. What your money pouch is filled with, shows what your heart is filled with. *In this way you will always be ready to stand before the Great Spirit with a clean heart."*

Keep Your Hearts Free From Greed

He then told them another story about always being ready.

"The men of a certain village were waiting for their chief to return from a distant wedding feast. Their regalia was laid out and ready to wear. Their torches were trimmed and burning bright as they watched for the chief. They were ready to greet him, whether he came late into the night *or early in the morning.*

"When the chief returned, they were ready and welcomed him into the village. He felt so honored that he took off his regalia and dressed himself in servant's clothes. He had them sit down at his own table and served them a great feast."

"Here is another way to see what I am saying. A wise father, *who cared deeply for his family,* stayed on the lookout for thieves who might come during the night. *He made sure to stay alert and watchful.* In the same way you must always be ready, looking for the True Human Being to return, for like the thieves in this story, he will come at a time you do not expect."

Hearing this, Stands On The Rock said to him, "Wisdomkeeper, is this story for us, or for all people?"

He answered him with another story.

"There was once a man who went on a long journey. He asked his brother, the uncle of the family, to care for them while he was away. When the father returned he found his family well cared for. He then honored that uncle, welcomed him into the family and shared with him all he had.

"But what if that uncle had said to himself, 'My brother is away and will not return soon, so I can do whatever I want.'—and then begins to abuse the family members, take the best food for himself and get drunk on the wine?

"I will tell you what will happen," Creator Sets Free continued. "The father will return at an unexpected time and find the uncle abusing his family. He will then put him out of the family and send him away to share the fate of the ones who wear false faces. There they will weep and grind their teeth together in anger and frustration."

"Who is the story for?" Creator Sets Free said to his followers. "It is for the ones who have been told the right things to do but fail to do them. They will be given the greatest punishment, for more is

required from the ones who are given and trusted with more. As for the ones who do not know, but still fail to do what is right, their punishment will not be as great."

My Message Will Bring Division

He also knew that his followers were not prepared for the effect his message would have on their nation and what would soon happen to him in Jerusalem.

"I came down from above to ignite a fire on this land, and how I long for it to burn!" he said *with a look of determination on his face.* "I have a purification ceremony *with fire* to accomplish—and I am desperate to finish it!

"Do you look for me to bring peace to this land? *Peace will come, but first* there will be great conflict. The message I bring will pierce like the blade of a long knife. It will even separate the members of a family. A family of five will take sides, three against two and two against three. Father against son, daughter against mother, and daughter-in-law against mother-in-law. In their own homes they will fight like enemies—*all because of me and my message.*

"The ones who choose their family members over me—dishonor me. The ones who fail to pick up their tree pole and walk the road with me, do not know my worth. The ones who care only for their own life, will fail to find it, but the ones who give up their own life, for the life I offer, will find the true life."

Who Has Bad Hearts?

Some people came and told Creator Sets Free about the people from Galilee who Pilate had put to death and mixed their blood with their ceremonial offerings.

He said to them, "Do you think it was because of their bad hearts and wrongdoings that they suffered? Do you think their hearts were worse than all the others in Galilee?

"What about the eighteen people on whom the tower in Siloam fell? Do you think they were worse than all others living in Jerusalem? No, I say to you! But if you, *the people of the Sacred Village of Peace,* do not change your ways of thinking *and walk the path of peace,*[104] you will all die in the same way."

So he told them this story, "There was a man who planted a fig tree in his garden, but when he came to find fruit, there was none. He said to the keeper of the garden, 'I have been looking for fruit on this tree for three seasons and have found none. Cut the tree down! Why waste good dirt on it?'

"But the garden keeper answered the man, 'Give me another season. I will dig around the tree, and fertilize it. If it has no fruit after that, then cut it down.'"

Conflict About the Day of Resting

Back in Galilee, on the Day of Resting, he was teaching at a gathering house. There was a woman there who had a spirit of weakness for eighteen winters. Her back was bent and twisted, so she could not stand up straight.

When Creator Sets Free saw her, he told her to come to him and said, "Honored woman you are set free from your weakness." He put his hands on her and right away she stood up straight and gave thanks to the Great Spirit.

The head man of the gathering house was offended because Creator Sets Free had healed on the Day of Resting. He stood up and told the people, "Are there not six other days to do your work?

Come on one of those days to be healed, not on the day of resting."

Creator Sets Free helped the woman back to her seat. He then turned to the head man with a look of sorrow mixed with anger on his face.

"You who wear false faces!" he rebuked the head man. "Is there anyone who would not let his donkey or oxen out of the stall on the Day of Resting, and take it to a watering hole? This woman is a daughter of Father Of Many Nations. The evil serpent has kept her tied up for eighteen winters. Why should she not be set free on the Day of Resting?"

The enemies of Creator Sets Free were put to shame by his words, but the hearts of the people jumped for joy, because of the wonderful things he was doing.

No Peace in the Village of Peace

At that time some of the Separated Ones came to him and said, "You should leave this place! Chief Looks Brave is looking for you, to put you to death."

"You can tell that sly coyote," he answered them, "Look out! I am forcing out the evil spirits and healing the sick, today and tomorrow. On the third day I will finish the work I came to do. That is why I will go from this place today, tomorrow and the day after. For a prophet cannot be put to death this far from Jerusalem!

"Jerusalem, O Village of Peace! You who kill the prophets and stone to death the ones sent to you! How I have longed to gather your children together, like the eagle gathers her young under her wings, but you would not have it.

"Listen to what I am saying to you! The people living today will have to give an answer, for all of these things will fall upon this generation. Look! Your house has fallen and will be left in ruins!

"I tell you from my heart, you will not see me again until you learn to say, 'Blessed is the one who comes representing the Great Spirit!'"

Who Will Eat at Grandfather's Table?

Creator Sets Free once again set out for Jerusalem. On the way, as he passed through the villages, he would stop and teach the people. At one of these villages a man asked him, "Wisdomkeeper, will only a few find their way onto the Good Road and be set free?"

"Yes," Creator Sets Free said to the man, "so make it your aim to enter in by the narrow way *that I have taught you.* There will be many who try to enter some other way, but will not be able. They will be like the ones who try to enter a Sacred Lodge meeting after the door has been closed. They will *pound on the door and* say to the head man, 'O Great One, O Holy One, open the door for us!'

"But since the head man does not know who they are, or where they are from, he will say to them, 'Go away, you do not belong here.'

"'Did we not eat and drink with you?' they will argue. 'Did you not teach on our village pathways?'

"But he will say to them, '*If you heard my teachings then* why are you still walking in the ways of your bad hearts? No, it is clear that I do not know you.'

"They will shed great tears and grind their teeth together in anger, for inside the Lodge are all the ancestors, Father Of Many

Nations, He Made Us Laugh, Heel Grabber and all the prophets of old, feasting in the Land of Grandfather's Good Road. Sitting at the table with them are people of many nations, from the East, South, West and North."

"So you see," Creator Sets Free said to the man, "the first will be last and the last first."

The man's face became pale as the meaning of the words of Creator Sets Free sank into his heart.

The Honorable Samaritan

As Creator Sets Free made his way to Jerusalem, he took the path between Samaria and Galilee. He went into a small village where ten men with a skin disease came across his path. They *kept a respectful distance from him and* called to him, "Creator Sets Free! Wisdomkeeper!" they pleaded, "be kind to us!"

Creator Sets Free looked at them and said, "Go to the holy men and show yourselves to them."

The great law instructed that a person healed of a skin disease must be pronounced clean by a holy man.

They did what he said, and as they were on the way they were healed. One of the ten men, when he saw he was healed, returned to Creator Sets Free. He thanked the Great Spirit out loud and then bowed down at the feet of Creator Sets Free and offered him thanks. The man was from Samaria *and all Samaritans were despised and looked down on by the tribes of Wrestles With Creator.*

Creator Sets Free said *to those who were watching,* "Were not ten men healed? Where then are the other nine? Was the only one who returned to give thanks to the Great Spirit a man from Samaria?"

Then he said to the man, "Stand up and be on your way. Your faith has made you whole."

Storytelling at a Feast

A while later Creator Sets Free was invited to eat at the house of one of the head men of the Separated Ones. He noticed how the spiritual leaders had chosen the best seats at the table, so he told them a story.

"A man was invited to a wedding feast and sat down in one of the seats of honor. A short time later someone with greater honor also came to the feast. The head man of the feast came to the first man and said, 'I'm sorry, but you must give your seat to this honored person.' The man hung his head, and in front of all the other guests, went to sit in the lowest seat.

"Another man came to the feast, but chose not to sit in one of the honored seats. Soon the head man of the feast came to the man and said, 'Honored friend please come and sit in the reserved seats.' And so, this man was honored in the eyes of all who were at the table."

Creator Sets Free looked around the table at all the guests and said, "The ones who put themselves above others will be brought down, but all who humble themselves will be lifted up."

Creator Sets Free turned to the head man who had invited him and said, "When you have a feast, do not invite only your friends, relatives and the ones with many possessions, who can repay you. Instead, invite the poor, the blind and the crippled, who cannot repay you. Then you will be honored when the ones with good hearts are brought back to life again."

One of the guests at the feast said to Creator Sets Free, "The blessing way rests on the ones who will feast at the table in the Land of Grandfather's Good Road!"

Creator Sets Free could see they still did not understand so he told them another story.

"There was a man who prepared a great feast and invited many people. When the feast was ready he sent a messenger to tell them, 'Come to the table, the feast is ready!' But one by one they all began to make excuses and made light of the wedding feast.

"One said, 'I must go and tend to my new field.'

"Another said, 'Please excuse me, I must try out the horses[105] I just traded for.'

"And another, 'I cannot come for I have just been married.'

"When the messenger told the man their answer, he became angry and said, 'The wedding feast is ready, but the ones invited have no honor. Waste no time! Go out into the village pathways and invite the ones who are poor, blind and lame.'

"The messenger did as he was told, but there was still room at the table. So he sent the messenger out again, with these instructions, 'Go out to the mountain trails, look behind all the bushes and urge them to come, so that my house may be filled with people. None of the ones I first invited will even taste of this feast!'"

Counting the Cost

As Creator Sets Free came near Jerusalem the crowds following him grew larger, too many to number, so he turned to them and said, "The ones who come to me must put me first, above all others. To walk the road with me they must love and respect me above their own fathers and mothers, wives and children, and brothers and sisters—even more than their own lives. If you are not prepared to carry your own tree pole[106] to die on, you are not ready to walk with me and learn my ways.

"Who would build a great lodge without first making sure he had enough trees to finish it? If he only built the floor and then ran out of trees, others would laugh at him and say, 'How will you finish what you started?'

"Would a chief go to war against another chief if he only had half as many warriors? No! He would send messengers ahead to make a peace treaty!

"You must count the cost of following me, for all who are not willing to give up all they have, are not ready to walk the road with me and learn my ways."

Sacred Lodge Purification Festival

Two moons had passed since he was last in Jerusalem. It was time for the people to celebrate the Feast of Dedication.[107] This festival was to remember the time when the Great Spirit's Sacred Lodge was cleansed after it had been made ceremonially unclean by an evil ruler. Creator Sets Free decided to go again to the Sacred Village Of Peace and attend this festival.

It was winter and Creator Sets Free was walking near the Sacred Lodge, under the entryway named after the great chief, Stands In Peace. The tribal leaders came to him and said, "How long will you make us wait? If you are the Chosen One, then tell us!"

"I already told you who I am," he said to them, "but you did not believe me. The things I do, representing my Father, speak the truth about me. As I told you before, you do not trust me because you are not my sheep. I know who my sheep are, for they know my voice and go where I lead them. My gift to them is the life of beauty and harmony, and they will never fade away or come to a bad end. My Father gave them to me and no one can take them from me, because no one is greater than my Father. My sheep are safe in his hands, for I and my Father are one."

The Tribal Leaders Reject Him

The tribal leaders *became furious and* picked up stones to throw at him and put him to death.

Creator Sets Free *stood his ground and* said to them, "I have done many good things, representing my Father. For which of these do you mean to stone me?"

They answered, "Not for any good thing you have done, but for speaking against the Great Spirit. How can you, a weak human being, say you are the Great Spirit."

Creator Sets Free answered them, "In your law it says, 'You are great spirits.'[108] The Sacred Writings are clear and cannot be changed. So how can you say that the one the Father has made holy and sent into the world is speaking against the Great Spirit when he says, "I am the Son of the Great Spirit?"

"If I am not doing what my Father does, then do not believe me. But even if you do not believe me, then at least believe in the powerful things I do. Then you will see clearly that I am in the Father and he is in me."

The tribal leaders moved toward him to take him by force, but he slipped through their hands and walked away.

Creator Sets Free Retreats

Creator Sets Free decided it was time to leave Jerusalem *again.* He went to the place, on the east side of the Jordan River, where He Shows Goodwill first performed the purification ceremony. He and his followers remained there *for a time.* Many people from the area came to listen to him *and hear the stories about the Good Road.*

CHAPTER THIRTEEN

Seeing the Good Road

The Worth of the Lost Ones

Tribal agents and outcasts would often gather around Creator Sets Free to listen to him tell his stories. But the Separated Ones and the scroll keepers would complain about this. They would say things like, "This man welcomes outcasts to join him at the table and eat with him."

On one of those occasions Creator Sets Free answered them, "Let me tell you a story," he said as the people gathered around. "A shepherd was watching over one-hundred sheep out in the desert wilderness. One of his lambs wandered away, so he left the ninety-nine and went to find the lost lamb. When he found it his heart was so glad that he invited his friends and family to his house for a celebration. He was happier about finding one lost lamb than he was about the ninety-nine who were safe. Would you not do the same thing this shepherd did?"

"Just like the shepherd in this story, the True Human Being has come to find and rescue the lost ones. Listen to me! The world above will celebrate more over one outcast who finds the way back to the Good Road, than for ninety-nine people with good hearts. Your Father, the Great Creator, does not want even one of these small ones to come to a bad end."

"Let me say it another way," he explained. "A man with ten eagle feathers[109] lost one of them. He lit a torch and searched everywhere in his house. He swept it clean and looked under all the furnishings, until he found it. Then, after he had found that lost eagle feather, he gathered his family and friends together for a celebration. In the same way, the spirit messengers from the world above will celebrate when one outcast finds the way back home."

Lost and Found

Creator Sets Free then told this story to help them see even more clearly.

"There was a man with two sons. The younger son said to his father, 'Father, give me now my share of what is coming to me.'"

This was a great insult to the father, for this would not have been done until the father had crossed over to death.

"But the Father, *who was good hearted and loved his sons,* divided all he had with his two sons anyway.

"Not many days later the younger son took his share and went far away to another land. He began to spend it all on wild living and soon had nothing left. The time came when there was not enough food in the land for everyone, and he found himself poor and hungry. So he went to work for a rancher, who sent him out to feed the pigs. He became so hungry he wanted to eat the husks he was feeding the pigs, but no one would even give him a meal.

"Soon the younger son came back to his right mind and said to himself, 'Look, here I am naked and starving, but the servants who work for my father are well fed! I am going back to humble myself to my father. I will tell him that I have dishonored both him and the Great Spirit, and I am no longer worthy to be called his son. I will ask him to just let me be a hired servant to work in his fields.'

"He then made up his mind and began to go home. While he was still far away his father saw him walking. The father's heart opened wide, he ran to his son, threw his arms around him and kissed him.

"The son said, 'Father, I have failed the Great Spirit and you, I am not worthy to be called your son.'

"But the father ignored his son's words, turned to his servants and said, 'Go! Find my best regalia and put it on him. Give him a headdress of feathers for his head and new moccasins for his feet! Go get the fattest calf and prepare a great feast for a celebration. This is my son! He was lost, but I have found him. He was dead to me, but now he is alive!' Then they all began to feast, sing and dance.

"Now, the older son was just returning from a hard days work in the field. He heard the music and dancing, so he asked one of the servants what was going on. The servant told him, 'Your brother has come home and your father has prepared a great feast for him, because he is alive and well.'

"Hearing this, the older brother became very angry and refused to go into the lodge. The father saw him *brooding outside,* so he went to him and urged him to come in.

"The older son said to his father, 'Why can't you see? I have worked hard for you all my life and done all that you have asked of me, but you have not even given me one small goat to have a feast with my friends. But when this son of yours comes home, who wasted all you gave him on loose women, you kill the fattest calf for him.'

"The father *looked kindly into his older son's face and said,* 'My son, you are always close to my heart and everything I have is yours. But it is a good thing for us to celebrate with glad hearts; for your brother was dead but now is alive. He was lost but now we have found him!'"

Possessions and the Good Road

He then told the ones who walked the road with him another story.

"There was a man with so many possessions, he had to have someone to manage them all. The rich man was told that his manager was mishandling his possessions. He sent for the man and said to him, 'Why am I hearing these things about you? Give me an account of all I possess, for I can no longer trust you to manage my belongings.'

"The man said to himself, 'What will I do? I am too old to dig ditches and too proud to beg from others.' *Then an idea came to his mind.* 'I know what to do so that others will help me and give me a place to live.' He went to each person who was in debt to the rich man.

"He said to the first one, 'How much do you owe?' 'One hundred containers of oil,' the man answered. 'Make it to be fifty,' the manager told him.

"He then said to another, 'How much do you owe?' 'One hundred baskets of wheat,' he answered. 'Make it to be eighty,' the manager said back to him.

"When the rich man found out what the dishonest manager had done, he *shook his head but* admired the man's craftiness.

"Do you see what this means?" Creator Sets Free asked. "The children of darkness are wiser in the ways of this world, than the children of light are in the ways of the world above.

So then, use the possessions of this world to help others in need. Then when possessions run out, you will always have a place to live in *the Land of Creator's Good Road.* If Creator cannot trust you with the possessions of this world, then how will he trust you with the treasures of the world above? But if you do well with the small things *of this world,* you will do well with the great things *of the world above.*

"That is why I told you no one can be loyal to two chiefs. He will have to choose between them, for either he will hate one chief and love the other or he will honor one and resent the other. You cannot be loyal to the Great Spirit and to possessions at the same time."

When the Separated Ones heard him they shrugged their shoulders and rolled their eyes, for they loved their many possessions.

Creator Sets Free said to them, "You always make yourselves look good to others, but the Great Spirit sees your heart. What many see as valuable he sees as worthless."

The Rich Man and the Beggar

He then told the Separated Ones this story to make his teaching about possessions clear.

"There was once a rich man who always dressed in the best clothes, had more than enough to eat, and lived a life of ease. Every day a beggar named Creator Helps Him was laid at the gate of his lodge. Dogs would come and lick the sores that covered his body as he begged for crumbs from the rich man's table.

"When the time came for the beggar to cross over to the world of the dead, spirit messengers carried him into the welcoming arms of his ancestor, Father Of Many Nations.

"At the same time the rich man also crossed over to death and his body was buried. In the world of the dead he was suffering and in pain. He looked up and saw his ancestor, Father Of Many Nations, far off in the distance. He could see Creator Helps Him being comforted in his arms.

"He lifted his voice and cried out loud, 'Father Of Many Nations, my ancestor, have pity on me. Send Creator Helps Him to dip the tip of his finger in the water and cool my thirsty tongue. Help me, for I am suffering in this flame.'

"Father Of Many Nations said to him, 'My son, don't you remember? All your days were filled with good things, but the days of Creator Helps Him were filled with sorrow and pain. It is now his time for comfort, but it is your time for sorrow and pain. Look! There is a great canyon between us, so wide that none can make the journey from here to there.'

"The rich man *hung his head* and said, 'Please, my ancestor, send him back to the lodge of my father and my five brothers. He can warn them of this place of suffering and pain, so they won't have to come here also.'

"Father Of Many Nations said to him, 'They have the words of Drawn From The Water and the words of the prophets, let your family listen to them.'

"'No!' the rich man cried out. 'If someone goes back to them from the world of the dead, they will listen.'

"Father Of Many Nations *shook his head and* said, 'If your family will not listen to their words, then they will not listen even to one who comes back to life from the dead.'"

Learning to Serve the Chief

Another time Creator Sets Free sat down with the ones who walked the road with him and asked, "Would a young man who is learning to serve his chief, come to him after a long day of hunting and say, 'My chief, here is the deer I hunted for you. Skin it and cook it so we can eat'?

"What do you think the elders of the tribe would say to him?"

Creator Sets Free looked around at his followers, waiting for an answer. When no one said anything he continued.

"Here is what they would say, 'Young man, you have much to learn about honoring your chief. Now get busy, skin and clean that deer, cook a meal with it and take it to the chief. Say to him, "I have dishonored you my chief, my place is to serve you, not have you serve me."'"

"In the same way, when you have done everything the Great Spirit expects of you, consider yourself to be his humble servant and do not expect to be rewarded for doing only what you should do."

The Good Road Has Come

Another time the Separated Ones asked him, "When will we see the Land of Creator's Good Road?"

He said to them, *"Creator's Good Road is not what you expect.* It does not come with the outward signs you are looking for. *You will need new eyes to see the Good Road.* No one will say, 'Here it is —I found it!' or 'Look—it is over there!' Open your eyes! Creator's Good Road is in you and all around you."

Praying For Justice

Creator Sets Free told them a story to show they should pray at all times and never lose heart.

"Listen!" he said. "There was a village that had a tribal council that did not fear the Great Spirit or respect human beings. A woman of that village, who had lost her husband, kept bothering them. She would say to them, 'Stand up for me against the one who has done me wrong!'

"The tribal council ignored her at first, but the woman kept demanding that they help her. The council grew weary, changed their thinking and said, 'This woman really troubles us. If we don't stand up for her and right this wrong she will never stop bothering us! Not because we respect human beings or even fear the Great Spirit, but only because she won't give up until we do it.'"

Creator Sets Free then said, "Can you hear the words of this bad-hearted tribal council? If a council like that will do what is right, how much more will the Great Spirit right the wrongs done to the ones who cry out to him day and night? Will he ignore their cries? No! I tell you, he will not be slow to bring justice to them. But when the True Human Being comes, will he find this kind of faith anywhere in this land?"

Arrogance and Humility

He then told this story to warn the ones who trusted in themselves and thought they were better than others.

"Two men, a Separated One and a tribal agent, went to the Great Spirit's Sacred Lodge to send up their prayers.

"The Separated One kept his distance from the tribal agent and prayed out loud. 'Creator,' he said, 'I thank you that I am not like the rest of mankind. Like the ones who use force to get from others what they want, or who are not faithful in marriage, or who have no understanding of right or wrong. I thank you also that I am not like this tribal agent standing here! I go without food twice a week for spiritual reasons and I give a tenth of all my gain.'

"Now the tribal agent hung his head down and would not even lift his face to the world above. He beat his hands against his chest and cried out, 'Grandfather! Be kind and have pity on me. I am a broken man, full of bad thoughts and wrongdoings!'

"Listen to me closely!" Creator Sets Free said. "The tribal agent returned home set free and cleansed from his bad heart, but the Separated One did not! The ones who think too highly of themselves will be brought down low; the ones who humble themselves will be lifted up."

Questions About Marriage

The Separated Ones began to surround him *like hungry wolves. They put him to the test with questions about the great law, hoping to trap him. They knew that among the spiritual leaders of the tribes there was sharp disagreement about the instructions of the great law concerning divorce.*

They asked him, "Does the law permit a man to put away his wife for any reason?"

"What did the great lawgiver, Drawn From The Water, instruct you to do?" he questioned back.

They stared at him and said nothing, so he answered, "Have you not read in the Sacred Scrolls, that in the beginning of creation, from one human being, the Great Spirit made two. One male and one female. This is why a man will leave his father and mother and be joined to his wife. Together they become one flesh, no longer two, but one body joined together. No human being should tear apart what Creator has put together."

The Separated Ones *smiled like sly coyotes and said*, "Why then does Drawn From the Water, in the great law, permit a man to put away his wife with divorce papers?"

"It is because of your cold hearts of stone that Drawn From the Water permitted this," he answered. "But this was not the Great Spirit's original plan for men and women."

Later, in private, his followers asked him again about this.

He said to them, "Any man who puts away his wife *without divorce papers* is making his wife unfaithful, unless she was unfaithful already. Then, anyone who marries her is guilty of taking another man's wife. A husband or a wife who ends a marriage, *without being divorced,* is guilty of being unfaithful if they marry another."

The ones who walked the road with him *shook their heads and* said, "If this is so, then it must be better not to marry."

He answered them, "It may be good for some not to marry, but not everyone has this gift. There are many reasons for not getting married. Some are born with no desire or ability for marriage. Some have lost their ability from what has been done to them. Others choose not to marry so they can put all their strength into walking the Good Road. The ones who have this gift are able to receive this wisdom."

Little Children and the Good Road

The people were bringing their little children to Creator Sets Free, so he would lay his hands on them and bless them, but his followers spoke harsh words to the ones bringing them.

When Creator Sets Free saw what his followers were doing he was deeply troubled and said to them, "Let the little children come to me! Do not turn them away. Grandfather's Good Road belongs to the ones who are like these children. I tell you from my heart, the only way onto the Good Road is to become just like them."

He then took the children into his arms, laid his hands on them and blessed them.

After hearing Creator Sets Free teach, tell his stories, heal the sick and force out evil spirits, the people were saying, "He Shows Goodwill never performed a miracle or did any powerful signs, but what he told us about this man is true."

And so, many of the people there believed *he was the Chosen One.*

CHAPTER FOURTEEN

The Power of Life Over Death

A Friend Crosses Over

A messenger came to Creator Sets Free with bad news from Head Woman and Bitter Tears, saying, "Our brother, Creator Helps Him, the one you care deeply about, is sick." Creator Helps Him lived in Judea in the village of Bethany, near Jerusalem, with his sisters.

When Creator Sets Free heard the message, he said, "This sickness will not end in death. Instead, this will bring honor to the Great Spirit and his Son."

Even though Creator Sets Free loved this family dearly, he stayed where he was for two more days. Then he said to his followers, "Let us go to Judea."

Their eyes grew wide and they shook their heads, saying, "Wisdomkeeper, the tribal members *in Judea* tried to throw stones at you to kill you! Why would you want to go there?"

He answered them, "Does not the sun give us a full day of light? The ones who walk during the day never stumble, because they see the light that shines on this world. But the ones who walk at night stumble in the darkness, because there is no light for them to see. *I am the light shining in this dark world, it is time to let my light shine even brighter."*

Let Us Wake Him Up

Creator Sets Free explained to them, "Our good friend, Creator Helps Him, has fallen asleep and I am going to wake him."

They said to him, "Wisdomkeeper, if he is only sleeping he will get well."

They didn't understand that Creator Sets Free meant that he had died. They thought he was sleeping naturally.

He then told them plainly, "Creator Helps Him has crossed over into the world of the dead. It is a good thing that I was not there, so you will believe. But we must go to him now."

Looks Like His Brother said to the others, "We should go and die with him."

When Creator Sets Free came to Bethany, he found out that Creator Helps Him had died four days earlier and was laid in a burial cave. The Village of Bethany was not far from Jerusalem. Many of the local tribal members had gathered, along with the women, to give comfort to Head Woman and Bitter Tears for the loss of their brother.

I Am the Rising From the Dead

When Head Woman heard that Creator Sets Free was coming she went out to greet him, but Bitter Tears stayed home. When she found Creator Sets Free she said to him, "Wisdomkeeper, if you had been here my brother would still be with us. Even so, I know if you ask anything of the Great Spirit, he will give it to you."

He *looked softly into her eyes and* said to her, "Your brother will live again."

"I know he will live again," she said, "when the dead rise up at the end of all days."

"I am the rising up from the dead and the life that follows," he told her. "The ones who trust me will live again, even after death. The ones who are alive and trust me will never die. Do you believe what I am saying to you?"

"Yes, Wisdomkeeper!" she *smiled and* said. "I believe you are the Chosen One, the Son of the Great Spirit. The one who came *down* into this world *from above.*"

Bitter Tears and Creator Sets Free Weep

After she said this, she left him and went secretly to her sister Bitter Tears and said to her, "The Wisdomkeeper is nearby, and wants you to come to him."

When Bitter Tears heard this she got up right away and went to see him. He was still waiting outside the village. The tribal members, who were comforting Bitter Tears, saw her get up and leave quickly, so they went with her thinking she was going to the burial cave to weep.

When Bitter Tears found Creator Sets Free, she crumpled at his feet and wept. "Wisdomkeeper!" she said *as tears ran down her face.* "If only you had been here my brother would still be alive."

Creator Sets Free stood there watching Bitter Tears weeping at his feet. He looked around and saw all the tribal members who came with her also weeping. A deep anguish began to well up inside him and he was troubled in his spirit.

He cried out! "Where did they bury him?"

"Come with us," they said to him, "we will show you."

Tears began to flow down his face. Creator Sets Free wept.

When the tribal members saw his tears, some said, "See how deeply he cared for him." But others said, "If this man could open the eyes of a blind man, why couldn't he have kept this man from dying?"

Power Over Death

Creator Sets Free, still deep in anguish, found his way to the family burial place. It was a cave and a large stone blocked the entrance.

Creator Sets Free cried out, "Take away the stone!"

Head Woman *came close to Creator Sets Free and* whispered, "Wisdomkeeper, he has been dead four days; there will be a terrible smell."

He *looked at her and* said, "Do you not remember what I told you? If you believed, you would see the Great Spirit show his mighty power and great beauty."

Head Woman could say nothing. She watched as some of the men rolled the stone away from the burial cave.

Creator Sets Free turned his eyes upward toward the sky and said, "I thank you Father, that you have already heard my prayers and always listen to me. The reason I say this out loud is so that all who are standing around me can hear and believe that you sent me."

The men and women gathered there stood silently, listening to his prayer.

Then the voice of Creator Sets Free pierced the silence as he cried out with a loud voice, "Creator Helps Him, come out of there!"

The sound of his voice echoed from out of the burial cave and then faded into the distance. The people looked at Creator Sets Free and then back to the cave. No one dared say anything, so they all waited.

Suddenly, gasps could be heard from the crowd. There was movement in the cave! Creator Helps Him came *stumbling* out from the darkness of the burial cave with his ceremonial wrappings still clinging to his head, hands and feet. *He was alive!*

Creator Sets Free told the people, "Take off his wrappings and set him free."

Head Woman and Bitter Tears wept for joy as they tore the ceremonial wrappings from their brother. They couldn't stop hugging and kissing him! All the people were full of joy and began to celebrate.

When many of the local tribal members saw what Creator Sets Free had done, they believed in him. But some of them went to find the Separated Ones, to tell them what had happened.

A War Council is Called

When the Separated Ones and the head holy men heard about this great miracle, they called the Grand Council together. "What are we going to do?" they asked each other. "This man has powerful medicine and performs many signs and wonders. If he is not stopped all the people will believe in him. Then the People of

Iron will come and take away our Sacred Lodge and our *power to rule this* nation."

Hollow In The Rock, the high holy man for that year, said to the council, "Is it too hard for you to see? It would be better for us if one man were to die for the people, than for our whole nation to be destroyed."

Hollow In The Rock was not aware that, as the high holy man for that year, he prophesied that Creator Sets Free would die for the nation. *Little did he know, that* he would not only die for their nation, but also to gather all of Creator's scattered children together and make them into one people.

From that day forward it was decided by the Grand Council to have him put to death.

Knowing this, Creator Sets Free no longer walked openly among the people. He went into the countryside near the desert wilderness in the region of Ephraim, *which means Fruitful Place.* There he stayed *for a time* with his close followers.

Possessions or the Great Spirit?

After some time had passed, Creator Sets Free set out from there and once again visited many villages, before returning to the Sacred Village of Peace.

As he was walking on the road a young head man, who had many possessions, ran up to Creator Sets Free and humbled himself. "Good Wisdomkeeper," he asked, "what must I do to find the life of beauty and harmony that does not fade away?"

"Why do you call me good?" he asked the man. "Only the Great Spirit is good. If you want this life, then follow the instructions *given by Drawn From the Water."*

"Which instructions?" the young head man asked.

"You already know them," Creator Sets Free answered. "Do not take away the life of another, do not be unfaithful in marriage, and do not take what is not yours. Be honest in all you say and do, and never cheat a fellow human being. Give honor and respect to your father and mother and love your fellow human beings as much as you love yourself."

"Wisdomkeeper," the man answered, "from my youth I have followed all of these instructions. What have I left undone?"

Creator Sets Free looked deeply into the man's face and felt great love for him. Then he said, "Only one thing remains. Take all of your possessions and give them to the ones who have none, then you will have great possessions in the world above. Come and walk the road with me, and be ready to carry the tree pole with me *to the place of ultimate sacrifice."*

The young man's heart fell to the ground. He hung his head and walked away, for he had many possessions.

Possessions and the Good Road

Creator Sets Free looked around at the people and then said to his followers, "Walking the Good Road is a hard thing for the ones who have many possessions."

His followers could not believe what they were hearing. *They thought having many possessions was a sign of Creator's blessing way.*

Creator Sets Free spoke kindly to them "Little children," he said, "the ones who trust in their many possessions will have a hard time finding their way onto the Good Road. It would be easier for a moose[110] to go through the eye of a needle."

They shook their heads in wonder, looked at each other and said, "How then can anyone walk the Good Road that sets all people free?"

Creator Sets Free looked at them and said, "This is only possible with the help of the Great Spirit."

Stands On The Rock spoke up, "We have left all our possessions, and our relatives, to walk the road with you? What will become of us?"

"I tell you from my heart," he answered, "in the world that is coming the True Human Being will sit in his place of honor and you who have walked the road with me will sit in twelve places of honor; choosing what is good and right for the twelve tribes of Wrestles With Creator.

"No one who has given up their homes and families[111] will go without. In this present world they will become part of an even greater family, with many homes and lands.[112] Even though they will be abused and mistreated, they will receive much more than they have lost. The life of beauty and harmony that never fades away will be theirs.

"But *remember,* many who are first in this present world, will be last in the world to come, and many who are last in this present world, will be first in the one to come."

The Last Will Be First

To help them understand what he was saying more clearly, Creator Sets Free told them another story about the Good Road.

"There was a man who was the manager of a large ranch. He went out early in the morning to find people to work in his field.

After they agreed with him on the amount for a full day's pay, he sent them to work.

"A few hours later he went to the trading post and saw people doing nothing. He told them, 'If you will join the workers in my field, I will pay you well.' So they went to work.

"About midday, and again at mid-afternoon, he went out and found others and did the same.

"Finally, when the day was nearly done, he found a few more people doing nothing. 'Why aren't you working?' he asked them. 'No one has hired us,' they answered. He agreed to pay them fairly, so they went to work.

"At the end of the day, the head man said to his manager, 'Bring the workers in from the field and pay them, beginning from last to first.'

"He paid the workers hired at the end of the day a full day's wage. When the workers who were hired at the start of the day were paid, they expected to receive more, but were paid the same amount. 'We have worked all day in the scorching heat,' they complained to the manager. 'Why should we be paid the same as the ones who only worked one hour?'

"'I am being fair with you, my friend,' he said to one of them, 'Did we not agree on the amount of a full day's wages? If I want to pay these men the same, what is that to you? Am I not permitted to be generous with what is mine? Or are you jealous because I have done a good thing? Take your pay and go in peace.'"

Creator Sets Free let his followers think about the story for a moment, then he said to them, "That is why I told you before, the last will be first and the first will be last."

The Good Road is About Serving

The mother of Heel Grabber and He Shows Goodwill, who are the sons of Gift of Creator, came close to Creator Sets Free and humbled herself before him.

"What do you want from me?" he asked.

"Promise me," she said, "that my two sons will have an honored place with you in the Land of the Good Road. One on your right hand, the other on your left."

"You do not know what you are asking," he said to her.

He turned to her two sons and asked, "Can you drink the cup of suffering that I will drink, or endure my purification ceremony?"

"We are able!" they answered.

"Yes," he said to them, "you will drink from my cup of suffering and you will endure my purification ceremony, but the place of honor on my right and left hand is not mine to give. My Father will give this honor to the ones he has chosen."

When the other ten message bearers heard this they began to look down on Heel Grabber and He Shows Goodwill.

Creator Sets Free *called them together and* said, "Other nations have rulers, like the People of Iron. They like to show their power over people and push them around. But this will not be the way of the ones who walk with me. The great ones will humble themselves and serve all the others. In the same way, the True Human Being did not come to be served by others, but to offer his life in the place of many lives, to set them free."

As they continued on their journey to Jerusalem, Creator Sets Free was walking ahead of them, leading the way. As they walked along the road, dread began to fall upon his followers and soon all who were traveling with them began to feel it.

Creator Sets Free took the twelve aside and told them again about what was coming on the road ahead.

"Consider closely what I am telling you," he reminded them. "We are on our way to Jerusalem, the Sacred Village of Peace, where the words of the ancient prophets will come to pass. The True Human Being will be taken and turned over to the head holy men and the scroll keepers. They will condemn him to death and hand him over to the People of Iron.[113] They will treat him shamefully, spit on him, whip him with chords, and put him to death by piercing his hands and feet to nail him to a tree pole. On the third day he will come back to life from the dead."

His followers did not understand what he was saying. The meaning was hidden from their eyes.

A Tribal Agent Sees the Good Road

On the way to Jerusalem they passed through Jericho. They were surrounded by a great crowd as he walked into the village. A man named Pure Of Heart, who was a head tribal agent with many possessions, lived there. When he saw the crowd coming he wondered who it was they were following, but he was too short to see over the crowd. So he ran ahead and climbed a sycamore tree to get a better view.

When Creator Sets Free came to the tree he looked up and said, "Pure Of Heart, come down from there and take me to your house, for I need a place to rest."

He quickly climbed down the tree and with a glad heart welcomed him into his house. But when the people saw this, *they shook their heads.* "What is he doing?" they grumbled out loud. "Why would he go into the house of an outcast?"

Pure of Heart stood up to the crowd and said to Creator Sets Free, "Hear me Wisdomkeeper, I will give half my possessions to the ones who have none. If I have cheated anyone, I will give them back four times as much."

Creator Sets Free smiled and said, "This a good day, because this man and his family have finally been set free, for he also is a descendent of Father Of Many Nations, *who had lost his way.* The True Human Being has come to find the ones who have lost their way, and guide them back again to the Good Road."

Two Blind Men See Again

They left the home of Pure Of Heart and the village of Jericho, continuing toward Jerusalem. A large crowd of people trailed after them. Not far from the village there were two blind men sitting by the road asking for money or food. One of the blind men was named Son of Honored One.

The blind men heard the sound of the approaching crowd and asked what was happening. They were told that Creator Sets Free, from the village of Nazareth, was passing by.

When they heard who it was, Son of Honored One, along with the other blind man, yelled out, "Creator Sets Free, descendant of Much Loved One, have pity on us!"

The people in the crowd scolded them and said, "Be quiet!"

That only made them cry out louder, "Wisdomkeeper! Descendant of Much Loved One, have pity on us!"

Creator Sets Free stopped walking, turned to the crowd and said, "Tell them to come to me."

They said to the men, "Have courage! He is calling for you. Get up and go to him."

Son of Honored One stood up and threw off his outer garment. Both men *stumbled toward the voice of Creator Sets Free, and with the help of others* came to him.

He asked them, "What do want from me?"

"Wisdomkeeper," they said, "open our eyes, so that we may see."

Creator Sets Free, feeling pity for them, laid his hands on their eyes and said to them, "Look at me and see."

As soon as he said this they could see! *The people were amazed as the men blinked their eyes and looked into their faces.* With grateful hearts all the people gave praise to the Great Spirit.

Then Son Of Honored One and the other man went to Creator Sets Free to thank him.

"You may go your way," he said to them with a gentle smile. "Your faith in me has made you whole."

But they couldn't leave him and chose instead to follow him down the road.

Story About Rejecting the New Chief

It was now six days before the Passover festival. Creator Sets Free and the ones who walked the road with him made their way toward Jerusalem. They stopped to lodge at Bethany, the home of Creator Helps Him, Head Woman and Bitter Tears. This was the same village where Creator Helps Him was brought back to life from the dead.

The Sacred Village of Peace was now about two miles away—a short walk. Since his followers thought that the Land of Creator's Good Road would appear as soon as they arrived, he told them this story. The people gathered around him and listened closely as he spoke.

"There was a man who was born to be chief of a large tribal nation. The time had come for him to take his place as chief. But first he had to take a long journey to another land, *to meet with a council of many nations,* to be approved.

"Before he left, he called together ten trusted tribal members who served him. He gave them each a woven blanket of great value. 'Go,' he told them, 'and trade well with these until I return.' *Then he left on his journey to the council.*

"But many of his own people despised him, so they sent some messengers ahead of him to speak with the council. 'We do not want this man to be our chief,' they said, *but the council did not listen to them.*

"*Much later,* after being appointed as chief, he returned to his own tribal nation. He called together the men to whom he had given the woven blankets, to see how well they had traded.

"The first to come to him said, 'Honored chief. Look, I now have ten blankets to return to you.'

"'You have done well my trusted servant,' he said to him, 'You did well with this small thing, now you will represent me in ten villages.'

"The second man to come to him, said, 'Look, my chief, your one blanket is now five.'

"'You will represent me in five villages,' the chief told him.

"Another came to him and said, 'See, honored one, I have returned to you the blanket you gave me. I folded it and hid it safely away. I dared not trade with it, for I know you to be harsh man and I was afraid. You take from others what is not yours and harvest food you did not plant.'

"'You worthless servant," he said to the man. 'Your own words will decide your fate! If you thought I was this way, why did you not turn over your blanket to the trading house, and at least have something to show for it when I returned?'

"The newly appointed chief turned to the ones who stood close by and said, 'Take the blanket from him and give it to the one who has ten.'

"They were confused by this. 'But honored one,' they said, 'he already has ten blankets!'

"The chief said to them, 'The ones who do well with what they have will be given more. But for the ones who do nothing, even what they have will be taken away.'

"'Now bring to me the ones who opposed my appointment as chief. They will die because they have made themselves my enemies.'"

He told them this so they would see that the Good Road would not come in the way they expected.

CHAPTER FIFTEEN

Jerusalem, O Village of Peace

Looking for Creator Sets Free

It was time for the traditional festival of bread with no yeast, called Passover. Tribal members would travel from their homelands to Jerusalem. Many would arrive early to perform a purification ceremony *to prepare for the festival.*

The head holy men and the Separated Ones were looking for a way to capture Creator Sets Free and have him put to death, for they feared his influence over the people. They put the word out that anyone who saw Creator Sets Free should report back to them.

As the people stood near the Sacred Lodge, many were talking about him. "What do you think," they asked each other, "will he even come to the festival?"

Preparation For His Grand Entry

The next day as they were coming into Jerusalem Creator Sets Free stopped near the Mountain of Olives. While there, he said to two of his followers, "Go to the village of Bethphage, just ahead of us. When you come into the village you will see a donkey with her colt tied next to her; a young donkey that no one has ever ridden.

Untie them and bring the young colt to me. If anyone asks what you are doing say this to them, 'Our Wisdomkeeper is in need of it,' and they will send you on your way."

His followers did as they were told. When they arrived at the village they found everything just as he had said. They started untying the donkeys when the owners asked them, "What are you doing?"

They answered the owners just as they had been instructed, so they were permitted to go. They brought the young donkey to Creator Sets Free, laid their outer garments on the colt, and sat him upon it.

O Sacred Village of Peace

Creator Sets Free began to ride the colt down the Mountain of Olives, being led by his twelve followers. He could see the Sacred Village of Peace and tears began to flow down his face.

As he opened his mouth to speak, his voice trembled with anguish and he could taste the salt from his tears.

"Jerusalem, *O Jerusalem*, you are the Sacred Village of Peace," he wept out loud. "Of all people, you should be the ones who would know the things that make for peace, but now they are hidden from your eyes.

"In the days ahead your enemies will encircle you and close in on you from every side. You will be crushed and trampled down, along with all your children. Every lodge will fall to the ground and not one log will be left standing against another. All of this, because you did not know it was your time for the Great Spirit to visit you."

His Grand Entry

When the people who had come to the Passover festival heard that Creator Sets Free was entering Jerusalem, a great crowd of them went out to greet him. Among this crowd were the ones who had seen Creator Sets Free bring Creator Helps Him back from *the world of the* dead. They were telling everyone about this great miracle and that is why the crowd was so large that day.

Creator Sets Free came riding into the Sacred Village of Peace down the Mountain of Olives toward the gate that is called Beautiful. His twelve followers encircled him and led the donkey forward.

He did not fit the powerful image of a conquering ruler, for he was not riding a warhorse; instead he rode a small, humble colt of a donkey. No mighty warriors rode next to him. No dignitaries from Jerusalem came out to meet him. It was mostly the common people who welcomed him that day.

Some of the people began to spread their outer garments on the road in front of Creator Sets Free. Others cut down palm branches from the trees and did the same. As he was coming down to the foot of the mountain the people began to dance and sing. They encircled him front and back, celebrating and giving thanks to the Great Spirit for the wonders they had seen.

As they came *through the Beautiful Gate* into the Sacred Village of Peace the whole village was in an uproar. "Who is this?" the people asked.

With one voice the crowd answered, "This is the prophet Creator Sets Free from the village of Nazareth in Galilee."

"Hosanna! Help us!" they cried out with glad hearts. "We honor you, O Grand Chief, who comes representing the Great Spirit. You shine down peace on us from the world above. You are the descendent of Much Loved One. You are the Grand Chief of the tribes of Wrestles With Creator!"

Some of the Separated Ones, who were in the crowd, could not believe their ears. "Wisdomkeeper!" they cried out. "Tell your followers to be silent and not say such things!"

"I will tell you this," he said to them. "If they were silenced the stones and rocks would lift their voices and cry out!"

The Separated Ones *huddled together near the crowd.* "Nothing we have done to stop him has worked," they complained. "Look! The whole world is now following him."

All this happened to show the full meaning of the ancient prophecy, "Do not fear, O daughter of Zion. Your Grand Chief is coming to you, in a humble way, riding upon a young donkey."[114]

At the time his followers did not understand these things. It was not until some time later, when he had entered his place of beauty and honor, that they remembered how the things done to him had first been written down by the ancient prophets long ago.

Creator Sets Free rode into Jerusalem until he came to the Sacred Lodge. He went into the Lodge and looked around at everything—then he left. It was time for the sun to set, so he returned to Bethany, along with his twelve followers, *to the place where they were lodging.*

The Fig Tree With No Fruit

The next morning, as Creator Sets Free was returning to Jerusalem from Bethany, he became hungry. He saw a fig tree with leaves on it in the distance and went to it thinking he might find some figs on it. But when he came to the tree he found only leaves, for it was not the season for figs.

He spoke to the tree, "No one will eat fruit from you again!" and his followers heard what he said.

Sacred Lodge Keeper

They went through the village gate, made their way through the crowded pathways, and went straight to the Sacred Lodge.

They came into the area in the Lodge called Gathering Place for the Nations. It was here that other nations could come to learn about the Great Spirit and his ways.

As Creator Sets Free entered the Lodge he saw people sitting at money tables. They were trading, buying and selling the ceremonial oxen, sheep and doves. *It was so crowded that there was no room for the people from other nations who had come to learn about the Great Spirit. They were not honoring the purpose of this holy place.*

Creator Sets Free took some leather straps and made a whip to drive them out of the Lodge. *He cracked the whip to startle and move the animals.* He tipped over the tables and scattered their money on the floor. He turned over the seats of those who were selling the ceremonial doves and blocked the way of the ones who were carrying goods through the Lodge.

"Go!" he roared at them. "Take these things out from here. Do not make my Father's Sacred Lodge into a trading post!"

His eyes flashed with fire and his voice trembled as he tried to make them understand.

206

"It is written," he cried out, "'My Lodge will be a house of prayer for all nations, but you have turned it into a hideout for thieves!'"[115]

The ones who walked the road with him listened and remembered the ancient prophecy, "My desire to honor your Sacred Lodge burns like a fire in my belly."[116]

"What gives you the right to do these things?" the people said to him. "Show us a sign!"

"Tear down this Sacred Lodge," he answered, "and in three days I will raise it up again."

The people *shook their heads and* said to him, "It took forty-six years to build this Great Lodge, and you will raise it up in three days?"

They did not understand that he was speaking about the Lodge of his own body. After he was raised from the dead his followers remembered what he said. This helped them believe the ancient Sacred Writings and the words he spoke to them.

After the day was over, they returned to their lodging place in Bethany.

The Dried Up Fig Tree

In the morning, as they were walking *again to Jerusalem,* they saw a fig tree dried up from the roots. Stands On the Rock remembered that it was the same tree Creator Sets Free had spoken to. "Wisdomkeeper!" he said. "Look, the fig tree you spoke to has dried up from the roots. How did it wither so quickly?"

"You must put all your trust in the Great Spirit," Creator Sets Free answered. "I tell you from my heart, speak to this mountain, tell it to lift up and go into the great waters, and it will. Do not doubt that the Maker of Life has already heard you, and what you have said will happen. In the same way, when you send your prayers to the Great Spirit, believe that he has heard you and the answer will come."

Conflict at the Sacred Lodge

Creator Sets Free came to the Sacred Lodge day by day, teaching the people and healing the sick among them. The ones who could not see or walk were brought to him and he made them whole.

Sounds of joy could be heard throughout the Lodge from the children as they shouted *and sang* out, "Hosanna, to the descendent of Much Loved One!"

When the head holy men and the scroll keepers saw his powerful medicine and heard the children, they burned with anger and said to him, "Do you hear what these children are saying?"

"I hear them," he said, "but have you not heard what the ancient Sacred Writings say? 'From the mouths of little children and nursing babies comes the greatest praise.'"

Hearing this, the head holy men, the scroll keepers, and the spiritual leaders among them, looked for new ways to put him to death. They were in fear *of his power over the people*, but could not figure out what to do, for the people were amazed at his teaching and hung on to every word he said.

The sun was setting, so Creator Sets Free left the Sacred Lodge and returned to Bethany where he was lodging.

The Spiritual Leaders Challenge Him

Creator Sets Free continued to walk about freely at the Sacred Lodge in Jerusalem. One day, when he was telling the people about Creator's Good Road, the head holy men and the scroll keepers came to him, along with the elders.

"By what right do you do these things?" they challenged. "Who gave you this right?"

"Answer my question and I will answer yours," he said to them. "The purification ceremony performed by He Shows Goodwill, was it from the world above, or did it come from human beings?"

The spiritual leaders looked at each other. They didn't know how to answer him. Creator Sets Free stood before them and held his ground.

"Give me your answer," he challenged back.

They put their heads together and talked it over. "If we say it is from the world above, he will ask us why we didn't listen to him. If we say it is from human beings, the people would stone us to death, for they think He Shows Goodwill is a great prophet."

The spiritual leaders were afraid of the people, so they said to him, "We don't know."

Creator Sets Free looked straight at them and said, "Then I will not answer your question either."

Since they would not answer him, Creator Sets Free told them the answer to his own question, with a story.

"A man with two sons came to one of his sons and said, 'Son, will you work in my vineyard today?' At first the son told him 'No,' but later changed his mind and went to work.

"Then the man went to his other son and asked him the same. He told his father, "Yes, I will,' but never went.

He looked right at the spiritual leaders and said, "Which of the two sons did what his father wanted? How do you see it?"

They said to him, "The first one."

"I tell you the truth, tribal agents and prostitutes will find their way into Creator's Good Road ahead of you! He Shows Goodwill came in a good way, but you refused to hear him. You saw how the tribal agents and prostitutes put their trust in him, but not even this changed your mind to believe him."

The Chief Center Pole Rejected

"Listen," he said to them, "and I will tell you another story."

"The owner of a large ranch planted a vineyard. He put a fence around it, dug a pit for the winepress, and put up a watchtower. He rented the vineyard out to some farmers for a share of the crops. He then traveled far away to another land to stay for a long time.

"When the time came to harvest the fruit, the ranch owner sent trusted messengers to gather his share of the crops. The farmers grabbed the messengers. They beat some with their fists and put them to death; others were whipped, wounded and mistreated in a shameful way.

"The ranch owner sent other messengers, a second and third time, but the farmers treated them the same way.

"Finally the ranch owner decided to send his much loved son thinking the farmers would honor him. When the farmers saw that he had sent his son, they put their heads together and came up with an evil plan. 'This vineyard will one day belong to this son,' they schemed. 'If we kill him, the vineyard will be ours.'

"So they took him by force, put him to death, and threw his dead body out of the vineyard."

Creator Sets Free turned to the spiritual leaders and said, "When the owner of the vineyard returns, what do you think he will do to those farmers?"

He waited for an answer, but no one said a word. Then he said, "He will put those dishonorable men to death and give the vineyard to others."

The spiritual leaders were insulted by this story. "This will never happen!" they said.

Creator Sets Free looked at the spiritual leaders and said, "Then what do the Sacred Writings mean when they say, 'The log the lodge builders threw away has become the chief center pole. The Great Spirit over the Lodge has planned for this and it will make many wonder'?[117] For when they stumble over this log it will break them into pieces, and when it falls on them they will be crushed *and scattered like dust in the wind."*

A look of sadness swept over his face as he said, "Creator's Good Road will be taken away from you and given to a people who will walk in its ways and show its true meaning."[118]

When the head holy men and the Separated Ones realized that this story was spoken against them, they looked for a way to arrest him, but they could not, for the people believed he was a prophet. They were afraid of what the people might do, so they left him alone.

A Rejected Invitation

Then he told them another story to help them see.

"There was a great chief who prepared a wedding feast for his son and invited many people. When the feast was ready he sent out trusted messengers to gather the ones who had been invited, but no one came.

"So he sent out others again with this message, 'Come to the table, the food is ready, the wedding feast for my son has been prepared!'

"Some ignored the messengers and returned to their work, while others mistreated them and even put them to death.

"When the chief found out what they had done, he was filled with rage and sent his warriors to kill those murderers and burn their village.

"Then the chief told his messengers, 'The wedding feast is ready but the ones invited have proved they have no honor. Waste no time, go out into the village pathways and invite all you find to come to the feast.'

"So they went and did as they were told and gathered as many as they could find, even the ones among the outcast. So the lodge was filled with many wedding guests for his son—*making the father's heart glad.*

"When the chief came in to see the guests, he saw someone who was not wearing the proper regalia that was provided for the guests at the feast. He said to the guest, 'Why have you dishonored my son by not wearing the outfit I provided for you?'

"The man had nothing to say. The chief called his warriors and said to them, 'Bind him with leather straps from head to foot and throw him outside into the darkness, to weep and grind his teeth in anger.'

"So you can see," Creator Sets Free said, "many are invited but few accept his invitation."[119]

The Separated Ones Attack

The Separated Ones began to council with one another against Creator Sets Free. They sent spies who pretended to be good hearted to trap him in his words, so they would have a reason to turn him over to the People of Iron. So the spies went out, along with some of the Friends of Looks Brave, to question him.

"Wisdomkeeper," they said to him. "We know you always speak the truth about the Great Spirit and represent him well. You respect all human beings and treat them the same, whether rich or poor, powerful or weak."

Creator Sets Free could see right through them, but he let them finish speaking.

"Tell us what is right," they asked him. "Should our tribal members pay taxes to the government of the People of Iron? Yes or no?"

"Why are you putting me to the test? I can see behind your false faces!" he answered. "Show me one of their silver coins and let me take a close look at it."

They found a silver coin and handed it to him. *He took a good long look, holding it up to the sky to see it clearly. Then he turned the face of the coin toward them and asked,* "Whose image and words are carved into this coin?"

"The chief of the People of Iron," they answered.

He *handed the coin back to them and* said, "Then give to this chief the things that are his, and give to the Great Spirit the things that belong to the Great Spirit."

The spiritual leaders had failed, right in front of the people, and could not use his words against him. They were amazed at his wisdom and *hung their heads in silence as* they walked away.

The Upright Ones Attack

Later that same day some of the Upright Ones, who say there is no life again after death, came to Creator Sets Free to question him also.

"Wisdomkeeper," they said, "in the great law, Drawn From the Water gave us these instructions, 'If a tribal member should die before having children, then his brother should marry his widow and give her children. This way the man will have descendants.'

"In a family of seven brothers, the oldest took a wife, but died without children. The next brother married her, but he also died with no children. A third brother married her and like his other brothers he died with no children. The same happened to all seven of them and last of all the woman also crossed over to death. When they all come back to life in the new world, whose wife would she be, since all seven brothers married her?"

"You are asking the wrong question," Creator Sets Free answered back. "You do not understand the Sacred Writings or the power of the Great Spirit. Marriage belongs to this present world and to the ones who live in it. There will be no marriage in the world that is coming. The ones who are chosen to rise to life in that world will not marry. They will be like the spirit messengers who have no wives. They will never die, for they are the children of the Great Spirit who raises them again to new life."

And then he added, "You say you do not believe the dead will rise again. But do you remember the time when Drawn From the Water heard the voice of the Great Spirit speaking from the bush that was on fire? He said, 'I am the Great Spirit of Father Of Many Nations, of He Made Us Laugh, and of Heel Grabber.'

"He is not the Great Spirit of the dead, but of the living—for to him all are alive."

All the people who heard him were amazed at his wisdom and even the scroll keepers said to him, "Wisdomkeeper, you have answered well."

After that none of the Upright Ones asked him any more questions.

He Silences His Adversaries

Later when Creator Sets Free was teaching at the Sacred Lodge, he saw the Separated Ones gathering near him. He walked up to them and asked them this question, "Who is the Chosen One descended from? Whose son is he?"

"He is the son who is descended from Much Loved One," they answered.

"How then can the scroll keepers call him the descendant of Much Loved One," he asked, "when Much Loved One himself, speaking by the power of the Spirit, called the Chosen One his Great Chief? For in the book of Sacred Songs he said, 'The Great Chief said to my Great Chief, "Sit down beside me at my right hand, *my place of greatest honor,* until I make your enemies a place to rest your feet.""'[120]

He let his words sink in and then said, "If Much Loved One calls the Chosen One, 'My Great Chief,' how can the Chosen One be his descendant?"

None of the spiritual leaders could answer him. From that time on, no one dared to challenge him with another question. *His great wisdom had silenced the ones who were against him.*

The Greatest of the Instructions

One of the scroll keepers overheard Creator Sets Free opposing the Upright Ones. When he heard the good answer he had given, with an open heart he asked, "Which instruction in the great law stands first?"

"The first and greatest instruction is this," Creator Sets Free answered. "Hear me, O tribes of Wrestles With Creator. There is only one Great Spirit and Maker of us all—the One Who Is And Was And Is To Come.[121]

"You must love the Great Spirit from deep within, with the strength of your arms, the thoughts of your mind, and the courage of your heart.

"The second great instruction is like the first," he added. "You must love your fellow human beings in the same way you love yourselves. The great law and the words of the prophets all find their full meaning in these two instructions."

"Wisdom Keeper," he smiled, "you have answered well! What you have said is greater than all ceremonies and offerings we make to the Great Spirit."

When Creator Sets Free heard the scroll keeper's wise answer, he said, "You are not far from the Good Road."

He Warns About the Spiritual Leaders

In the mornings Creator Sets Free would come to the Sacred Lodge. Many of the tribal members would meet with him and listen with glad hearts as he spoke openly with all. *He cared deeply for the people, so he began to warn them about the spiritual leaders.*

"Beware of the Separated Ones and the scroll keepers," he said, *"they are leading you down the wrong path!* When they speak, they represent the great lawgiver Drawn From the Water, so listen to the truth they speak and do what they say, but do not walk in their ways.

"They fail to do the things they demand of others, and even worse they misuse their authority to control people for their own gain. They put heavy loads on their backs, too much for them to carry, but will not lift even one finger to help them.

"With many words they make long, empty prayers to trick widows into giving them their homes and possessions. The good deeds they do are only for show. When Creator brings everything full circle, they will find themselves in a bad place.

"Beware of the ones who try to look spiritual by wearing large and fancy medicine pouches and long fringes on their outfits. They love to dress up in fine regalia, sit in the seats of honor at the gathering houses, and have people call them 'wisdomkeeper' at the trading posts."

Then he turned and said to the ones who walked the road with him, "Titles like 'wisdomkeeper' and 'chief,' are not for you. There is only one true Wisdomkeeper and Chief, the Chosen One, and you all belong to his family; so call no one on earth 'father' for only the Great Spirit is truly the Father of us all.

When he finished speaking one of the scroll keepers said to him, "Wisdomkeeper, your words are an insult to all scroll keepers!"

He Confronts the Spiritual Leaders

Then he began to boldly confront the spiritual leaders, right in front of the crowds.

"You spiritual leaders hide behind false faces, but sorrow and trouble will catch up with you. You are not walking the Good Road and you stand in the way of the ones who want to enter it.

"You journey far and wide, across the great waters to find one person who will change to your ways. When you have won him over he becomes twice as bad as you are, a true son of the Valley of Smoldering Fire.

"You are spiritually blind guides, for you say, 'A promise made outside the Lodge can be broken, but one made inside must be kept.' Are you so foolish! It is not the Lodge that makes the promise good, but it is the Great Spirit over the Lodge who sees and hears all promises.

"Or you say, 'A promise made before a ceremony can be broken but one made during a ceremony must be kept.' Are you so blind? Can you not see that the Great Spirit sees and hears all promises and expects you to keep them?

"It doesn't matter if a promise is made inside or outside the Lodge, or before or during a ceremony. All promises on the earth below or in the world above are made before the eyes of the Great Spirit, who sees and hears everything.

"You are careful to do what the great law says by giving a tenth of each little herb in your garden, as you should, but you ignore the more important instructions like justice, kindness and honesty. *You fail to love people with the love Grandfather has shown to you.* You are spiritually blind guides, for you strain out a small flea from your water pouch, but swallow a whole moose.[122]

"Sorrow and trouble will be waiting at the end of the trail for you Separated Ones and scroll keepers, for you hide behind false faces. You are like unmarked burial grounds that others walk over without even noticing. You are like tombs that have been painted white to look good on the outside, but on the inside you are full of dead and rotting bones. You may look good to others, but you are full of falsehood and worthless ways.

"You scroll keepers have kept for yourselves the secrets of how to walk in the good pathways of wisdom and understanding. You have failed to walk in them yourselves and *even worse* you have barred the way for others who were trying to get in.

"You carve statues on the burial grounds of the prophets of old to honor them. But when you honor the prophets you show your false faces, for it was your ancestors who put them to death. You nest of poisonous snakes! How will you escape the Valley of Smoldering Fire?"

You say, 'If we had lived in the days of our ancestors we would not have participated with them when they shed the blood of the prophets.' But you are speaking against yourselves, for what you do proves you are the descendants of the ones who killed them, and you will finish what your ancestors started!

"But here is what the Great Spirit, in his wisdom, says to you, 'I will send to you prophets[123] and message bearers, wisdomkeepers and scroll keepers. You will whip some of them in your gathering houses, others you will nail to a tree pole. You will threaten them and pursue them from village to village until you shed their blood. Then you will be guilty of the blood of all the prophets from His Breath Goes Up,[124] *who was killed by his brother,* to Creator Will Remember, who was put to death in the courtyard of the Sacred Lodge.[125]

"The people living today will have to give an answer for shedding the blood of all the ones with good hearts, who have lived upon this earth since the beginning of the world."

When the scroll keepers and Separated Ones heard these words, spoken against them, their anger grew fierce, *but the people honored him, so what could they do?* So they kept scheming and waited for a better time.

A Sacrificial Gift

Creator Sets Free found a place to sit and rest near the storehouse of the Sacred Lodge. He watched as people came to put their gifts on the offering blanket. The ones with many possessions were putting down more than others. Then he saw a poor widow come to the blanket and place two small copper coins on it, worth almost nothing.

He gathered his followers around him, and told them about the widow's gift. "I tell you from my heart," he said, "this widow has given more than all the others. When they gave to the Great Spirit, they gave only a small part of their many possessions, but this poor widow has given all she had to live on."

Greeks Seek Him

Along with the tribal members of Wrestles With Creator, who came to participate in the Passover festival, there were also many outsiders from other nations who would come.

There were Greeks from these nations who came to celebrate the Festival. *Greeks are people who pride themselves in their study of wisdom and knowledge.* They went up to Friend Of Horses who was from Bethsaida in Galilee *and knowing him to be one who walked with Creator Sets Free,* they said to him, "Honored friend, we would like to see Creator Sets Free, your Wisdomkeeper, *to learn from him.*

Friend Of Horses *didn't know what to do with this request,* so he found Stands With Courage *and asked him what he thought.* Then together they both went to see Creator Sets Free and told him that the Greeks wished to see him.

He answered them, "It is time for the True Human Being to be lifted up to his place of honor, *by being nailed to a tree pole. This will sound foolish to those Greeks,*[126] *but go tell them this wise saying,* "If a seed is unplanted it remains only one seed, but if it dies, falls to the earth and enters the ground, it will then grow and become many seeds.

"The ones who love the life *the wisdom of* this world gives, will lose the life they seek, but the ones who let go *of their life in this world, and follow my ways,* will find the life of beauty and harmony that will never fade away.

"*Tell these Greeks to walk the road with me*; anyone who wants to serve me will walk in my footsteps and I will take them to the same place I am going. If they give up their lives to serve me in this way, my Father will honor them."

The Time of Honor Has Come

A look of sorrow came over the face of Creator Sets Free and he said, "But now I am deeply troubled and in anguish! Should I ask my Father to rescue me from this hour that has now come? No! I came into the world for this purpose."

He lifted his face, looked up to the sky and sent his words to the Great Spirit. "Father," he prayed, "honor your name and show the world the beauty of it."

Suddenly, a voice from above spoke out of the sky, "I have honored my name, *for it represents who I am,* and I will once again honor and show the beauty of it."

Some of the people standing nearby heard the voice and said, "Was that thunder?" Others said, "No, a spirit messenger has spoken to him."

Creator Sets free said to them, "This voice you heard was not for my sake, but for yours. It is a sign to you that it is now time for the Great Spirit to make his final decision about this world. The evil one who now rules this world will be defeated and thrown down. But I, the True Human Being, will be lifted up from the ground, *and nailed to a tree pole.* This is the way I will bring all *things, in the world above and the earth below,*[127] to myself." Creator Sets Free said this to show the kind of death he would die *and what his death would accomplish.*

The people who heard him said, "How can this be? We have been told from the great law that the Chosen One, when he comes, will remain beyond the end of all days. How can you say the True Human Being will be lifted up like this? Who are you talking about?"

Creator Sets Free spoke to them *with sadness in his voice,* "My light will shine on you for only a little while longer, so walk in my light before the darkness comes, for the ones who walk in darkness cannot see the path. Put your trust in the one who gives you light and then you will become children of light."

My Message Will Decide

Then he lifted his voice and cried out to the people, "If you trust me, you are not only trusting me, but the one who sent me. When you see me, you see the one who sent me. I came into this dark world as a shining light, so the ones who trust me will no longer have to stumble in the darkness.

"I have not come to decide against the ones who are not walking in my message, or to decide against the *people of this* world. Instead, I have come to rescue the *people of this* world and set them free. A day is coming when the ones who have turned away from me and my words will be decided against. In the end, it will be the message I have spoken that will decide for or against them.

"The message I have spoken is not from myself, it is from the one who sent me. I have spoken only what my Father gave me to speak, nothing more. The instructions he gave me lead to the life of beauty and harmony that does not fade away."

"That is all I have to say," he told them. *He then* went away and hid himself from the crowds.

Blind Eyes and Hard Hearts

Even though Creator Sets Free had *healed the sick, brought the dead back to life, and* shown the people powerful medicine from the Great Spirit, his own tribal nation still did not believe him or trust him.

This showed the full meaning of the ancient prophecy, "Who will believe such a thing? That Grandfather's great power would be shown in weakness."[128] And, "His great light has blinded their eyes and his great love has hardened their hearts. If only they would open their hearts to him, then they would see clearly and he would make them whole."[129]

The prophet Creator Will Help Us saw the true beauty of Creator Sets Free long ago and prophesied the reasons the people would not believe. But even so, many tribal leaders did believe in him, but would not tell anyone because they feared the Separated

Ones. They knew if they openly confessed their faith in him they would be put out of the gathering houses. In the end, their reputation with the people was more important to them than bringing honor to the Maker of Life.

CHAPTER SIXTEEN

Prophet of the End of the Age

What Will Be the Sign of Your Coming?

Creator Sets Free and his twelve message bearers were on their way out of the Sacred Lodge. They began to point out to him the size and beauty of the Great Lodge with all its surrounding buildings. "Look, Wisdomkeeper!" one of them said to him. "What handsomely carved logs and great stones!"

Creator Sets Free stopped walking and looked around at all the buildings of the Great Lodge. A look of great sadness came over his face and with a deep sigh he said to them, "Take a good long look, for I tell you the truth, in the days ahead all of this will fall to the ground. Not one log will be left standing against another."

Later that day Creator Sets Free sat down to rest on the Mountain of Olives. *He gazed across the valley looking at the walls of Jerusalem and the Sacred Lodge.* Stands On The Rock and Heel Grabber, along with He Shows Goodwill and Stands With Courage, came to him privately.

They *looked at him with worried faces and* asked, "Wisdomkeeper, when will this happen? What will be the sign of your coming that will bring an end to this age we live in?"

He answered them, "In the time of trouble ahead, you will long for the days when the True Human Being walked among you. Those days will be no more. But before this time comes he will first suffer many things and be turned away by the people living today.

The Sign of False Prophets

"Beware of the ones who would lead you down the wrong path," he warned them. "Many will come claiming to be the Chosen One and say, 'I am the Chosen One, *follow me*, there is no time left!' False prophets will emerge among the people. They will perform great signs and wonders to mislead the people.

"Be on the lookout, for even the ones who walk the Good Road will be tempted to believe them.

"Remember these words, for I am warning you ahead of time! Many will go with them to a bad end, so do not go along with them. When they say to you, 'Look, he is here!' and 'Look, he is over there!' ignore them! If they say, 'The Chosen One is in the desert wilderness,' do not go with them there. Or if they say, 'The Chosen One is hidden in a secret place,' do not believe them. When the True Human Being appears, it will be like lightning when it flashes across the sky from the east to the west."

The Sign of War, Famine and Plagues

"There will be wars and stories of war breaking out, but do not fear, for all of this must happen first. The end will not come all at once. There will be tribal wars and nation will make war against nation. Food will be scarce and sickness will spread everywhere.

"When you see the earth shake in many places and fearful signs in the world above, remember—this is only the beginning of the time of sorrow, like a woman who is giving birth.

The Sign of Tribal Betrayal

"Before all of this happens you will face troubled times. Because of me you will be hated by all kinds of people from many nations. Your own tribes will mistreat you and even kill you. They will hunt you down, drag you into their gathering houses, bring you before their tribal councils, and put you in their prisons. Even in their gathering houses they will whip you with leather cords.

"When they drag you before government rulers and officials, this will be your chance to tell them about me. Do not worry about what to say ahead of time. Speak what is given to you right then. The words you speak will not be your own, but will come to you from the Holy Spirit. I will give you the mouth of a wisdomkeeper and no enemy will be able to answer you or prove you wrong.

The Sign of Family Betrayal

"All of this will cause many to stumble in their walk and stray from the path. People will hate, betray and even kill each other. Brother will rise against brother and father against child. Children will turn on their parents and have them put to death.

"Evil will grow strong and the love in many hearts will grow cold. But the ones who stand firm *in their faith* to the end—will overcome.

"You will not lose even one hair from your heads, all because you stood strong and never gave up trusting me. The Good News about Creator's Good Road will be told all over the world, so all nations can hear about it—then the end will come.

Signs in the World Above and Earth Below

"In the days ahead, after this time of trouble and sorrow, there will be signs in the sun, moon and stars. When the people see the sun grow dim, the moon darken, and the stars fall from the sky, their knees will grow weak. When they see the powers from the world above tremble and shake, their hearts will fall to the ground.

"When they feel the earth shake, hear the great waters of the sea roar and see the waves swell, confusion and terror will fall on the nations. Human beings will tremble and weep when they see what is coming upon them.

"Then all the tribes of the land will mourn when they look up and see the sign of the True Human Being. He will be riding on the clouds showing his great power and beauty. He will blow his eagle whistle[130] loud and strong and send his spirit messengers to gather his chosen ones together from the four directions, from the world above and the earth below.

The Sign of the Horrible Thing That Destroys

"When you see Jerusalem encircled by the armies *of the People of Iron,* you will know that the time of her destruction has come. Then you will understand the meaning of what the prophet Creator Will Decide saw when he spoke of the horrible thing that brings destruction making its stand in the place that is holy. The people of Judea should run to the mountains for safety and the ones who are inside the walls of Jerusalem must get out and the ones outside should not go in. If you are on your rooftop, go—without taking time to get anything from your house. Workers in the fields should not even go back to get their coats. It will be a terrible time for women who are pregnant or nursing their babies. Pray that it will not happen in winter or on a Day of Resting, for it will be a time of great trouble on the land.

"The full meaning of the Sacred Writings are clear. It will be the day of destruction that Creator in his anger spoke about long ago; a time of trouble and sorrow like no other. A worse time has not been seen since the Great Spirit created the world up to this day and will never be seen again.

"If the Great Spirit did not cut those days short, no one would survive, but for the sake of the ones who walk the road with him, he will cut those days short.

"And so, when Jerusalem falls, cut down by the long knives, the people will be taken captive and scattered into all the nations. *Because they did not know the way of peace,*[131] this great Village of Peace will be trampled down by the nations until their time has come to an end.

"When you see all these things begin to happen, *stand strong my followers*—lift up your heads, for the time of your captivity will soon come to an end!

How the Great Spirit Will Decide

"When the True Human Being comes in all of his power and beauty, he will sit down in his place of honor. His spirit messengers will be with him and all nations will be gathered around him. He will choose between them like a shepherd separates the sheep from the goats. He will put the sheep on his right side and the goats to his left.

"Then the Chief will say to the sheep on his right, 'The blessing way of my Father rests on you. Come into the Land of Creator's Good Road that has been prepared for you from the beginning of the world. For I was thirsty and you gave me drink, I was hungry and you fed me, I was a stranger and you gave me lodging. When I needed clothes you gave me something to wear and you visited me in prison.'

"'When did we do these things for you?' the good hearted ones asked.

"'I tell you from my heart,' he answered them, 'whatever you did for my fellow human beings[132] who needed help, you did for me.'

"Then the Chief will say to the goats on his left, 'Go away from me, you who have bad hearts, into the fire that burns everything up; made for the evil serpent and his messengers. When I was hungry you gave me nothing to eat, when I was thirsty you gave me no drink, and when I was a stranger you turned me away. When I needed clothes you gave me nothing to wear and when I was in prison you failed to visit me.'

"'Honored One,' they questioned, 'when was it that we saw you like this and did nothing?'

"'Listen closely,' he answered back, 'When you did not help the ones who needed it most, you failed to help me.'

"Then the goats will go away to their final punishment and the sheep will enter the land of beauty and harmony that does not fade away."

The Sign of the Fig Tree and All Trees

Then he told them this wisdom story, "Look at this fig tree or any tree and see what it is saying to you. When the branches of a tree get soft and leaves appear, you know that it is nearly summer.

"In the same way when you see these things happening, know that Creator's Good Road is about to come into full bloom.

"Listen closely! All of this will happen to this generation, during the lifetime of the people who live today. What I am telling you is more sure than the morning sunrise.

No One Knows the Day or Hour

"No one knows the day or hour these things will take place, not the spirit messengers from the world above, not even the Son— only my Father knows.

"When the True Human Being comes it will be like it was in the days before the great flood. The people were eating and drinking and getting married until the day that One Who Rests entered the great wooden boat. No one knew what was coming until the flood waters came, washed them away and drowned them all.

"It will be the same as it was in the days of Covers His Head. The people were eating and drinking, trading goods, planting seeds, and building their lodges until the day came that Covers His Head left the village of Sodom. Then rocks burning with fire fell from the sky and destroyed them all.

"Listen! Two people will be in bed at night, one will be taken away and the other left. In the field two women will be husking grain, one will be taken and the other left. Two men will be working in the field, one will be taken and the other left.

"Taken where?" his followers asked.

"To the place where the *dead* bodies lie and the vultures gather over them," he answered.

So Always Be Ready

"That day will fall suddenly on all the people, like a beaver snared in a trap. Keep walking the Good Road so you will be prepared. You will not be ready if strong drink controls you and possessions rule over you. For the True Human Being will come at a time you do not expect. Pray that you will be found worthy, *walking the*

Good Road, to escape all these things and to stand strong when that day comes.

He told them a story to help them understand.

"A chief was going away on a long journey. He gathered the young men of the village together and put them in charge while he was gone. He gave each of them their work to do and set warriors to guard the village gate. The young men must always be ready, for they do not know when he will return. It may be when the sun sets, or when the moon is high. It may be when the rooster crows, or at the first light of day. But they know they must be wide awake when the chief returns. In the same way you must always be ready for your chief to return—so stay awake and watch!"

Then he told them another story to make sure they understood.

"When that day comes, *the ones who are walking* the Good Road will be like ten unmarried women who are part of a wedding ceremony. Five of them were foolish and five were wise. They all took their ceremonial oil lamps with them to welcome the groom. The wise women took a pouch of oil along, but the foolish ones did not bother to bring any.

"While they waited for the groom to come they all fell asleep. Then suddenly, in the dark of the night, someone cried out, 'Look! The groom is coming, let us go welcome him!' All the women woke up and prepared their lamps so they would shine bright, but the oil in the lamps had run out.

"The foolish ones said to the wise, 'Give us some of your oil so our lamps won't go out.'

"The wise ones answered back, 'There is not enough for all of us. *Hurry,* go to the village and trade for some more.'

"They hurried away to get more oil, but while they were gone the groom came and all the guests went into the lodge for the wedding feast and the door was closed. A while later the other women came to the door and said to the gatekeeper, 'Honored one, open the door and let us come in.' But he said to them, 'I do not even know who you are—*why should I let you in?*'"

Creator Sets Free finished the story with these words of wisdom. "Here is what I am saying to you, be prepared *like the wise women in this story,* for you do not know when the True Human Being will come."

CHAPTER SEVENTEEN

His Last Meal With His Followers

Preparation for His Burial

After Creator Sets Free had finished speaking all these things, he said to the twelve, "Passover is only two days away. This is when the True Human Being will be turned over to the government to be put to death on the tree pole."

Creator Sets Free and the ones who walked the road with him then returned one last time to Bethany, where they were lodging.

That night, they had a meal to honor Creator Sets Free in the home of a man with a skin disease, whose name was One Who Hears. Head Woman was preparing the meal, and Her brother, Creator Helps Him, was sitting with the Wisdomkeeper and the other guests.

Bitter Tears, *the sister of Head Woman*, took a pottery jar which held a small amount of costly oil. She came up to Creator Sets Free as he sat at the table, broke the pottery jar and poured the sweet smelling oil over his head. Then she rubbed some on his feet and wiped them with her hair. The scent of the sweet smelling oil filled the whole house.

Some of his followers, who saw this, became angry and said to each other, "Why waste this costly oil? It could have been traded for food and goods to give to the ones who have none."

All in the house began to speak harshly to her. Speaks Well Of, who was in charge of the money pouch, said, "This could have been traded for a year's wages and given to the poor." He said this, not because he cared for the poor, but because he was a thief and was stealing from the money pouch.

Creator Sets Free heard everything and said to them, "Let her be! Why are you troubling her? She has done a good thing, saving this for the day of my burial. You can help the poor any time, for they will always be with you, but I will not. This was her gift to prepare me for my burial. I tell you from my heart, when the Good News is told all over the world, what she has done will also be told in memory of her."

Word got out that Creator Sets Free was there. People came from all around to see him, not only him but also Creator Helps Him, the one he had brought back from the dead.

Betrayal

Back in Jerusalem in the lodge of Hollow In The Rock, who was the head holy man, the elders of the tribal council came together in secret. They were making a plan to kill Creator Helps Him, for because of him many of the tribal members believed in Creator Sets Free. They were also making a plan to capture Creator Sets Free—and kill him.

"We should not do it during the festival," they said, "for the people might turn against us and fight."

At the same time in Bethany, Speaks Well Of left the house, still angry about the waste of the costly ointment and the rebuke of

Creator Sets Free. The Accuser, who is the evil serpent, entered his heart, *so in anger he walked quickly to Jerusalem* and went to the Lodge of Hollow In The Rock, *where they were still in council.* He went to the head holy men and the other spiritual leaders and told them of his plan to betray Creator Sets Free.

"How much is he worth to you?" he said to the spiritual leaders. "What is the price you will pay me to hand him over?"

They couldn't believe their ears! With glad hearts they agreed to pay him. The amount they settled on was thirty pieces of silver."[133]

He agreed to the amount and began to look for a chance to betray Creator Sets Free at a time when there were no crowds around him."

Preparing for the Ceremonial Meal

It was now the first day of the festival of Passover also called festival of Bread With No Yeast. This was when the ceremonial Passover lamb would be killed *and eaten.*

"His followers came to Creator Sets Free and asked, "Where do you want us to go and prepare for the eating of the ceremonial meal?"

"Go into the village," he instructed them, "where you will meet a man carrying a pouch of water. He will take you to a house. Go in with him and say to the head man of the house, 'Our Wisdomkeeper wants to know where the room is to eat the Passover meal with his followers?' He will then take you to a large upper room that will be ready for you."

They did as he said and found everything was just as he told them, so they prepared the room for the ceremonial meal.

The Ceremonial Meal Begins

When the sun was setting, Creator Sets Free and his twelve message bearers went to the room that had been prepared and they all sat down around the table.

Creator Sets Free *looked into the faces of his followers.* "How I have longed to sit and eat this Passover meal with you before I suffer," he said with a heavy heart. "I will not eat of it again until it finds its full meaning in the Land of Grandfather's Good Road."

Creator Sets Free knew it was time to leave this world and go back to his Father. He had come from the Great Spirit and was returning to him. He knew his Father had entrusted everything to him. He also knew that the evil serpent had twisted the heart of Speaks Well Of to betray him. His love for the ones who walked the road with him had always been great and now at the end, his love for them remained strong.

Foot Washing Ceremony

Knowing all of this, Creator Sets Free got up from the table, took off his outer garments, and wrapped a towel around himself like a sash. He poured water into a vessel and one by one, he began to wash the feet of his followers and dry them with his towel.

This was a task reserved for only the lowest servant of the household.

He came to Stands On The Rock, who said to him, "Wisdomkeeper, are you washing my feet?"

"You will not understand now, but later you will," he answered.

"No!" Stands On The Rock lifted his voice, "This can never be!"

Creator Sets Free *looked deep into his eyes and* said, "If you refuse this, then you have no part in who I am."

"Wisdomkeeper," he answered back, "*If this is so,* then wash my hands and head also!"

Creator Sets Free *smiled and* said, "If you have already had a bath, only your feet need washing and then you will be clean all over. Now, you are all clean—except for one." He said this because he knew who would betray him.

After he had finished washing all their feet, he put his outer garments back on and sat down again at the table. "Do you see what I have done?" he said to them. "From now on do the same for each other. You are right to call me Wisdomkeeper and Chief—because I am. If I, your Wisdomkeeper and Chief, have washed your feet, then you should wash each others feet.

"I tell you the truth, the one who serves is not greater than the one who is served. A messenger is not greater than the one who sent him. If you walk in this way of blessing, you will do well and it will return to you—full circle. I tell you from my heart, the one who welcomes the one I send, welcomes me. The one who welcomes me, welcomes the one who sent me.

One of You Will Betray Me

"I am not talking about all of you, for I know the hearts of the ones I have chosen. Now you will see the full meaning of the Sacred Writings that said, 'The one who ate with me has turned against me.'[134] I am telling you this ahead of time, so when it happens you will believe that I am *the Chosen One."*

When he finished saying this Creator Sets Free became deeply troubled in his spirit. *As sorrow moved over his face,* he said to all,

"The one who will betray me is sitting at this table and has dipped his bread into the dish with me."

His followers' hearts fell to the ground. They looked around at each other, wondering who would do such a thing. They all, one by one, asked Creator Sets Free, "Am I the one?"

He Shows Goodwill was sitting next to Creator Sets Free. Stands On The Rock motioned him to ask Creator Sets Free who it was. So he leaned in close and whispered in his ear, "Wisdomkeeper, who is it?"

"It is one of the twelve sitting here," he answered. "When I dip my bread into the dish, I will give it to the one who will turn against me." He did as he said and handed the bread to Speaks Well Of, the son of He Hears. When Speaks Well Of took the bread, the evil serpent took hold of his heart.

"The True Human Being will walk the path that has been chosen for him," Creator Sets Free said out loud. "The Sacred Writings have made it clear, but it will not go well for the one who turns against him. It would be better if that one had never been born."

Speaks Well Of looked at Creator Sets Free and asked, "Wisdomkeeper, do you think I am the one?"

"You know *if* you are the one," he answered, and then said, "Go now!—and do what you have planned."

Right then Speaks Well Of got up from the table and went out into the night.

None of the others understood what Creator Sets Free was saying to him. Since he was the keeper of the money pouch, they thought he was going to pay for the meal or give something to the poor.

After he left, Creator Sets Free said to them all, "The time has now come for the True Human Being to show the beauty of the Great Spirit and to be honored by him. As soon as the Son gives him honor, he will give honor back to the Son."

A New Ceremony For A New Peace Treaty

During the meal Creator Sets Free took some of the bread, lifted it up and gave thanks. He broke it into pieces, gave some to each of his followers and said, "This is my body, my gift to you, take it and eat it. Do this to remember me."

After the meal was over, he took a cup of wine, lifted it up and gave thanks. He gave it to his followers and said, "This wine is for the New Peace Treaty.[135] It is my life-blood poured out for many people, to heal their brokenness, and take away their bad hearts and wrongdoings. Take it now and drink all of it."

The cup was passed from Creator Sets Free to each of them and one by one they all drank from it.

Creator Sets Free said to them, "I tell you from my heart, I will not drink from the fruit of this vine again until I drink it with you in a fresh and new way, in the Land of my Father's Good Road.

"You have stood with me even in my time of sorrow and testing. My Father has made me the gatekeeper of the Good Road. As the gatekeeper, I open the way for you to sit at my table and to eat and drink in the Land of the Good Road. There you will sit in twelve places of honor and decide all things for the tribes of Wrestles With Creator."

Who Is the Greatest?

When they heard what he said, they began to argue about which one of them was to be seen as the greatest.

"Do you not remember what I told you before," he said. "Rulers from the Nations show their power by forcing people around, saying they are helping them. This will not be the way of the ones who walk my road. The great ones will be humble like a child, and the rulers will be the ones who serve."

He let his words sink into their hearts. "Who is greater?" he asked. "The one who is being served or the one who serves?"

They all hung their heads and would not look him in the eye.

"You would say it is the one being served," he said clearly, "but this night I was the one serving you."

The voice of Creator Sets Free was full of compassion and love. His followers lifted their heads up and looked at their Wisdomkeeper.

"I am showing you a new road," he said. "In the same way I have loved you—you are to love each other. This kind of love will be the sign for all people that you are walking the road with me."

All Of You Will Turn Away

The Passover meal was coming to an end. It was time to close the ceremony and face the dark night ahead.

"My little children," he said to them, "my time with you is almost gone. You will look for me, but where I am going you cannot follow. This is the same thing I said to the other tribal members and I now say to you."

At the end of the ceremonial meal, they sang a song to honor Grandfather, and then walked to the Mountain of Olives.

Stands On The Rock said to Creator Sets Free, "Wisdomkeeper, where are you going?"

"The path I walk tonight, you cannot walk with me" he answered, "but you will walk it later."

"Wisdomkeeper!" he said with a loud voice. "Why can't I walk with you now? I am ready to give my life for you!"

"Yes!" all the others agreed. "We will give our lives for you."

"Will you lay down your lives for me?" Creator Sets Free asked. "The Accuser, that evil serpent, has claimed his right to put you all to the test, like one who separates the grain from the husks."

But turning to Stands On The Rock, he spoke to him using his family name, "O One Who Hears, I have prayed for you, that your failure will not turn you from the Good Road. When you turn back once again, then help the others to do the same."

But One Who Hears *could not hear, so he* said, "Wisdomkeeper, can you not see! I am ready to go with you to both prison and death. Even if they all turn away from you, I will not!"

Creator Sets Free *looked at him with sad eyes and* said to Stands On The Rock, *"One Who Hears*—listen to me! Before the rooster crows, this very night, you will deny that you know who I am. Not once, not twice, but three times."

Then he said to his followers, "All of you will turn away from me. It was written long ago, 'Attack the shepherd and the sheep will scatter.'[136]

"But when I rise from the dead, I will go ahead of you to Galilee."

No Other Guide

His followers hung their heads as his words sank deep into their hearts. Creator Sets Free gathered them together and had them sit down in a circle, like an eagle gathering her young under her wings. He spoke softly but clearly to them as the light of the moon made shadows on the ground and the sounds of the night whispered in their ears.

"Don't let your hearts fall to the ground," he encouraged them. "Trust the Great Spirit and trust me. My Father's Lodge has room for everyone. I would not tell you this if it were not so.

"Where I am going, *and what I am about to do,* will make a place for you. When I come back I will receive you to myself, *make my home in you,*[137] and you will always be with me. You already know the path to where I am going."

Looks Like His Brother interrupted and said, "Wisdomkeeper, if we don't know where you are going, how can we know the path?"

"I am the *Great Spirit's* pathway, the truth *about who he really is,* and the life *of beauty and harmony he offers to all.* There is no other guide who can take you to the Father. To know me is to know my Father, so from now on you know him and have seen him."

Show Us The Father

Friend Of Horses said to him, "Wisdomkeeper, show us the Father and that will be enough."

"Friend Of Horses," Creator Sets Free said, "how long have you walked with me, and still you do not know me? How can you say 'Show us the Father?' The ones who have seen me have seen the

Father. Do you not believe that the Father is in me and I am in the Father?

"The words I speak to you are not my own, it is the Father speaking in me. Trust me, for I am in the Father and he is in me; or trust in the works my Father does through me.

"Listen to what I am saying to you. The ones who trust me will do the same things I do, and even greater things, for I am going away to my Father. When you ask the Father for anything, ask it in my name, representing who I am. When you ask in this way, I will do it to bring honor to my Father.

Promise Of The Great Spirit Guide

"If you love me you will walk in my ways. I will ask the Father to send one who will always walk beside you and guide you *on the Good Road.* He is the Spirit of truth, the one this world is not able to accept, because it does not see or know him. But you know him, for he is with you now and will soon be in you.

"I will not leave you like a child with no parents—I will come back to you. Soon this world will no longer see me, but you will see me. Because I will live again, you will also live. When that day comes, you will know that I am in the Father, that you are in me and I am in you. The ones who walk in my ways and stay true to my message love me. They will be loved by my Father and I will love them and show them my true self."

Speaks Well Of (not the one who betrayed him) asked, "Wisdomkeeper, how will you show yourself to us and not to the rest of the world?"

"I will show myself to the ones who love me and are staying true to my message. They will be loved by my Father and we will come and make our home in and among them. The ones who do not *return my* love will not walk in my message. This message is not only mine. It is from the one who sent me—my Father.

"I have told you these things while I am still with you, but there is one who the Father is sending to represent me. He will walk beside you and be your Spirit Guide. He is the Holy Spirit. He will be your Wisdomkeeper and will help you remember all that I have told you.

"I leave you now with my great peace—it is my gift to you. It is not the kind of peace the world gives. Keep your hearts off the ground and do not let fear hold you back. I told you I am going away and that I will come back. This should make your hearts glad if you truly love me, for I am going to the one who is greater than I am— to my Father, the One Above Us All.

"I have told you all these things before hand, so when you see them happen you will believe. There is little time left to talk with you. The dark ruler of this world is coming. His power over me is nothing, but I must walk the path the Father has for me, so the world will know the great love I have for him.

The True Vine and the Vine Keeper

"I am the true vine. My Father is the Vine Keeper. He cuts off the branches that have no fruit. He carefully trims back the branches with fruit, so they will grow more fruit.

"My message purifies you, but you must stay joined to me in the same way a branch is joined to the vine. A branch cannot grow fruit unless it is joined to the vine and it is the same with you and me.

"I am the vine and you are the branches. The ones who stay joined to me will grow much fruit, for without me nothing grows.

The ones who do not stay joined to me are broken off and dry up, then they are gathered up and used to make a fire.

"If you are joined to me and my message lives in you, you can ask me for anything and it will be done. When you grow a harvest of fruit, this will show that you are walking my road and bring great honor to my Father.

The Good Road is the Way of Love

"In the same way the Father loves me I have loved you. Make this love your dwelling place. By doing what the Father has told me, I have remained in his love. As you walk in my ways, my love will remain in you. I am saying this so your hearts will be filled with the same joy I have.

"To walk the road with me, you must love each other in the same way I have loved you. There is no greater way to show love to friends than to die in their place. You are my friends if you do what I am telling you. I no longer see you as my servants but as friends. Masters do not share their hearts and plans with their servants, but I have told you everything my Father told me.

"You think you chose me, but I am the one who chose you. You are my new garden where I will grow a great harvest of my love— the fruit that remains. When you bear this fruit, the Father can give you whatever you ask for. I am telling you this so you will walk the road of love with each other.

The World Will Hate You

"If you are hated by the world, remember, it hated me first. The ones who walk in the ways of this world, love the ones who do the same, but look down on and hate the ones who do not. I chose you to walk in my ways, and that is why the ones who walk in the ways of the world hate you. Remember, I told you a servant is not greater than the one he serves. If I was hunted down, it will be the same for you. If they walk in my message, they will walk in yours.

"The *people who walk in the ways of this* world will do this to you, because you walk in my ways, representing me. This shows they do not know the one who sent me.

"If I had not come and told the people who walk in the ways of this world the truth, they would not be guilty of this, but now their guilt remains. If I had not done the things no one else has done, they would have no guilt, but now they have seen with their own eyes and hated me and my Father. The full meaning of their own law has become clear, 'They hated me for no reason.'[138]

"The Spirit of Truth is coming from the Father to tell about who I truly am. He is the one I am sending to you. He will guide you on the road of life and will help you show others who I truly am, for you have walked with me from the first.

"I am telling you these things to keep you from stumbling away from the path. They will force you out of their gathering houses. The time will come when they will put you to death thinking they are doing what the Great Spirit wants. All because they do not know me or my Father. I am telling you this so when the time comes you will remember I told you ahead of time. I did not tell these things from the first because I was with you—but now I am going away.

It Is Better For You If I Go Away

"I am returning to the one who sent me, but none of you are asking, 'Where are you going?' *You are thinking only of yourselves* because my words have made your hearts fall to the ground. But listen closely, it is better for you that I go away. If I remain, the one who will guide you will not come, but if I go, I will send him to you.

"When the Holy Spirit comes, he will show the people who walk in the ways of this world the truth about their wrong ways. He will show the right ways of the Great Spirit, and also where the world will end up if it continues on its dark path. The worthless ways of this world will come to an end when they trust in me and my way. The right way of the Great Spirit will come, when I return to the Father and you no longer see me. The world will see where the dark path is taking them, when I bring an end to the ruler of this world.

"There are many more things I want to say to you, but your hearts are not strong enough to hear them now. When the Spirit of Truth comes, he will be the one to tell you. He will be your Spirit Guide and will lead you down the path of truth. He will fully represent me and only tell you what I have told him. The Spirit will show you what is coming on the road ahead. He will honor me by showing you who I am and what I have done for you. All that I am and all that I have comes from the Father. He has not held back one thing from me and the Spirit will not hold back anything from you. He will show you who I truly am.

"Soon I will be gone and you will not be able to see me, and then after a little while you will see me again." His followers began to whisper to each other, "What is he saying? We don't know what he means by 'a little while' and 'not seeing him and seeing him again.' What does he mean by 'I go to the Father?'"

Creator Sets Free knew what they wanted to ask him, so he said, "You want to know what I meant when when I said soon you will not see me, but then you will see me again.

"Listen to me closely. Your hearts will fall to the ground and your tears will be many, but the world around you will have glad hearts. All of you will be filled with sorrow, but your sorrow will turn to dancing!

"When a woman is giving birth she has sorrow, for her time of pain has come. But when she gives birth to her child she forgets her pain, for a new human being has been born into the world. It will be the same for you. You will have sorrow for now, but when I see you again you will dance for joy—and no one will be able to take your joy from you.

A New Way of Asking

"When that time comes your questions will be answered. Not by asking me, but by asking the Father himself. You will ask the Father in my name, fully representing me. I know you have never asked in this way before, but it is now time. When you ask in this new way, the Father will answer, and your hearts will know the full meaning of joy.

"I have told you truths from the world above, using earthly stories. The time is coming when I will not have to use stories, but will tell you plainly about the Father. When that time comes, you will not need me to ask the Father for you, because you will ask him yourself. When you ask in my name, you are representing me, and your love and trust in me will bring the Father's love to you—full circle. I came into this world from the Father, and now I am leaving this world and returning to the Father."

His followers said to him, "Now you are speaking plainly to us, instead of using stories! We now see that you know all things, and can answer a question before it is asked. This helps us to believe that you came from the Father above."

"You say you believe now," he said to them, "but soon you will all be scattered and return to your families. You will leave me alone, but I will not be alone, for my Father is with me. I have told you all these things so you will have my peace. This world is full of sorrow, pain and trouble, but have strong hearts, for I have defeated the world."

He Prays for Himself and His Followers

When Creator Sets Free was finished speaking to his followers, he lifted his eyes to the world above and sent his words to the Great Spirit.

"O Great Father," he prayed, "it is time for you to bring honor to your Son, so he may bring honor to you. You have put all human beings under the care of your Son, so he can give them the life of beauty and harmony that does not fade away. This life comes from knowing you, the only true and Great Spirit, and from knowing the Chosen One, Creator Sets Free, the one you have sent into this world.

"I have brought you honor on earth by finishing the work you sent me to do. It is now time, my Father, for you to honor me with the beauty I shared with you before you created all things.

"I have shown who you truly are to the ones you gave me from this world. They were yours and you trusted me with them. They have walked in your ways and now know that I and my message[139] come from you.

"The message you gave to me I have given to them. They know the truth about who I am and trust that you sent me.

"I am not praying for the ones who walk in the ways of the world, but for the ones who belong to you. My followers bring honor to me, they are a gift from you, a gift we share together.

"I am now returning to you and will no longer be in the world, but my followers will still be here. O Father of all that is holy, watch over them with the loving care that we share with one another. In this way they will also share the love that makes us one.

"During my time on earth I kept them safe in your loving care. Not one of them has been lost, except for the one foretold in the Sacred Scrolls, the one doomed to a bad end.

"I am returning to you now, but while I am still here I pray for my followers, so they may share in my joy. Your message, that I gave them, has taken root in their hearts. Like me, they have chosen not to walk in the ways of this world, and so the world hates them.

"I am not asking you to remove them from the world, but that you keep them safe from the evil one and his ways. You sent me into the world and now, in the same way, I send them into the world. Make them holy through the beautiful message of your truth. I offer up my life for them, a sacred sacrifice, *like the smoke of burning sage,* so they can walk in the beauty of your truth.

"My prayers are not only for them, but for all who will trust in me through their message. I pray that all who walk with me will be joined together as one. In the same way that you, Father, are in me and I am in you; that they may be one in us. This is how the world will believe that you have sent me.

"The beauty you gave to me I have given to them, this will join them together in us. In the same way you are in me, I will be in them, beautifully joined together as one. This is the reason you sent me into this world, to show that you love them just as you love me.

"O Great Father, I want the ones you have given to me to share this place of beauty with me so they can see the beauty of your love for me, a love that we shared before you created all things. O Father of all that is good and right, the world does not know you, but I know you and so do the ones you sent to me. I have represented, and will always represent, who you truly are; so that the love you have for me will be in them, and I will live in them."

Troubled Times Ahead

After Creator Sets Free *had prayed he gathered his followers around him. He knew they would soon face troubled times, so he* said, "When I sent you out *to tell the Good News to the villages,* you took no money pouch, no traveling bundle, not even extra moccasins. Did you need anything?"

"Nothing," they answered.

"That is good," he said, "but now take your money pouch and your traveling bundle with you."

Then he spoke of what they would face that very night.

"Also, if you have no long knife, then trade for one using your outer garment, for there is another one of the Sacred Writings that tell what will happen to me, that says, 'He was numbered with the rebels.'[140] This also must find its full meaning in me."

"Wisdomkeeper!" they said, "Look, here are two long knives."

"That will be enough," he answered.

CHAPTER EIGHTEEN

End of the Trail

Prayer of Suffering

Creator Sets Free and his followers left there and went over the Kidron brook to a garden called Gethsemane near the bottom of the Mountain of Olives, a place where he often prayed. *Gethsemane means Where the Olives Are Pressed.*

When they arrived he said to them, "Wait here while I go and pray."

He then took with him Stands on the Rock and the two brothers, Heel Grabber and He Shows Goodwill, *to a place not far from the others.* Creator Sets Free became deeply troubled. Sorrow and pain began to show on his face. "My heart is sick with sorrow to the point of death," he said to them. "Stay close and pray for me. Pray also for yourselves, that you will have the strength to face the rough trail ahead of you."

He went from them about as far as one can throw a stone. He lowered himself to the ground, fell on his face and prayed, "O Great Father, will you remove from me this time of suffering and pain? Grandfather,[141] my Father! All things are possible with you. Take this cup of suffering and bitterness away from me!"

The night was silent and cold as Creator Sets Free trembled and prayed. The powers of darkness were pressing in hard.

"*O Great Father!*" he cried out, "if this is the only way, then I will drink deeply of this bitter cup, for I want your way, not mine."

After a while he got up and found his followers sleeping and said to them, "Stands On The Rock, are you sleeping? Can you not stay awake and pray with me for even one hour? Your human body is weak but your spirit is strong, so stay awake and pray."

Creator Sets Free went a second time away from them and prayed, "My Father, if this is the only way then let your will be done."

Then he got up again and found his followers sleeping, for their eyes were heavy, so he left them and went to pray a third time saying the same things. While he prayed a spirit messenger from the world above appeared, giving him strength. In his agony he prayed with desperation and his sweat fell like great drops of blood and soaked the ground.

He sent his words to Grandfather with tears and loud cries. Creator was the only one who could *bring him back to life and rescue him from death.* Because of his great respect his prayers were heard. Even though he was the Son of the Great Spirit, he still had to learn, through suffering, how hard it is to walk in the sacred ways.[142]

When he finished praying he again found his followers sleeping, for they were worn out and full of sorrow. He woke them up and said, "Why are you still sleeping? The time is upon us! The True Human Being has been betrayed into the hands of the ones with bad hearts. Get up! We must go! The one who has turned against me is at the gate!"

I AM is Betrayed

Right then, while Creator Sets Free was speaking, a crowd of people stormed into the garden. Speaks Well Of, one of the twelve, was leading the way, for he knew this was a place Creator Sets Free would come to rest *and pray* with his followers. Behind the betrayer came a band of soldiers sent from the scroll keepers, head holy men and Separated Ones, representing the elders of the tribal council. *The air was filled with the smell of burning torches as* the crowd pushed their way forward carrying clubs and long knives. The betrayer had told the soldiers, "Arrest the one I greet with a kiss and guard him close." Speaks Well Of walked up to Creator Sets Free to greet him.

Creator Sets Free looked at him and said, "My friend, why are you here?"

He ignored him and said, "Wisdomkeeper, I greet you," and kissed the side of his face.

"Speaks Well Of," he said to him, "will you betray the True Human Being with a kiss?"

Creator Sets Free knew all this would happen, so he turned to the soldiers and asked, "Who have you come for?"

With one voice they answered back, "Creator Sets Free from Nazareth!"

He said to them, "I AM." At the sound of his voice the soldiers moved back and fell to the ground.

He asked them again, "Who have you come for?"

They answered, "Creator Sets Free from Nazareth."

"I told you already, I am the one you are looking for," he said. "Let these other men go."

He said this to fulfill his promise, "None of the ones you gave to me have been lost."

Live by Violence ~ Die by Violence

The soldiers grabbed hold of him to take him away. When his followers saw what was happening they said, "Wisdomkeeper, should we fight?"

Before he could answer them, Stands On The Rock drew his long knife from its sheath and cut off the right ear of the servant of the head holy man. The servant's name was Chieftain.

Creator Sets Free *asked the soldiers to let him help the man, so they loosened their hold on him. He bent down, picked up the man's ear and holding it to his head,* touched and healed him.

He turned to Stands On The Rock and said, "No more of this! Put your long knife back in its sheath. All those who take up weapons will die by them! Do you not know that if I called out to my Father, he would send thousands of spirit messengers. But if I did, how would the ancient prophecies find their full meaning? I must drink the cup of suffering my Father has asked of me."

Creator Sets Free turned to the ones who had come to take him and said, "Why do you come at me with clubs and long knives as if I was a thief? Did I not sit with you every day in the Sacred Lodge? Why did you not take me then? But now the words of the prophets have come true, and you have given the powers of darkness their day."

After Creator Sets Free said this, all his followers turned and ran away. The head man and his soldiers bound Creator Sets Free with ropes and took him away. A young man dressed only in an under cloth trailed from behind. The people tried to grab hold of him, but the cloth tore and the young man ran away naked into the night.

Questioned by a High Holy Man

They took Creator Sets Free to Walks Humbly, one of the high holy men. He was the father of the wife of Hollow In The Rock, the head high holy man who had said, "It will be better if one man dies for all the people."

He questioned Creator Sets Free about his followers and his teachings. Creator Sets Free said to him, "I have spoken openly to all, in the gathering houses and the Sacred Lodge. I said nothing in secret. Why ask me? Ask the ones who heard me—they will know."

One of the head soldiers struck him with the palm of his hand and said, "Is that how you answer a head holy man?"

Creator Sets Free answered him back, "If I have spoken wrongly, tell me what I said wrong. If I spoke what is true, then by what right do you strike me?"

Walks Humbly decided to send Creator Sets Free to Hollow In The Rock, the head high holy man. They took him, still bound by ropes, to the house of Hollow In The Rock, where all the head holy men, the scroll keepers and the council of elders had gathered.

Stands On The Rock—Falls

Stands On The Rock and He Shows Goodwill had been watching from a distance. Since He Shows Goodwill was known by the head holy man, he entered the courtyard of the house, but Stands On The Rock stood outside the gate. He Shows Goodwill spoke to the gatekeeper, a young woman, who let Stands On The Rock in. She looked at him and said, "This man was with Creator Sets Free of Nazareth." Then she looked at him closely and said to him, "Are you not one of his followers?"

"Woman, I don't know what you mean," he said to her. "I am not his follower!"

The night was growing cold, so some of the men, along with the soldier guards from the Lodge, built a fire in the courtyard. As they warmed themselves by the fire Stands On The Rock came close and sat down with them. The woman gatekeeper came up to the men and said, "This man is a follower of Creator Sets Free."

"They asked him, "Are you one of his followers?" But he denied it saying, "No, I am not."

The Grand Council Questions Him

They brought Creator Sets Free before the head holy men and the Grand Council[143] of elders. They kept trying to find someone who would speak against him falsely, but found no one. Many spoke against him, but their stories did not agree with each other.

Finally two men came forward. The first one said, "I heard him say, 'I can tear down the Sacred Lodge and build it again in three days.'" The second said, "I heard him say, 'I will tear down this Sacred Lodge made with hands, and build a new one in three days, not made with hands.'" And so their stories did not agree either.

Hollow In the Rock, the head high holy man, became frustrated and stood up before all. He said to Creator Sets Free, "Have you no answer? What do you have to say about this? Defend yourself!"

Creator Sets Free stood silently before all—and said nothing.

The face of Hollow In The Rock became red with anger and his voice thundered, "I demand of you, before the living Creator—speak the truth! Tell us if you are the Chosen One, the Son of the Great Spirit!"

The room became silent. Time seemed to stand still. The air was filled with tension as they waited for his answer. When he spoke, every ear and eye in the room was fixed on him.

"I AM," he answered them. "From now on you will see the True Human Being sitting at the right hand of the Great Power. He will come riding the clouds across the sky."[144]

They could not believe their ears! The head high holy man tore his outer garments in two and cried out, "He is guilty! His words have insulted the Great Spirit!"

He turned to the council of elders and said, "You have heard it with your own ears! What does the council have to say?"

With one voice the council answered, "Death to him! He must be put to death."

The soldiers began to spit in his face and strike him with their fists. They put a blindfold over his eyes and slapped his face. "Prophecy to us!" they taunted him. "Tell us who struck you!" They kept hitting him and saying, "Prophesy, Chosen One." They mocked him and insulted him with cruel words and twisted faces.

When they were done they bound the ropes around him again. All the ones who had gathered there got up and followed as they took Creator Sets Free to the governor of the People of Iron, Pontius Pilate, *whose name means "Spear of the Great Waters."*

The Rooster Crows

Outside in the courtyard, Stands On The Rock was still warming himself by the fire. Some others, who were standing by, came up to him and said, "You must be one of his followers. You talk like someone from Galilee."

One of the servants of the head holy man, a relative of the man whose ear had been cut off, looked at him and said, "Yes! I saw you in the garden with him!"

Stands On The Rock cursed and swore out loud, "What are you all saying? I don't know this man you are talking about."

As the Lodge soldiers were bringing Creator Sets Free out through the gate, a rooster crowed twice. Stands On The Rock looked up just in time to see Creator Sets Free gazing back at him. *A chill shot through his body and he hung his head in shame,* remembering what he had been told earlier, "Before the rooster crows, you will deny three times that you know me."

Stands on the rock ran out of the gate, *at the first light of dawn,* and wept bitter tears *as he stumbled down the road.*

The Betrayer Takes His Own Life

When Speaks Well Of, the one who betrayed Creator Sets Free, saw they had decided to put him to death, he was overcome with sorrow. He took the thirty silver coins back to the head holy men and the elders.

"I have done wrong!" he told them. "I have betrayed the blood of an innocent man."

"What do we care?" they said back to him. "You did this to yourself."

He threw the thirty silver coins on the floor of the Lodge and ran away in sorrow. *As the light of the sunrise grew brighter on the horizon,* the lifeless body of Speaks Well Of could be seen hanging from the branch of a tree. *He could not live with what he had done.*

The head holy men didn't know what to do with the silver coins. They said, "It is not permitted to put them in the storehouse of the Sacred Lodge, for it is blood money." So they counseled together and purchased a field with it. From that time on it has been called the Field of Blood.

This gave full meaning to the words of the prophet Lifted By Creator, "He was sold out for thirty pieces of silver by the tribes of Wrestles With Creator. This is how much they thought his life was worth. With the silver they bought a potter's field, as instructed by the Great Spirit."[145]

Turned Over to the People of Iron

Creator Sets Free was taken from the house of the head high holy man to the council house of the People of Iron. The tribal people stayed outside, for they did not want to become ceremonially unclean by going inside the council house. It was early in the morning and many of them had not yet eaten the ceremonial meal of Passover.

Pilate came outside to meet them. They stood Creator Sets Free in front of him. Pilate looked at him, turned to them and said, "What has this man done wrong?"

"If he was not a criminal would we have brought him to you?" they answered.

"Take him away!" Pilate said to them, "and use your own law to decide what to do."

"Your law will not permit us to put him to death," they answered.

This proved that Creator Sets Free was right when he said he would be nailed to a tree pole.

They continued to accuse him, "We caught this man misleading our nation and telling people not to pay taxes to the government of the People of Iron. He tells the people that he is the Chosen One, a Grand Chief."

As they continued to accuse him, Creator Sets Free stood silent and said nothing.

"Why are you silent?" Pilate said to him, "Do you not hear their accusations?"

But Creator Sets Free answered not one word. The governor was caught off guard by this.

Pilate took Creator Sets Free into the council house to question him. Once inside he said to him, "Are you Grand Chief of the tribes of Wrestles With Creator?"

"Is this your question," he asked, "or are you listening to others?"

"I am not from your tribes," Pilate answered. "It is your own people and their head holy men who have turned you over to me. What have you done to offend them? Are you a chief?"

"I am a chief, but my chiefly rule is not in the ways of this world. If it were, my followers would have fought to keep me from being taken."

Pilate said you him, "So then, you are a chief?"

"You are right to say so," he answered. "I was born for this and have come into the world for this purpose—to tell about the truth. The ones who belong to the truth will listen to me."

Pilate looked at him and said, "What is truth?"

Taken to Chief Looks Brave

Pilate went outside to the head holy men and the people and said to them, "I find no guilt in this man."

But they kept accusing him and saying, "He is making trouble with the people of Judea, from Galilee to Jerusalem."

When Pilate heard he was from Galilee he decided to send him to Chief Looks Brave, who was in Jerusalem for the festival, for he was chief of the territory of Galilee.

Chief Looks Brave was glad to see him. He had waited a long time for this, for he had heard much about Creator Sets Free. He was hoping to see him do a powerful sign. The head holy men and scroll keepers made strong accusations against him, so Looks Brave dug deep with many questions.

Creator Sets Free stood silent.

Chief Looks brave mocked him along with his soldiers. They dressed him in a fancy outfit and sent him back to Pilate. Looks Brave and Pilate hated each other, but on that day they became friends.

Back to the People of Iron

They brought Creator Sets Free back to Pilate. He gathered the head holy men, the head men, and the people together and said to them, "You told me this man was a troublemaker, but I questioned him and found him not guilty of your accusations. Looks Brave, *one of your own people,* also questioned him, found nothing wrong with him and sent him back to the People of Iron."

Pilate knew that the head holy men and elders had brought Creator Sets Free to him because they were jealous *of his reputation with the people.* While he was deciding what to do Pilate's wife sent word to him, saying, "Do no harm to this innocent man, for today I had a dream about him that troubles me." *So Pilate did not want to put him to death and was looking for a way out.*

Pilate then spoke to the crowd, "He has done nothing to deserve death! By your own tradition we set free one criminal during your Passover festival. I will have him whipped and then release him to you."

The agreement of releasing one criminal during the festival required the approval of the people. So Pilate brought a man forward who had a bad reputation, a prisoner named Son Of His Father.[146] He was a troublemaker who had caused an uprising in Jerusalem, the Sacred Village of Peace, and had been imprisoned for murder.

Pilate *stood Creator Sets Free and Son Of His Father in front of the crowd and said* to them, "Which one should I release to you?"

The crowd roared with one voice, "Son Of His Father!"

Pilate was amazed by their answer. He didn't know that the head holy men and elders had been going through the crowd turning them against Creator Sets Free.

Pilate once again said to the people, "What of Creator Sets Free who is called your Chosen One, the Grand Chief of your tribes?"

"Nail him to a tree pole!" they cried out together. Then the crowd began shouting, "Death! Death on a tree pole."

Pilate *quieted the crowd, and* a third time said, "Why! What evil has he done? I have not found him guilty or worthy of death. I will have him beaten and then set him free."

At the Stone of Deciding

Pilate turned Creator Sets Free over to his soldiers to have him beaten. The soldiers made a headdress for him from a thorn bush and pressed the thorns into his head. They stripped off his clothes, wrapped a purple and red blanket around him, and put a chief's staff in his hand. They bowed down low before him, making a big show of it and said, "Honor! Honor to the Grand Chief of the tribes of Wrestles With Creator." They took his chief's staff, clubbed him with it, and then took turns beating him with their fists *until his face was bruised and bloodied.*

Pilate stood before the crowd again and said, "I bring to you the one I have found no guilt in."

Creator Sets Free was brought forward, blood flowing down his bruised face. He was wearing the headdress of thorns and the purple cloth around him. He stood silently before the crowd.

"Behold, the man!" Pilate said to them. *"Take a good long look at him!"*

The crowd stared at him in stunned silence, but the head holy men and the Lodge guards began to shout, "Death! Death on a tree pole!"

"Would you have me nail your grand chief to a tree pole?" he asked them.

"We have no other grand chief than the grand chief of the People of Iron," they shouted back.

"Then you take him and put him to death yourselves. I find no guilt in him!"

They answered him back, "Our law tells us he must die, for he has represented himself as the Son of the Great Spirit."

When Pilate heard this it troubled him, so he took Creator Sets Free back inside the council house.

"Don't you know I have the power of life and death over you? I can have you killed or set you free," he threatened him. "Have you no words to say?"

"The only power you have is what has been given you from above," he answered. "The ones who turned you over to me carry the greater guilt."

Pilate tried harder to have Creator Sets Free released, but the people would not have it. They stood their ground, saying, "If you release a man who says he is a grand chief, you are not honoring the chief of your people."

Pilate saw that their minds would not be changed. He was worried that the crowd might turn violent, so he decided to give them what they wanted. Pilate washed his hands in a vessel of water in front of all the people and said, "This man's blood is not on my hands. It is on yours!"

"Let his blood be on us and on our descendants!" they answered him back.

Pilate went to the Stone of Deciding and sat down on it.

He ordered that *the man of violence,* Son Of The Father, be released; and that Creator Sets Free, *the man of peace*, be put to death on a tree pole.

The sun was rising in the east *as the soldiers of the People of Iron took hold of Creator Sets free and dragged him away.* They took him to their headquarters, where a large company of soldiers was assigned to guard him. They stripped him down to his under garments and whipped him with a leather cord.

The People of Iron used a whip with many strips of leather, each braided together with bone and metal. The victim would be tied to a large rock exposing his bare back, and then lashed. The pieces of bone and metal would rip and tear the skin from the body leaving the victim almost lifeless.

When they were finished they put his own clothes back on him, and marched him away to be nailed to a tree pole until dead. They tied a large tree pole to his bleeding back and forced him to carry it as they marched him down the road.

CHAPTER NINETEEN

Ultimate Sacrifice

His Trail Of Tears

Creator Sets Free stumbled under the weight of the tree pole. His body was weak from the beating he had endured, too weak to bear the burden.

A man named He Hears, from the village of Cyrene *in northern Africa,* was just entering Jerusalem. The soldiers forced him to walk behind Creator Sets Free and carry his tree pole for him.

A large crowd of people trailed behind. Some of the women were walking beside him, wailing and crying out loud. Creator Sets Free turned to them and said, "O Daughters of Jerusalem, weep not for me but for yourselves and your children. Listen to me! The time is coming soon when people will say, 'It is better for the women who have borne no children, *for they will not have to watch them die.'* People will say to the mountains and the hills, 'Fall on us and cover us over.'

"If I, a green and living tree, have to pass through this fire, think of what the fire will do to the trees that are dead and dry?"

Two other men, both of them criminals, were being forced to carry tree poles, along with Creator Sets Free, to a hill just outside of the Sacred Village of Peace, known as Skull Mountain.[147]

Skull Mountain

When they came to Skull Mountain it was still mid-morning, for the sun had risen only three hours earlier. *The soldiers took the tree pole from He Hears and threw it to the ground.* They stripped Creator Sets Free of his clothes and forced him down on the tree pole. They roped a crossbeam at the place of his shoulders and fastened him to the tree pole. The People of Iron then drove large iron nails through his hands and feet. Several soldiers lifted the pole up high, dropped it into a hole in the ground and packed dirt around it to make it stand.

Two other men were with him, thieves, who were carrying their tree poles. The soldiers also nailed them to the tree poles and placed them, one on his left, the other on his right. This gave final meaning to the Sacred Writing that said, "He was numbered with the criminals."[148]

Pilate had given them instructions to fasten a sign above his head with these words carved into it.

Creator Sets Free
Grand Chief
Of the tribes of Wrestles With Creator

The tree poles stood near the village pathway where all could see. The people walking by could read what the sign said, for it was written in both the language of the tribes and the languages of the People of Iron.

The tribal head holy men said to Pilate, "Don't write 'Grand Chief of the tribes.' Instead write, 'He said he is Grand Chief.'" But Pilate answered, "What I have written will stand."

Father, Forgive Them

The soldiers offered Creator Sets Free wine mixed with bitter herbs. He tasted it but would not drink it. They mocked him saying things like, "O Grand Chief of the Tribes," to shame and scorn him. When they became tired of that, they sat down to keep watch over him and tore one of his garments into four pieces, one for each guard. His long outer garment was woven together into one piece, so they gambled with each other to see who would keep it. This gave full meaning to the Sacred Writing that said, "They divided my clothes between them and gambled for my garment."[149]

As people walked by and saw him, they spoke arrogantly to him. They wagged their heads and said, "You think you can tear down the Lodge and rebuild it in three days? Hah! You can't even come down off that tree pole. Son of the Great Spirit, are you? Then set yourself free."

The head holy men, the scroll keepers and the elders all joined in, "He set others free," they said, "why can't he free himself? If you are the Chosen One, O Grand Chief, then come down from there. If you are the Son of the Great Spirit, then why doesn't he help you!"

The people passing by, the spiritual leaders and the soldiers, kept throwing insults over and over again as he hung there, bleeding and in great pain and anguish.

Creator Sets Free could hear their words as they laughed at him. He pushed against the nails in his feet, and gasping for air, his voice trembled as he cried out, "O Great Father—forgive them! They do not know what they do."

A Bad Heart Finds the Good Road

One of the thieves next to him spewed out angry words, "If you are the Chosen One, then help yourself and us!" He kept repeating it over and over again. Finally, the other thief spoke up and said, "Do you have no fear or respect for the Great Spirit? We are suffering for our own wrongdoings, but this man has done nothing wrong!"

The man turned to Creator Sets Free and said to him, "Wisdomkeeper, remember me when the Land of your Good Road comes."

Creator Sets Free looked at the man and said, "I tell you from my heart, before the sun sets today, you will walk with me in the beautiful garden."[150]

His Mother Comes To Him

Bitter Tears, the mother of Creator Sets Free, had come to see him, along with her sister. Two other women[151] also named Bitter Tears came with her, along with He Shows Goodwill, the much loved follower of Creator Sets Free.

When Creator Sets Free looked down and saw his mother standing with He Shows Goodwill, he said to her, "Honored woman, look to your son." Then he said to He Shows Goodwill, "Look to your mother." From that time He Shows Goodwill took Bitter Tears into his family and cared for her.

His Last Words

It was now midday, for the sun had reached the center of the sky. *Creator Sets Free had hung on the tree pole since the middle of the morning.* A great shadow of darkness had covered the land like a blanket, and the light of the sun grew dim. The sky remained dark until mid-afternoon when suddenly Creator Sets Free, speaking his native language, cried out in a loud voice, "Eloi, Eloi lama sabachthani," which means, "O Great Father, Maker of Life, have you left me alone?"[152]

Some of the people standing there thought he was calling on the prophet, Great Spirit Is Creator, to help him.

Creator Sets Free, knowing he had done all the ancient Sacred Writings had foretold, said, "I thirst."

There was a vessel of sour and bitter wine standing nearby. One of the soldiers ran and dipped a cloth in it to soak up some wine. He wrapped the cloth around the tip of a hyssop branch and held it up to Creator Sets Free. The people said, "Let him drink it and see if the prophet, Great Spirit Is Creator, will come and rescue him."

Creator Sets Free drank of the bitter wine, turned his head to the sky and cried out loud, "It is done! O Great Father, my life is in your hands!" He lowered his head to his chest and with his last breath, gave up his spirit.

Creator Sets Free was dead.

The Sacred Lodge Opens to All

One of the head soldiers of the People of Iron, who was standing near him, heard the words of Creator Sets Free as he breathed his last. He honored the Great Spirit by saying, "He must have been a man of honor, not deserving death."

Suddenly the earth began to quake. *The Sacred Village of Peace trembled and rocked.* In the Great Spirit's Sacred Lodge *the ceremonial items shook and fell to the floor.* The great heavy blanket that hung over the entry to the most holy place was torn from top to bottom. *For the first time the inner chamber, where only the high holy man could go, was open to all.*

Large rocks broke in half and stones rolled away from the burial caves of many holy ancestors. After Creator Sets Free came back to life, some of their bodies came back to life and appeared to people in the Sacred Village of Peace.

When the head soldiers of the People of Iron felt the earth shake and saw what was happening all around them, they trembled with fear and said, "This man must truly be the Son of the Great Spirit."

A large crowd had gathered to watch. When they saw and heard all that was happening, they began to wail and beat their fists against their chests as they walked home.

Many friends of Creator Sets Free stood watching from a distance. The women who had walked the road with him from the time he was in Galilee were there, along with many more women. These were the women of Galilee who loved him and stood by his side, serving him during his journeys.[153]

Preparation for His Burial

Soon the sun would set and the Day of Resting would begin, when no work could be done. It was time to prepare for this day, so the tribal members asked Pilate to have the legs of the men on the tree poles broken, which would make them die sooner. Then they could prepare their bodies for burial.

The soldiers came and broke the legs of the two men on each side of Creator Sets Free, but when they came to him they saw he was already dead. Instead of breaking his legs, one of the soldiers took a spear and pierced his side. Blood and water flowed out from the wound.

He Shows Goodwill saw this with his own eyes, and tells the truth about it—so you can believe. This was foretold in the ancient Sacred Writings that say, "Not one of his bones were broken."[154] And "They will look upon the one they have pierced."[155]

He Gives Sons of Arimathea, a man with many possessions, was a follower of Creator Sets Free, but in secret, because he feared the Spiritual Leaders. He had a good reputation in the Grand Council of elders, but had not agreed with their decision to put Creator Sets Free to death. He was a good hearted man who looked for the Good Road of the Great Spirit. Since it would soon be sunset when the Day of Resting would begin, he went boldly to Pilate and asked for the body of Creator Sets Free.

Pilate, wondering if he was dead yet, consulted with one of the head soldiers in charge. When he assured Pilate of the death of Creator Sets Free, he released his body to He Gives Sons.

He Gives Sons purchased a new soft cloth to wrap the body in. He then went and took Creator Sets Free down from the tree pole. Conquers The People, the one who came in secret by night to Creator Sets Free, brought a mixture of myrrh and oils weighing about seventy five pounds. Together they ceremonially wrapped his body for burial, in the traditional way, using the new and clean cloths and the myrrh and oils.

They took his body to the nearby garden, where He Gives Sons had carved into the rock cliff a burial cave that had never been used. The Day of Resting was about to begin, so they laid the body of Creator Sets Free in the burial cave. They rolled a great stone over the entryway of the cave and left.

The women from Galilee had followed them. They sat close by and watched as the men laid his body in the burial cave. Then they went to where they were staying and followed the tradition of the Day of Resting.

They Set Guards At the Burial Cave

The next day, after the Day of Preparing, the head holy men and the Separated Ones came to Pilate and reminded him that Creator Sets Free had said, "On the third day I will come back from the dead." We must put an end to his lies or his followers could take his body away and tell the people he has come back from the dead, making things worse for all of us. Order your soldiers to guard the burial cave. Pilate said to them, "Take with you a good number of my soldiers and set them to guard the burial cave." So they went and placed a seal over the great stone and set the guards to watch.

CHAPTER TWENTY

The Suffering Servant of Creator

Creator Sets Free Was Dead

Creator Sets Free had crossed over into the land of the dead. He said he would come back on the third day, but his followers' great fear had blinded them, and they had forgotten his words. They were now in hiding, behind locked doors, not knowing what to do.

If they had understood the words of the ancient prophets they would have had hope. The prophet, Creator Will Help Us, over eight-hundred years earlier, spoke of one who would be sent by the Great Spirit to walk a path of suffering and death, to set all people free.

As we wait to hear the rest of this story, let us stop and think about the meaning of his death, through the eyes of the Great Spirit, and the mouth of his prophet.[156]

The Prophecy of Creator Will Help Us

"You will see what the one who does everything I want will accomplish. He will be honored and highly respected. *But before this he will be misunderstood and mistreated.*

"Many were struck speechless when they saw him, beaten and bloodied, so disfigured one would barely know he was a human being. This will cause many nations to stop in their tracks, unable to say a word. Grand Chiefs will stand speechless in his presence. They will see and understand things they never saw or understood before.

"Who could believe such a thing? Would the Almighty show his great power in weakness?

"As the Great Spirit watched over him, he grew up like a young plant taking root in dry ground. He looked so ordinary we hardly noticed him. He was looked down on and unwanted, mistreated, and familiar with sorrow and suffering. We turned our faces and looked the other way as he passed by.

"We thought the Great Spirit was punishing him for his own wrongdoing. But he was sick and weighed down with our bad hearts. Because of us he was tortured and suffered great pain. He was wounded by our worthless ways and beaten down because of our guilt. The abuse he suffered healed us and brought our lives back into balance with the Maker of Life.

"Like sheep that wander away we chose our own path. We were guilty, but Creator permitted us to put our guilt on him. He never complained when he was mistreated and oppressed. Like a lamb led to the slaughter or like a sheep being sheered, he took it humbly and quietly.

"He was arrested and condemned to die without a fair trial, cut down in the prime of his life. No one imagined he would have a future. It was for our peoples' wrongdoings that he was put to death. He never hurt or deceived anyone, but still they put him to death along with the criminals, and laid him in the burial ground of a wealthy man.

"It was the Great Spirit's plan to let him be crushed and have his heart broken. Even though his life was offered up *like the smoke of burning sage,* he will have many descendants and enjoy a long life. His sacrifice will honor and complete the great plan of Creator. When he sees all that has been accomplished by his suffering, he will find satisfaction and great joy.

"Because my humble servant carried the weight of all their bad hearts many will be given new hearts. I will give him the honor of the great and mighty chiefs, because he counted coup[157] with death. He was considered a criminal, but the truth is he carried the weight of their wrongdoing and prayed for them while he was dying."

CHAPTER TWENTY-ONE

A New Day For All the World

A New Sunrise

All through the night the soldiers had kept close watch over the burial cave. As the light of the sunrise crept over the hills the earth began to tremble and quake. The soldiers looked up and saw a spirit messenger coming down from the world above. His face was shining as bright as a flash of lightning and his outfit was pure white like snow. The soldiers staggered back, trembling with fear and fell to the ground like dead men. The spirit messenger rolled the great stone away from the entryway of the burial cave and sat down on it.

He Has Risen From the Dead

A number of women were on their way to the burial cave. They were bringing spices and oils to rub on the body of Creator Sets Free. There was Bitter Tears of Magdala and Bitter Tears who was the mother of Heel Grabber, along with Daughter Of Peace and Woman Of His Goodwill. As they came near they were asking each other about how they could move the large stone from the burial cave. But when they looked up they saw the stone had been rolled away!

They made their way inside the cave and saw a young man dressed in pure white sitting to the right side of the stone slab. Their eyes grew wide and they shook with fear.

"Do not fear," the spirit messenger said. "The one you are looking for is not here. Creator Sets Free of Nazareth, who was put to death on the tree pole, has come back to life again—just as he said. Look! Here is where they laid him. Now go quickly and tell his followers that he has risen from the dead. Tell them he is going ahead of them to Galilee and they will see him there.

The women could see the body of Creator Sets Free was gone. They were standing there in amazement and wonder when suddenly two men appeared beside them dressed in shining white outfits. The women, trembling with fear, bowed down low to the ground on their faces.

The men said, "Why do you look for the living in the place of the dead? He is not here, he has returned to life. Do you not remember what he told you in Galilee? The True Human Being will be turned over to the ones with bad hearts. They will put him to death on a tree pole, but he will come back to life on the third day. Then the women remembered what he had said.

Some of the women ran away from that place and told no one about the things they had seen, for terror and amazement had taken hold of their hearts.

The First Message Bearer

But Bitter Tears of Magdala ran as fast as she could and found Stands On The Rock and He Shows Goodwill. She told them, "They have taken the body of our Wisdomkeeper away and we don't know where he is!"

Stands On The Rock raced to the burial cave, but He Shows Goodwill outran him and came there first. He stooped low to look inside, but did not go in all the way. He saw strips of cloth lying there, but the cloth that had been wrapped around the head of Creator Sets Free was rolled into a bundle lying by itself.

Stands On The Rock ran behind him. When he came to the cave he went inside and saw the same things. He Shows Goodwill now found the courage to go inside all the way. He saw the burial cave was empty, and believed. But they still didn't understand from the Sacred Writings that he would return from the dead. So they went back to the place where they were staying.

A Woman Sees Him First

After the men left, Bitter Tears went back to the garden. Her heart was on the ground as she stood outside the cave weeping. As the tears ran down her face she looked inside. There she saw two spirit messengers dressed in white. They were sitting, one at the head, the other at the feet, of where the body of Creator Sets Free had once lain.

They looked at her and said, "Honored woman, why do you weep?"

"My Wisdomkeeper is gone," she answered, "and I don't know where they have taken him."

She turned around to see a man standing behind her. It was Creator Sets Free, but she didn't recognize him.

"Honored woman, why the tears?" he said to her. "Who are you looking for?"

She thought he was the keeper of the garden, so she said, "If you have carried him away, tell me where, and I will find him."

"Bitter Tears," he said to her *in a soft and kind voice.*

She looked closer at him *and her eyes grew wide.* Then she hugged him close and whispered in his ear in her native language, "Rabbouni!" meaning Wisdomkeeper.

"You must let me go," he said back to her, "I have not yet gone up to the Father. Go to my brothers who walked the road with me, and give them this message, 'I am going up to my Father and your Father, to the one who is the Great Father of us all.'"

Creator Sets Free had chosen to show himself first to a woman, Bitter Tears of Magdala, the one he had set free from seven evil spirits.

More Women See Him

The other women came and joined her as she was leaving the garden. Their hearts were full of joy, but they were also afraid. Suddenly, Creator Sets Free was standing in front of them. "Greetings!" he *smiled and* said to them. They bowed down low to honor him and touched his feet. "Don't be afraid," he told them. "Go and tell the others they will see me in Galilee."

The women who had seen Creator Sets Free went with Bitter Tears and found the eleven message bearers. Bitter Tears spoke out and said to them, "We have seen our Wisdomkeeper!" and she told them everything. But they did not believe the women, thinking it was only empty talk.

The Soldiers are Bribed

After the women had left the burial cave, some of the soldiers who were guarding the place went into Jerusalem and reported everything to the head holy men, who gathered a council together to make a plan. They decided to pay the soldiers to make up a story, "Tell the people that his followers took his body while you were sleeping. Don't worry about Pilate hearing about this, we will pay him whatever it takes to keep you from trouble."

So the soldiers took the money and did as they were told. Their story has been told far and wide among all the tribes, up to this day.

He Walks With Two Men On the Road

On the same day, two of the followers of Creator Sets Free were walking to the village of Emmaus, seven miles out from Jerusalem. As they walked along they were talking about all that had happened. Creator Sets Free came along side them as they walked, but their eyes were kept from seeing who he was.

He said to them, "What are you talking about?"

They stopped walking and a look of sadness fell over their faces. One of the men, Honored By His Father, answered him, "How can you not know about the things that have happened here? You must be coming from far away."

"What things are you talking about?" he asked.

"About Creator Sets Free from the village of Nazareth. He is a prophet of the Great Spirit, with powerful medicine, who did many good things among all the people. The head holy men and other leaders handed him over to the People of Iron to be put to death on a tree pole. We had hoped that he would free the tribes of Wrestles With Creator from the People of Iron. It is now the third day since he died, but today some women told us an amazing story. Early this morning they went to his burial cave and found that his body was not there. They told us about visions of spirit messengers who told them he was alive! Some of our men went to see with their own eyes and found the empty cave, but they did not see Creator Sets Free."

"Why are your hearts so slow to believe the words of the prophets?" he said. "It should be clear to you that the Chosen One would suffer first before he would be lifted up and honored above all."

So Creator Sets Free told them the story, beginning with Drawn From the Water and all the Prophets. He showed them how all the ancient Sacred Writings were about the Chosen One and pointed the way to him.

They still didn't know it was Creator Sets Free talking to them. As they entered the village, he walked on as if to go further. They said to him, "Please, stay with us. It is late and the sun will soon set." So he went into the lodging house with them.

When they sat down to eat a meal together, Creator Sets Free took some bread into his hands. He gave thanks and broke it, giving each of them a piece. Suddenly, their eyes were opened and they knew who he was, but he vanished right in front of them.

The men were stunned. They looked at each other in wide eyed wonder and said, "Did it not feel like our hearts were on fire when he was talking with us on the road, showing us the meaning of the Sacred Writings?"

They got up without finishing their meal and walked back to Jerusalem, as fast as they could, for the sun was setting. They found where the eleven had gathered together with the others. The eleven were saying, "Our Wisdomkeeper is alive! He has shown himself to Stands On The Rock."

So the two men told them what happened on the road and how their eyes were opened when Creator Sets Free broke the bread into pieces.

But even after all this, some still did not believe.

The Message Bearers See Him

It was now late in the same day, the first day of the week. His followers were all hiding behind locked doors in fear of being captured by their own people.

Suddenly, Creator Sets Free himself was standing in front of them. "Peace be with you!" he said to them. Filled with fear, they all moved back from him, thinking he was a ghost.

"Why are you afraid?" he asked. "Why do you doubt? Look at my hands and feet. Touch me. A ghost does not have flesh and bone —as I have."

They looked at him with glad but fearful hearts, so he said to them, "Give me something to eat."

They gave him some cooked fish and he ate it in front of them, but still some doubted. He then sat and ate a meal with them and *gently* scolded them for their hard hearts and failure to believe the word of the others who had seen him after he had come back to life.

Put Away Your Doubts

Looks Like His Brother, one of the original twelve followers, was not there when Creator Sets Free showed himself to the others. They told him, "We have seen the Wisdomkeeper with our own eyes." But he said to them, "Unless I see the nail marks in his hands and put my hand into the hole in his side, I will not believe."

Eight days later his followers were gathered together again, and Looks Like His Brother was with them. The doors were all locked, but Creator Sets Free came in and stood before them all.

"Peace be with you," he said. Then he turned to Looks Like His Brother and said, "Look at my hands and put your finger into my scars. Put your hand into the wound in my side. Put away your doubts and trust in me."

His eyes were wide with wonder as he touched Creator Sets Free and said, "You are my Great Chief and my Creator."

"Now you believe, because you have seen me?" he said to him. "A greater blessing way will rest on the ones who have not seen, but still believe."

Back to Fishing in Galilee

A while later, back in Galilee, Stands On The Rock gathered with other followers of Creator Sets Free. With him were Looks Like His Brother, Creator Gives—from Cana, the two sons of Gift Of Creator, along with two other followers.

Stands On The Rock said to them, "I'm going fishing."

They all agreed and said, "Take us with you."

So they took a canoe out onto the lake. Under the light of the moon and stars they worked hard all night. Again and again they threw out their nets and drew them back in—empty.

Just as the first light of day was dawning Creator Sets Free came and stood on the shore, but they did not know it was him.

"Friends!" he called out to them, "have you netted any fish?"

"No!" they answered, *"and we are worn out from fishing all night."*

"Throw out your nets to the right of your canoe," he shouted to them. "You will find some fish there."

They did as he said and the net was filled with so many fish they could not pull it into the canoe. He Shows Goodwill said to Stands On The Rock, "It is our Wisdomkeeper!"

Stands On The Rock had taken off his outer garment to fish. He put it back on and dove into the water. The shore was not far, so the others made their way in, dragging the net full of fish behind the canoe.

They came to the shore and stepped out of the canoe. They saw a warm fire with fish cooking over the coals and some bread to eat. Creator Sets Free stood up from cooking and said, "Bring me some of the fish you caught."

Stands On The Rock climbed into the canoe and pulled the net to shore. The fish were large, and they counted them, one hundred and fifty three in all. But even with so many fish the net did not tear.

Creator Sets Free said, "Lets eat." They all sat down to eat but no one dared ask, "Who are you?" For they knew it must be their Wisdomkeeper.

He took the bread and gave some to each of them, along with a piece of fish. This was the third time he had shown himself to them after coming back to life from the dead.

Stands On The Rock Restored

When they had finished eating, Creator Sets Free took Stands On The Rock *and sat down with him by the lake.* He spoke to him, using his family name, "One Who Hears, son of He Shows Goodwill, do you love me more than these?"

"Wisdomkeeper," he answered, "you know I am your friend."

"Then feed my lambs," he said.

They sat, looking out over the water, and listening to the sound of the waves coming in to the shore.

Then a second time Creator Sets Free asked, "One Who Hears, Son of He Shows Goodwill, do you love me?"

"Wisdomkeeper," he answered him again, "You know how much I care for you."

"Then watch over my sheep," he said.

The sound of the water birds could be heard in the distance and the sun felt warm as it rose higher in the sky.

Creator Sets Free asked him a third time, "One Who Hears, Son of He Shows Goodwill, are you my friend?"

Stands On The Rock felt his heart sink, because he asked the third time, "Are you my friend?"

"Wisdomkeeper!" he said, "you know all things, you must know how much I care for you as a friend!"

Creator Sets Free said to him again, "Feed my sheep."

Three times Stands On The Rock had denied that he knew his Wisdomkeeper, even after he said he would die for him. Now he was asked, three times, if he truly loved him.

Creator Sets Free *put his arm around his shoulder and* said, *"Stands On The Rock,* I tell you from my heart, when you were a young man you dressed yourself and walked wherever you wanted. But when you grow old, you will stretch out your hands and someone else will dress you and take you to a place you do not want to go." He was telling him the kind of death he would die, to bring honor to Creator.

Then he said to Stands On The Rock, "Come, walk the road with me."

This was the same invitation he had given years earlier to Stands On The Rock in Galilee after the canoes had been filled with fish.

Stands On The Rock looked over at He Shows Goodwill, the much loved follower of Creator Sets Free. The same follower who, during the meal, had leaned back and asked, "Wisdomkeeper, who will betray you?"

When Stands On The Rock saw him, he said to Creator Sets Free, "Wisdomkeeper, what about this man, *how will he die?"*

Creator Sets Free answered him, "If I want him to remain alive until I return, why would it matter? You must walk the road I have chosen for you."

When the others heard what Creator Sets Free had said about He Shows Goodwill, talk began to go around that he would never die. But Creator Sets Free did not say he would not die. He said, "If I want him to remain alive until I return, why would it matter."

He Shows Himself to Many People

After coming back to life again from the dead, Creator Sets Free showed himself to all of his message bearers at a mountain in Galilee, where he had told them to go. When they saw him they all bowed down before him. After that he showed himself to over five hundred[158] of his followers who saw him with their own eyes. For forty days he continued to show himself, giving proof that he was alive, and sharing his final words about the Land of Creator's Good Road.[159]

He later gathered them together at the Mountain of Olives near Bethany and said to them, "When I was with you before, I told you that all the words of Drawn From The Water, the Prophets, and the Book of Songs must find their full meaning in me."

He then opened their minds and hearts so they could see the full meaning of the Sacred Writings.

He said, "It was foretold long ago, the Chosen One would walk the path of suffering, he would die and rise to life on the third day.

"You have seen these things with your own eyes. The time has now come for you to carry my message to the people of all nations. *You will no longer consider these nations as outsiders.* Beginning in the Sacred Village of Peace you will tell my story to all of Judea, then to the Samaritans, *who you will no longer despise,* and from there to all the world.

"This message will turn them back to the Maker of Life, heal their broken ways, and release them from their bad hearts. I leave you with my peace. In the same way the Father has sent me, I am sending you."

Go and Tell the Good News to all Creation

It was now time for Creator Sets Free to return to the world above. It had been forty days since he had come back to life again. So he gathered his followers on the Mountain of Olives, one last time, to give them their final instructions.

"Wisdomkeeper," they asked him, "will you now give the Good Road back to the tribes of Wrestles With Creator?"

"Times and seasons are in the Fathers's hands," he answered, "Do not trouble your minds with things that are not your concern. It is now time to set your hearts and minds on the Holy Spirit. He will give you strong medicine when he comes and you will tell my story in all Judea, then Samaria and on to the furthest parts of the earth. *You are now to be concerned with all nations.*

"Stay here in the Sacred Village of Peace until I send you the Holy Spirit, the one my Father has promised. He Shows Goodwill performed the purification ceremony with water, but not many days from now, you will receive the purification ceremony with the Spirit."

He blew his breath on them and said, "*You will* breathe in the Holy Spirit. *With his wisdom and guidance,* if you release others from their bad hearts, they are released. If you do not release them, they are not released.

"All authority in the world above and the earth below has been given to me. I am sending you to represent me to all the world. Go and tell all creation the Good News about me and my Good Road, and help the people of all nations walk the road with me. As my wisdomkeepers, you will give all nations the same instructions I gave you.

"You will perform the purification ceremony, *initiating them into the community of love and life,* in harmony with[160] the Father, Son and Holy Spirit.

"The ones who believe in me will participate in the purification ceremony, making them whole *and joining them with others who walk my Good Road.* The ones who choose not to walk this road will come to a bad end.

"Powerful signs will follow the ones who follow me. Here are some of the things they will do in my name, representing who I am; they will force out evil spirits, pick up and throw out serpents, and even the deadly poison of the enemy[161] will not harm them. They will speak in new languages and heal the sick by laying hands on them."

He Goes Back Up to the Father

Creator Sets Free lifted up his hands toward his followers and spoke these blessing words over them, "Know this, I am always by your side, walking with you in my Spirit, till the time comes for Creator to bring all things full circle."

As he spoke these words, he was taken up and went into a cloud where they could no longer see him. In the world above he sat down at the right hand, the place of greatest honor, of the One Above Us All.

His followers bowed down low to honor him and then, full of wonder and awe, they stood there looking up into the sky.

As they were looking up, two men appeared before them in pure white garments. "Men of Galilee!" they said. "Why are you looking up into the sky? This same Creator Sets Free, who you saw going up into the world above, will return one day, in the same manner you have seen him go."

With glad hearts they returned to the Sacred Village of Peace. Day by day they gathered at the Sacred Lodge to pray and give thanks to the Great Spirit.

They went out far and wide telling about the Good News and the Holy Spirit went with them showing his approval by powerful signs.

The Purpose of This Story

Many more things could be told about Creator Sets Free, the message of his Good Road, and the people his life touched. I have told this story and written it down in a book. But I have not written about everything, for he did so many things, if they were all written down in books, the whole world might not have room for them.

I have told this story, so you will believe that Creator Sets Free is the Chosen One, the Son of the Great Spirit. When you put your trust in him, the life of beauty and harmony he has promised to all —will be yours.

Now we have been told the full truth, by the ones who saw it with their own eyes, written down in a book.

This has been the story of the time when the Great Spirit walked among us.

The Greatest Story of All!

Miigwech Bizandowiyeg
(Thank you for listening)

Peace and blessing ways to you!

Terry M. Wildman
Gitchi Animiki Meno Mashkikki Manido
Voice of the Great Thunder With a Good Medicine Spirit

Glossary of Names

Names and Titles Used in this Book

Bitter Tears—Mary
Chief Looks Brave—King Herod
Chieftain—Malchus
Chosen One—Christ, Messiah
Conquers The People—Nicodemus
Covers His Head—Lot
Creator Gives—Nathaniel
Creator Hears—Simeon
Creator Helps Him—Lazarus
Creator Is My Promise—Elizabeth
Creator Is With Us—Emmanuel
Creator's Mighty One—Gabriel
Creator Saves Us—Elisha
Creator Sets Free—Jesus
Creator Shows Goodwill—John
Creator Will Decide—Daniel
Creator Will Help Us—Isaiah
Creator Will Remember—Zechariah
Drawn From The Water—Moses
Evil Serpent—Satan, Devil, Accuser
Father of Many Nations—Abraham
First To Change—Alphaeus
Friend Of Creator—Theophilis
Friend Of Horses—Phillip

Gathering House—Synagogue
Gift From Above—Zebedee
Good Road—Kingdom of God/Heaven
Great Spirit Is Creator—Elijah
He Brings Together—Levi (Matthew)
He Gives Sons—Joseph
He Made Us Laugh—Isaac
Head Holy Men—Chief Priests
Head Woman—Martha
Heel Grabber—Jacob, James
He Gives Light—Jairus
He Hears—Simon (the Cyrene)
High Holy Man—High Priest
Holy Man/Woman—Priest
Honored Dwelling—Zebulon
Honored By His Father—Cleophas
Honored Father—Abram
I Will Wrestle—Naphtali
Lifted By Creator—Jeremiah
Looks Like His Brother—Thomas (Didymus)
Much Loved One—David
One Who Rests—Noah
One Who Hears—Simon (Peter)
One Who Listens—Simon the Zealot
People Of Iron—Roman Empire
Pure Of Heart—Zachaeus
Sacred Lodge—Holy Temple
Son Of Ground Digger—Bartholomew
Son Of Honored One—Bartimaeus
Speaks Well Of—Judas
Spirit Messenger—Angel
Stands In Peace—Solomon
Stands On The Rock—Peter (Simon, Cephas)
Stands With Courage—Andrew
Story, Storyteller—Word, Message
True Human Being—Son of Man

Walks Humbly—Annas
Water Flower—Susanna
Wings Of Dove—Jonah
Woman Of Goodwill—Anna
Woman Of His Goodwill—Joanna
Wisdomkeeper—Rabbi, Teacher
Wisdomkeepers—Wise Men, Magi
Wrestles With Creator—Israel

Culture and Context

Setting the Story in Context

To help the reader with the historical and cultural context I am including some background information. While this is not comprehensive, it should provide guidance to help set the story in its proper context. The Bible is a book that spans several millennia and by the time of Jesus many thousands of years of history had already passed.

1. Names and Titles for God

When referring to God, I have used many different names and titles. I chose several that are common to Native Americans. No particular rule was followed, I simply used artistic preference. Whenever practical I coordinated with Biblical titles, such as, Most High might become One Above Us All.

Creator, Great Spirit, Grandfather, One Above Us All, Maker Of Life, Giver Of Breath, Great Mystery, Great and Holy One, and Great Father, are some of the names and titles for God used in this story.

2. Creator Sets Free (Jesus)

The name Jesus was a common name in first century Palestine. Jesus' name finds its roots in the Hebrew language. His name in

Hebrew is *Yeshua,* (pronounced yeh-shoo-wah). The name comes from two words: the first is Yah, the shortened form of Yahweh, the Hebrew name for God. The second comes from a word that means to rescue, deliver or simply set free—Yahweh sets free. From the Hebrew to the Greek of the New Testament Yeshua became *Iesous* (pronounced yeh-soos). From the Greek to the English, Iesous became Jesus. In this paraphrase I have chosen to call him *Creator Sets Free,* which is the basic meaning of his name.

3. The Chosen One (Christ)

God spoke to Israel through many prophets. These prophets spoke of a coming deliverer called the Messiah, which means the *Anointed One.* From the Greek language of the New Testament Messiah is translated in English as *Christ,* which means the same thing. This Messiah, or Christ, was to be God's Chosen One to set his people free. In this retelling of the story of Jesus I use the term *Chosen One* in place of Christ since few English-speaking people understand the meaning of the word Christ. Scripture uses the term *Chosen One* to refer to Jesus in many English translations—see Luke 9:35.

4. The True Human Being (Son of Man)

Jesus most often referred to himself as the *Son of Man.* This title is full of meaning from the Old Testament Scriptures. In the book of Ezekiel it is used over 90 times, and simply means a human being. There, it is not meant to be a title of prestige, but of humility. In using this title Jesus is presenting himself as a common human being—as one of us.

In the book of Daniel the title Son of Man takes on a expanded meaning. Daniel sees a vision of one like a son of man coming before the Ancient of Days (God) on the clouds of heaven. This person is given authority, glory and sovereign power from God.

His rule is over all peoples and languages and his kingdom will never come to an end. Even though he is a human being he will be worshiped—See Daniel 7:13-14.

So Jesus as the Son of Man shows us that the Kingdom of God is a kingdom of humility, love and service to others. He is a common man and at the same time the almighty Creator who alone is worthy of worship. As Son of God he is divine, as Son of Man he is human.

I have the used the title *True Human Being* for Son of Man. For he is one of us, and what a human being should truly be like. As we walk the road with him we are on the path of a true human being.

5. The Good Road (Kingdom of God)

For many Native Americans the word *kingdom* evokes images of colonial governments that illegally took the land from them and destroyed their way of life.

Jesus uses the word *kingdom*, but gives it a whole new meaning. His kingdom would not be like the kingdoms of the world that use force and violence to conquer others. Rather, it would be a peaceable kingdom whose leaders served others instead of ruling over them.

One way to see his kingdom is to see it as God's new form of government, one that releases people to be who he created them to be, and with them all of creation—see Romans 8:19-21. The church is intended to be the assembly or community of those who have chosen to live together in this new way.

Today, many Native American tribes speak of the *red road* or the *good way* as a way to understand a way of life that seeks to live in harmony with the Great Spirit's plan for all of creation. To live in harmony with fellow human beings and all of creation could be called *walking the good road.*

With the advice of some of my Native American friends and the insights from the prominent American Indian theologian, George E. Tinker,[162] I have chosen to paraphrase *the Kingdom of God* as *the Good Road.* Jesus came to call us to walk in a new way, a way of beauty and harmony, that reflects the government of God/ Heaven. Walking the road in the Jesus Way is to be on this path.

6. The Tribes of Wrestles With Creator (Israel)

Long before the time of Jesus, God made a covenant with a man named Abram (Honored Father), and gave him a new name, Abraham (Father Of Many Nations). Abraham is considered to be the father of faith and today many religions trace their beginnings to him. God promised Abraham he would make him into a great nation. When he and his wife Sarah were too old to have children, God gave them a miracle child, and they called him Isaac (He Made Us Laugh). Isaac had a son named Jacob (Heel Grabber) and God changed his name to Israel (Wrestles With Creator), because he wrestled with the Angel of God. Israel had twelve sons who became the twelve tribes of Israel. After four hundred years of slavery under the Egyptians, God set them free through the great lawgiver, Moses (Drawn From The Water).

Israel eventually became a great nation, but its history is filled with failure and heartbreak. God had chosen them to represent him to the nations. But over and over again they failed to keep the covenant, and ended up misrepresenting him. He would send them deliverers to turn them back to his right ways, but eventually they would turn against God and break his covenant again.

About one thousand years before the coming of Jesus, Israel was divided into two kingdoms: Israel (Wrestles With Creator) and Judah (Give Him Honor). Both kingdoms became corrupt and eventually God allowed them to be taken captive. Israel was taken captive by the Empire of Assyria and about 250 years later Judah was taken captive by the Empire of Babylon. After spending seventy years in exile, God brought them again back to their own land.

Over the next 450 years or so, Israel struggled to maintain faithfulness to God—and failed. They were conquered by other nations and eventually by the Roman Empire. It was during this time that God sent them his final deliverer—Jesus, the Christ.

7. The Sacred Village of Peace (Jerusalem)

Jerusalem means *Village of Peace*. It was also sometimes called *the City of David*. It is an ancient city that dates back to the time of Abraham. Jerusalem eventually became the civil and religious headquarters of the nation of Israel.

Like many ancient cities, Jerusalem had stone walls built around it to protect the people from invaders. Large gates made from tree logs were built into the walls that could be closed at night or in a time of war. In the time of Jesus, Jerusalem had eleven gates, each of the gates named for their purpose. In the book of Revelation, the New Jerusalem has twelve gates.

Jesus wept over Jerusalem and warned them that if they did not learn the ways of peace they would be destroyed (Luke 19:42-44). This was the point of many of his stories (parables).

In 70 CE, less than forty years after Jesus, Jerusalem was destroyed by the Romans in the Siege of Jerusalem. The Jewish people had revolted against Rome and expelled the Romans from Jerusalem. But the Roman Emperor sent generals to retake the city. It took 3 years as they starved out the people inside the walls. The Roman catapults launched large hailstones into and over the walls to bombard the people. Jerusalem fell in a terrible slaughter and the Temple was burned to the ground and the stones removed. Jesus had prophesied this would happen and warned his followers about it. According to history the followers of Jesus heeded his warning, and when they saw the armies coming they fled from the city.

The Nation of Israel came to an end and most of the people scattered to other nations. Over the last two-thousand years Jerusalem has been largely inhabited by the Arabs and ruled by many different nations. Today, this ancient village still stands, and is divided into four quarters; the Jewish, the Muslim, the Christian and the Armenian.

The Jewish people began to return to the land in the late 1800's. After a war to establish control over the land, in 1948, the modern nation/state of Israel was established, and a large part of Jerusalem came under Jewish control once again.

This author continues to pray that all the people living there will learn to walk in the ways of peace and restorative justice—for all the inhabitants of the land.

8. Council of Wisdomkeepers (Church)

The word *church* in the Greek of the New Testament simply means *gathering* or *assembly*. It is used in the book of Acts as the village council in Ephesus—see Acts 19:39-41. A village council would come together to discuss things related to the community of people living there. So the church of Jesus would be the ones who believe in him, and gather together in worship and in the discussion of how to live in and serve their communities. For church in this version I use *village council* and *Council of Wisdom Keepers.*

9. Purification Ceremony With Water (Baptism)

In the time of Jesus, baptism in water was a cultural practice among the Jewish people. Baptism was a sacred ceremony symbolizing purification or cleansing. It also was used as an initiation rite into the spiritual and social community. To be baptized in the name of someone was to accept their teachings and become identified with them. Baptism was most often practiced by immersing a person in flowing water, which is why rivers were often used. In this paraphrase I have chosen to call baptism *the purification ceremony.*

10. Spirit Messengers (Angels)

In the language of the Bible the word angel comes from the Hebrew and Greek words that mean messenger. This word is used in the Bible to refer to human beings or to spirit beings who were sent by God. So in the First Nations Version I have chosen to call angels simply *spirit messengers.*

11. The Evil Serpent (Satan)

In Old Testament *satan* was not a formal name, but the description of a spirit being who opposed God. The word *satan* means accuser or adversary, and eventually this became a formal name to refer to this spirit being. Satan is sometimes called the devil which is a word that also means accuser or adversary. He is called the ancient serpent in the book of Revelation, referring to the serpent who came into the Garden of Eden to twist the hearts of the first man and woman—Adam and Eve. In this paraphrased version of the Gospels I call Satan *the evil serpent.*

12. Spiritual Leaders

In the time of Jesus, Israel was divided into many different religious groups with differing beliefs. The members of these religious groups had set themselves up as the spiritual leaders of Israel.

A. The Pharisees are mentioned most often. The title Pharisees means *separated ones.* The Pharisees were the most vocal and influential of the spiritual leaders and held a very strict interpretation of the Law of Moses. As their name indicates they separated themselves from those they deemed to be *sinners* and pressured others to do the same. I have paraphrased Pharisees as *Separated Ones.*

B. The Sadducees, which means *righteous ones* were often rich and held positions of power within Israel's religious and political establishments. They differ from the Pharisees in several ways. Most significantly they did not believe in spirits or in a resurrection from the dead. I have paraphrased the Sadducees as *Upright Ones.*

C. The scribes and lawyers are mentioned quite often in the Gospels, and both titles describe the same group. The scribes were the keepers of the Sacred Scrolls, the Scriptures. Since they knew how to write they became scroll copiers, making copies of the Scriptures. Since they spent so much time reading and writing the Scriptures, they became experts in the interpretation of the Law of Moses. I have paraphrased scribes as *scroll keepers.*

D. The Herodians are believed to be a small group that supported the family dynasty and political interests of King Herod. The Heriodians were Jews. I have paraphrased the Herodians as *Friends of Herod.*

E. The Zealots are indirectly referred to in the Gospels. Zealot means *to be on fire* or *full of zeal.* However, in practice the Zealots were insurrectionists using violent terrorist methods. Many of the Zealots were openly rebellious against Rome and wanted to lead a violent uprising against the Romans. Barabbas was most likely a

Zealot, and one of Jesus' own followers appears to have been a former Zealot (Simon the Zealot). Some historians speculate that Judas, who betrayed Jesus, may have also been a Zealot. I have not offered a translation other than for Simon the Zealot, referring to him as *One Who Listens—the Man On Fire*.

13. Gathering Houses (Synagogues)

In the time of the Gospel story the Jewish people usually had a village meeting place called the synagogue, which simply means *gathering place*. The synagogue was used primarily for religious purposes, such as the study of the Scriptures and prayer. I have chosen to call the synagogues simply *gathering houses*.

14. The Great Spirit's Sacred Lodge (Holy Temple)

Under King David God instructed the nation of Israel to build a temple in Jerusalem. This temple would be a permanent structure to replace the tent, also called the tabernacle, that was used when Israel was wandering in the wilderness. However, God did not allow David to build it because he was a man of violence and warfare.

The first Temple was built by King David's son, King Solomon, and later destroyed by the Babylonians. When they returned from their exile in Babylon a second Temple was built, but it was smaller and much less impressive. Leading up to the time of Jesus, King Herod the Great had used his fantastic wealth to further rebuild the temple and restore much of its ancient glory. Herod's Temple, as it was called in the time of Jesus, contained 4 courtyards: The Court of the Priests, the Court of Israel, the Court of the Women, and the Court of the Gentiles. Most scholars agree that it was in the Court of the Gentiles that Jesus drove out the money changers.

In this paraphrase I have translated Holy Temple *the Great Spirit's Sacred Lodge.*

The Holy Place was another inner chamber within the Temple, connected to the Most Holy Place and separated by a double curtain. The holy place was entered often by priests performing daily ceremonies and for morning and evening prayers.

The Most Holy Place, also called the Holy of Holies, was the innermost chamber of the temple, a small room separated from the Holy Place by a thick double curtain. It contained sacred objects from their tribal history. No one was allowed to see behind this curtain except the High Priest, and then only once a year when he entered for a special ceremony. It was this curtain that was torn in two, from top to bottom, when Jesus gave up his spirit.

15. Grand Council and Tribal Councils (Sanhedrin)

In the time of Jesus there was a council of elders called the Sanhedrin. It was a council of seventy men consisting of the high priest, the chief priests, and scribes and elders from the community. The Sanhedrin was like a Supreme Court that decided criminal and civil cases. They had their own police force and could make arrests. There were also local councils in each of the villages, probably connected to the Synagogue. In this book I call the Sanhedrin the *Grand Council* and the local councils *tribal councils.*

16. Outcasts (Sinners)

The Pharisees identified certain people as *sinners.* This word carries a more disturbing meaning than just someone who sins. These *sinners* were the outcasts of Jewish society and designated as such by the Pharisees' oppressive interpretation of the Law of Moses. These outcasts were not permitted to enter the gathering houses and were despised by the Separated Ones. Outcasts included tribal agents, prostitutes, people who ate and drank too much, those with diseases that made them ceremonially unclean, and all Gentiles (non-Jews).

17. Tribal Agents (Tax Collectors)

Tax collectors were often Jewish tribal members who contracted with the Roman government for the procurement of taxes. They could force the people, under the threat of violence, to pay them. They often became extremely rich off the suffering of the people and were hated by everyone. I have chosen to call them *tribal agents* of the colonial Roman Government.

18. One Who Hears (Simon and Peter)

Jesus gave to Simon the name Cephas, in Aramaic, which is translated from Greek to English as Peter. When Jesus first met Peter in John's Gospel (John 1:42), he said to Simon, "you will be called Peter," which could have indicated a future event. In Matthew 16, when Peter confesses Jesus as the Son of God, Jesus confers on Simon the name Peter. For storytelling purposes I have waited until this time to refer to Simon as Peter (Stands On The Rock), hoping to highlight this dramatic shift in Simon's understanding of who Jesus is.

19. The Valley of Smoldering Fire (Gehenna)

Gehenna means Valley of Hinnom and is often translated incorrectly as *hell* in most English translations. It refers to a valley in Israel just south of Jerusalem. In Ancient Israel, some apostate Israelites sacrificed their children by throwing them into fire (2 Chronicles 28:3 and 33:6). Later, through the prophet Jeremiah, God calls this valley a place of slaughter and carnage (Jeremiah 30:32-34). This valley then becomes a metaphor of destruction and devastation. In Jesus' day the Hinnom Valley was a literal garbage dump for the city waste, a huge compost pile that smoldered. Bodies of criminals were thrown into this valley to waste away and be eaten by worms. In this paraphrase I have chosen to call Gehenna *the Valley Of Smoldering Fire.*

20. The Dark Underworld of Death (Hades)

Most English translations have rendered the Greek word *Hades* (hay-dees) as *Hell.* The Greek translation of the Old Testament uses Hades for the Hebrew word *Sheol,* which primarily means the grave. So Hades and Sheol could both be rendered *the place where the dead go.* In Christianity there is much speculation and disagreement over the exact interpretation of this word. It is only used twice by Jesus in the Gospels. I have chosen to call Hades *the Dark Underworld of Death.*

21. Nailed to a Tree Pole (Crucifixion)

In the time of Jesus the Romans used a form of torture and death, called crucifixion, as the ultimate punishment for crimes. To be crucified was to have one's hands and feet nailed to a large wooden cross. Crucifixion is considered by many to be one of the most painful ways to die ever devised by human beings. In addition to this, from the Jewish perspective, any one crucified was under a curse, based on Deuteronomy 21:23. I have chosen to call the cross, *the tree pole.*

22. Genealogy and Ancestry

From the Gospel of Matthew 1:1-17.

Here is the record of his *chiefly* ancestry, from the ancient scrolls.

The first fourteen generations begin with Father Of Many Nations, He Made Us Laugh, and Heel Grabber. Then there was Give Him Honor and his brothers; followed by He Breaks Through and his brother Rising Sun, by their mother, Fruit Of Palm Tree; then

Circle Of Teepees, He Is Lifted Up and Noble Relative. After that there was Talks With Snakes and He Makes Peace; then Moves With Strength, by his mother, Boastful Woman. Finally there was He Works Hard and Original Man. Original Man was the father of the great chief Much Loved One.

The second fourteen generations begin with Much Loved One and his son, Stands In Peace, by the wife of Fire From Creator. Then there was Big People Maker, Creator Is My Father, Gathers The People and He Makes Wrongs Right Again; then Creator Is Above, My Great Power, Creator Has No Equal, and Held By Creator. These were followed by He Will Be Strong, He Made Them Forget, Burden Bearer, and Good Medicine. Then there was He Will Stand Strong and his brothers at the time of the great removal to Babylon.

The next fourteen generations begin with He Will Stand Strong and his son Ask Creator; then Born In Babylon, Father Boasts In Him, and Creator Lifts Up. Then came He Helps Him, Stands With A Good Heart, and Makes Him Strong. After this was Power Of Creator, Creator Helps Him, and Gifted By Creator; and finally there was Heel Grabber, the father of He Gives Sons who was the husband of Bitter Tears. Bitter Tears gave birth to Creator Sets Free, who is the Chosen One.

From the Gospel of Luke 3:23-38.

Here is the family tree of Creator Sets Free, the Chosen One.

Creator Sets Free was about thirty years old when he began his great work. He was the son, so it was thought, of He Gives Sons.

He Gives Sons was the son of One Above Us, son of Gift From Creator, son of One Who Joins Together, son of My Chief, son of He Grows Strong, son of He Gives Sons, son of Gift From Above, son of Burden Bearer, son of He Gives Comfort, son of Creator Is

Near, son of Light Bringer, son of Small One, son of Gift From Above, son of He Hears, son of Creator Gives More, son of Gives Honor, son of Shows Goodwill, son of Born In Babylon, son of Ask Creator, son of My Chief, son of Clothed In Beauty, son of Talks To Spirits, son of Counts How Much, son of Creator Sets Free, son of He Helps Him, son of Honored By Creator, son of Gift From Creator, son of He Brings Together, son of Has Plenty, son of He Is Ready, son of Gift Giver, son of He Gives, son of Much Loved One, son of Original Man, son of He Works Hard, son of Moves With Strength, son of He Makes Peace, son of Talks With Snakes, son of Noble Relative, son of Red Flower, son of He Is Lifted Up, son of Circle Of Teepees, son of He Breaks Through, son of Give Him Honor, son of Heel Grabber, son of He Made Us Laugh, son of Father Of Many Nations, son of He Made Them Wait, son of Man Who Snorts, son of Growing Stem, son of Faithful Friend, son of Where The Water Divides, son of Over The River, son of Winding Branch, son of Strong Wall Of Babel, son of His Name Is Known, son of One Who Rests, son of Strong Wild Man, son of Long Arrow, son of He Will Teach, son of He Came Down, son of Beauty Of Creator, son of Birth Of Sorrow, son of Human Being, son of Took His Place, son of Red Clay, son of the Great Spirit.

From the Author

An Unexpected Journey

Over twenty years ago, God, whom I have learned to call Creator, Great Spirit and Grandfather, changed the course of my life when he made it clear to me that I was to become involved in the lives of the First Nations People of North America, often called American Indians.

This journey eventually led my wife and I to live among the Hopi Indians in the high desert of northern Arizona. Since I had Native American heritage from both the Ojibwe and Yaqui Indians I had hoped that I would fit right in, but I had much to learn then, and my learning continues to this day.

As we began to share the Gospel with the Hopi, I soon learned that a doctrinal based study of Scripture, often taken out of the context of the narrative of the Bible, was not a clear message. A New Testament had been translated into their language, but because the Hopi traditionally had no written language, most could not read it. Later we found this to be true for a majority of the North American tribes.

As we lived in a Native setting we began to learn from them the beauty and value of traditional storytelling. Over the years I began to present the Bible in the form of storytelling. This led to the release of our RainSong CD called *The Great Story From the*

Sacred Book, a condensed narrative of the Bible story from Creation to Christ, retold for Native Americans. This CD has been well received by many traditional and non-traditional Natives. It also won the *2009 Native American Music Award* for *Best Spoken Word.*

From that time forward I began to reword many of my favorite Scripture passages and share them at our live RainSong concerts. Many people began to ask if I would be doing an entire New Testament or even the whole Bible in this manner. Even though that sounded like a good thing, I couldn't imagine myself taking on such an overwhelming task.

After much research I could not find any English translations that had been done specifically with Native Americans in mind. A still, small voice keep gently nudging me, in the back of my mind, that I should attempt a paraphrase of the New Testament for Native Americans and English speaking First Nations People. Finally in the fall of 2012, with what I felt was clear confirmation from Creator, I committed myself to this task.

Even though this journey was one I never expected to embark on, it has been a captivating and eye opening adventure. With that in mind I humbly submit this sacred task and labor of love to our First Nations peoples and to all who seek to walk the Good Road following Jesus.

The Story of the Great Storyteller

The story of Jesus has often been called the greatest story ever told. Jesus grew up in the village of Nazareth in the land of Israel, the area of the world we now call the Middle East. He was a Jewish man who was born into the culture of his tribe and people. Yet he was no ordinary man as you will see when you hear his story. Today, over two billion people identify themselves as followers of Jesus.

His story, called the Gospel, is told in four separate accounts historically attributed to Matthew, Mark, Luke and John. Three of these men were Jewish and eyewitnesses—Matthew, Mark and John. Though Luke was neither Jewish nor an eyewitness, he personally talked to many eyewitnesses as he put the story into an orderly account. Each of these storytellers told the story from their own perspectives. These four stories have been preserved and handed down to us in ancient manuscripts written in the Greek language.

Four Gospels ~ One Story

This book is a harmony of the four Gospels, blended together into one narrative. Harmonies of the Gospels have been put together since the second century. This version is new because it is done with a particular people in mind, the First Nations People of North America.

Great care and effort have been taken to include every verse, without repetition, in all four Gospels; but at times, to make the meaning as clear as possible, they had to be reworded and blended together in ways that might make them unrecognizable as individual verses.

From a storytelling perspective, the genealogies of Matthew and Luke seemed to slow down the narrative. I was advised by other storytellers, and a few involved friends, not to include them in the narrative, but because of their historical importance they were placed in the Culture and Context section of this book.

As any serious student of the Gospel knows, the events depicted in the four Gospels, and their sequence, can vary significantly. Debatable geographic locations were taken in to account along with the help of harmonies designed by others. The final and overriding factor considered in this harmony is the flow of the story. In the end it is the story within the narrative that is most important—and a storyteller knows this! With the help of other harmonies, and some valuable input from a passionately involved friend, I have submitted this imperfect but heartfelt version to the reader.

This is the second book of the *First Nations Version Project* by this author. It retells the story of the Bible using words and phrases that relate to the First Nations People, then also for English speaking indigenous peoples from all nations, and finally to all who want to hear the story in a fresh and unique way. You can learn more about the *First Nations Version Project* at our website www.firstnationsversion.com.

Artistic, Poetic and Dramatic License

In an attempt to present the scriptures as a living and moving narrative I sometimes added reasonably implied statements. For this I used my imagination and took a few liberties as I tried to picture what may have been the reaction in the voices and faces of the participants. I also at times inserted comments on the history, culture and geography to add depth to the story. None of the additions add or take away from the meaning of the text of Scripture. *These insertions are in italics.*

Paraphrase or Translation

The word *translation* doesn't completely describe this project. Rather, it is a retelling of the Scriptures in the tradition of the storytellers of oral cultures—some might call it a paraphrase. It is similar, in concept, to *The Message* by Eugene Peterson[163] and *The Living Bible* by Kenneth N. Taylor.[164] But it is different in the sense that it attempts to convey the rhythm and feel of an oral storyteller.

Even though this is a paraphrase of the Scriptures, I have taken great care to convey the original meaning of the text, to the best of my ability, by using the most current scholarship and translation tools available to me. On some of the most difficult passages I enlisted the help of a seminary professor who is skilled in the knowledge of New Testament Greek. However, any and all mistakes are mine alone.

The First Nations Version is not intended to replace standard translations but to present the scriptures with phrases and word choices that relate in a general way to Native Americans and other First Nations English speaking people. It is not intended to be culturally or tribally specific.

About the Author

Terry M. Wildman

Born and raised in lower Michigan, Terry is of Ojibwe (Chippewa) and Yaqui ancestry. Terry is a recording artist, songwriter, storyteller, speaker and published writer.

Terry is the "Chief" of Rain Ministries, a nonprofit organization based in Arizona. Since the year 2000 as "RainSong" he and his wife Darlene have invested their lives in sharing the message of Jesus with Native Americans.

They have produced four music CD's, Sacred Warrior, Rising Sun, Rise Up and Dance and Hoop of Life. Their music style is a folk rock blend with Native American instruments and melodies.

In 2004 RainSong was nominated for a Grammy award and two Nammy awards. In 2005 they won the "American Christian Music Award" for the category of "Favorite Band/Duo–Breakout." In 2008 they were nominated for two Nammy Awards, one for "Best Song of the Year," All Colors Together, and for "Best Gospel Recording" for their CD Rise Up and Dance. Terry and Darlene were presenters that year at the awards ceremony held in Niagara Falls, New York.

They have also produced a storytelling CD with a musical background called The Great Story from the Sacred Book. This

CD won the Nammy (Native American Music Award) for "Best Spoken Word" in 2009. Soon after they released a booklet to compliment the CD through Indian Life Ministries based in Manitoba, Canada, (indianlife.org).

Other books by this author: Sign Language: A Look at the Historic and Prophetic Landscape of America, and Birth of the Chosen One.

Endnotes

[1] Grandfather is used by many tribes as a respectful way to refer to God.

[2] Jesus, see Culture and Context section 2.

[3] See Genesis chapter 1 for the story.

[4] Garden of Eden, see Genesis 2:8-15 for the story.

[5] Satan or the Devil, see Culture and Context section 11.

[6] Noah, see Genesis chapters 6 to 9 for the story.

[7] Abram, see Genesis chapter 12:1-3 for the story.

[8] Covenant.

[9] Abraham, see Genesis 17:1-8 for the story.

[10] Isaac, see Genesis 18:1-15 for the story.

[11] Jacob, see Genesis 25:21-26 for the story.

[12] Israel, see Genesis 32:22-32 for the story.

[13] Moses, see Exodus 2:1-10 for the story.

[14] David, see 1 Samuel 16:1-13 and 2 Samuel 5:1-4 for the story.

[15] Roman empire.

[16] Synagogue, see Culture and Context section 13.

[17] Holy Temple, see Culture and Context section 14.

[18] Christ or Messiah, see Culture and Context section 3.

[19] Gospel, meaning good news.

[20] Jesus, see Culture and Context section 2.

[21] See Culture and Context section 22 for complete genealogy.

[22] Angel, see Culture and Context section 10.

[23] "Counting Coup" is a Native American practice among the plains tribes, of touching an enemy with a "coup stick" as an act of courage during battle, to show he could have killed him, but chose to spare him instead.

[24] This shows they were poor, for this was the offering a poor family was permitted to bring.

[25] Judea: Much of the southern sector of the Land of Promise.

[26] See Isaiah 53:2.

[27] See Isaiah 53:3.

[28] High Priest. The high priesthood was transferring from Annas to Caiaphas that year. See Luke 3:2a.

[29] The Apache and a few other Southwestern tribes have burden baskets. They are often used in a coming of age ceremony, symbolizing the transition from the old generation to the new. Here I use it for John the Baptist who is called by God to carry the burden of transition from the old covenant to the new.

[30] See Isaiah 40:3-5.

[31] Baptism, see Culture and Context section 9.

[32] Pharisees and Sadducees, see Culture and Context section 12-A and B.

[33] Tax collectors, see Culture and Context section 17.

[34] See Isaiah 40:3-4.

[35] Satan, see Culture and Context section 11.

[36] Rabbi, meaning Teacher.

[37] Simon (aka Peter, Cephas) see Culture and Context section 18.

38 Son of Man, see Culture and Context section 4.

39 Decapolis. A region on the east side of the Sea of Galilee where there was a mixture of nations and religious practices.

40 Lit. Salvation.

41 Sabbath.

42 Jubilee, see Leviticus 25:8-17.

43 See Isaiah 61:1-2

44 The brothers of Jesus: James, Joses, Judah and Simon.

45 See 1 Kings 17:8-24 for the story.

46 See 2 Kings 5:1-19 for the story.

47 See Isaiah 9:1-2.

48 See Isaiah 53:4.

49 Herodians, see Culture and Context section 12-D.

50 See Isaiah 42:1-4.

51 Apostles, meaning sent ones.

52 The twelve Apostles: Peter (aka Simon), Andrew, James, John, Phillip, Bartholomew, Thomas, Matthew (aka Levi) James, Thaddaeus (aka Judas), Simon the Zealot and Judas (who betrayed Christ).

53 See 2 Kings 2:19-22.

54 Leviticus 2:13, Ezekiel 43:24.

55 See Exodus 20:13.

56 In the culture of the time saying "you fool" may have been like calling a person godless and condemned or cursed.

[57] Valley of Hinnom—Gehenna, see Culture and Context section 19.

[58] See Exodus 20:14.

[59] Lit. Offends you.

[60] Lit. Offends you.

[61] See Deuteronomy 24:1.

[62] At that time men would "put away" their wives without divorcing them, leaving them destitute and unable to properly remarry.

[63] See Exodus 21:24 and Leviticus 24:20.

[64] See Leviticus 19:18.

[65] See Romans 14:16

[66] Lit. To dogs who will turn on you and tear you apart.

[67] Lit. Throw pearls to pigs.

[68] Lit. I never knew you.

[69] Centurion, a Roman officer.

[70] Lit. East and West.

[71] The mustard plant was used as an herbal medicine. Once the seed was planted it would grow and take over an entire field.

[72] See Jeremiah 5:21.

[73] See Isaiah 6:9-10.

[74] Lit. Legion. A segment of the occupying Roman army of about 5000 soldiers.

[75] Beelzebul, another name for Satan.

[76] Also called Sea of Tiberias.

[77] Lit. At the last day.

[78] Lit. Flesh.

[79] Lit. devil, adversary.

[80] See Isaiah 29:13.

[81] Lit. Parable.

[82] Jonah, who spent three days and nights in the belly of a great fish. See Jonah 1:17-2:10 for the story.

[83] Elijah or Jeremiah or one of the prophets.

[84] Jonah, aka John.

[85] Peter, see Culture and Context section 18.

[86] Church, see Culture and Context section 8.

[87] Hades or Hell, see Culture and Context section 20.

[88] Lit. I give you the keys of the Kingdom of Heaven.

[89] Chief priests.

[90] Here Jesus refers to Peter as Satan, recognizing who is influencing Peter.

[91] Church, see Culture and Context section 8.

[92] See Deuteronomy 6:5.

[93] See Leviticus 19:18.

[94] The people of Samaria were mixed bloods who had changed the traditional ceremonial ways and were despised by the Jewish people.

[95] Beelzeebul, another name for Satan.

[96] Queen of Sheba.

[97] Lit. Circumcision, identifying the men as belonging to the nation of Israel.

[98] See Isaiah 12:3.

[99] See Jeremiah 2:13.

[100] The flesh.

[101] Lit. Me.

[102] To say "I AM" is to use the name reserved for God alone, Exodus 3:14.

[103] Jesus (Creator Sets Free) was a common name among the tribes of Israel in that day.

[104] See Luke 1:79 and 19:42

[105] Lit. Oxen.

[106] Cross, see Culture and Context section 21.

[107] Also called Hanukkah and Festival of Lights.

[108] Lit. "You are gods."

[109] Lit. A woman with ten silver coins.

[110] Lit. Camel.

[111] Lit. Or brothers and sisters, or father and mother, or wife and children, or their lands.

[112] Lit. One hundred times more brothers and sisters, mothers and children, and lands. They now belong to the new family of God that will care for them.

[113] Lit. Gentiles.

[114] See Zechariah 9:9-10.

[115] See Isaiah 56:7, Jeremiah 7:11.

[116] See Psalm 69:9

[117] See Psalm 118:22-23.

[118] Lit. Bear its fruit.

[119] Lit. Few are chosen.

[120] See Psalm 110:1.

[121] English translations use Lord. In the Hebrew language this is the name of God—Yahweh. This name means I AM—the Eternal One.

[122] Lit. Camel.

[123] See Jeremiah 44:4.

[124] Abel. Adam's second son, his name means breath or vapor. He was the first human being to be killed by another. See Genesis 4:1-16 for the story.

[125] Lit. between the alter and the sanctuary. See 2 Chronicles 24:20-22.

[126] See 1 Corinthians 1:18-25.

[127] See Colossians 1:19-20

[128] See Isaiah 53:1.

[129] See Isaiah 6:10

[130] Lit. Shofar: the Jewish trumpet.

[131] See Luke 19:41-44

[132] Lit. Brothers.

[133] This was equal to about 6 months wages.

[134] See Psalm 41:9.

[135] New Covenant.

[136] See Zechariah 13:7.

[137] See John 14:3 and 14:23.

[138] See Psalm 69:4

[139] Lit. All that I have.

[140] See Isaiah 53:12.

[141] Lit. Abba in the Aramaic. Papa, a term of endearment.

[142] See Hebrews 5:7-8

[143] The Sanhedrin, see Culture and Context section 15.

[144] Many scholars believe that this was a reference to Daniel 7. "Coming with the clouds" was a word picture of the one who would come to the Ancient of Days and receive the authority to judge the world.

[145] See Jeremiah 32:6-9

[146] The man's name was Jesus Barabbas or Creator Sets Free Son Of His Father.

[147] Hebrew: Golgotha, Greek: Calvary. Both mean Place of the Skull.

[148] See Isaiah 53:12.

[149] See Psalm 22:18.

[150] Paradise.

[151] Mary of Magdala and Mary the wife of Clopas.

[152] See Psalm 22:1.

[153] Mary Magdalene, Mary the Mother of James the younger and Joses, and Solome the mother of the sons of Zebadee.

[154] See Psalm 34:20.

[155] See Zechariah 12:10.

[156] See Isaiah 52:13 to 53:12

[157] "Counting Coup" was a Native American practice among the plains tribes of touching an enemy with a "coup stick." It is an act of great courage during the battle to spare the enemy but to show he could have killed him. In this case Jesus showed the greatest courage, by not killing his enemies, but letting them kill him, and in this way defeat the true enemies of violence and death, when he rose from the grave. This is implying that the cross was Jesus' coup stick.

[158] See 1 Corinthians 15:5-6

[159] See Acts 1:3

[160] Lit. In the name of.

[161] Luke 10:17-19. The enemy is Satan and his demons (serpents and scorpions).

[162] See George E. Tinker, *Spirit and Resistance*, Chap. 7, pages 91-99. Fortress Press, Minneapolis MN.

[163] *The Message: The Bible in Contemporary Language.* Eugene Peterson. NavPress.

[164] *The Living Bible.* Kenneth N. Taylor. Tyndale House Publishers, Inc. Wheaton, IL 60189.

CPSIA information can be obtained
at www.ICGtesting.com
Printed in the USA
BVHW041537011021
617921BV00008B/89